George Eliot
Her Beliefs and Her Art

In the same series

Novelists and Their World
General Editor: Graham Hough
Professor of English at the University of Cambridge

George Eliot
Her Beliefs and Her Art

NEIL ROBERTS

 Paul Elek   London

To my Father and Mother

Published in Great Britain in 1975 by
Elek Books Ltd.
54–58 Caledonian Road, London N1 9RN

ISBN 0-236-15486-9

Printed in Great Britain
by John Sherratt & Son, Ltd., Park Road, Altrincham
Cheshire WA14 5QQ.
and set in 11 on 12 Baskerville

Preface

Behind George Eliot's novels there is a powerful and coherent intellectual and moral life. This creates critical problems which—while George Eliot has been unusually well served by critics and intellectual historians—have not been fully faced. Only a small proportion of the work on her has attempted critically to examine the relation between her thought and her art. The intellectual historian tends to treat the novels simply as dramatisations of preconceived ideas, while many of the best critical studies pay little attention to the intellectual background.

My purpose is to examine George Eliot's moral, social and religious ideas as elements in her artistic creation; to consider to what extent they contribute to the strengths or weaknesses of the novels; where they are affirmed by her imagination; where questioned or denied. This is primarily, therefore, a critical study. The background information that I have given does not pretend to be exhaustive but, while George Eliot's intellectual interests were considerably wider than what is discussed here, I do believe that an introduction to Comte, Feuerbach, Evangelical Christianity and evolutionary theory indicates the most important and abiding influences. If I had had the space to discuss further influences, I should have paid considerably more attention to her literary predecessors, particularly the English Romantic poets.

Parts of Chapters 1, 4, 7 and 8 were originally parts of a Cambridge Ph.D. thesis of quite different scope. My research supervisor was Professor Raymond Williams, without whose advice and encouragement the thesis and consequently the book would never have been completed. I am also grateful to Professor Graham Hough for suggestions which have

7

resulted in the book's being better than my unaided judgement would have made it; and to my wife for many laborious hours spent in typing and checking the manuscript.

Acknowledgements are due to Messrs Routledge and Kegan Paul Ltd and to Yale University Press for permission to quote copyright material from George Eliot's essays and letters respectively.

Introduction

For some decades after her death it was not uncommon for well-educated people to speak of George Eliot with amused contempt, sometimes even suggesting that her life's work could be explained by referring to her supposed ugliness.[1] Today she is among the most widely respected and revered English novelists. There has of course been a stabilisation of attitudes towards all the achievements of the 'High' Victorian age, which more or less corresponded with George Eliot's mature life; but it will be better to avoid cultural generalisations and to ask why George Eliot in particular should be held in such esteem.

In her writing we hear the sincere and intelligent voice of profound human experience in an age which for the sensitive and intelligent was one of uncertainty, contradiction and conflict. Even if we did not have her novels, her life would repay study, for it was representative in the way that only an exceptional life can be. Because of her honesty and intelligence, the central conflicts of her age impressed themselves directly upon her life. An atheist of a strongly religious temperament, an adultress who believed in marital fidelity, a believer in progress who loved the past, an intellectual who glorified feeling: these are glib paradoxes, which nevertheless indicate the qualities of a life and mind that attempted to live through the contradictions with which they were presented and to reject nothing, however apparently discredited, which fostered the cardinal values of sympathy and reverence. Of one dominating influence on her age—the growth of industry, concentration of men and women in large towns, and conflict between property-owners and workers—George Eliot knew and understood little. But of the moral and spiritual experience of educated people, she is a uniquely complete witness.

Furthermore, what George Eliot represents is of more than passing antiquarian interest. It is fair to assume that for most of her admirers the questions which preoccupied her are still subject for concern. People still wish to preserve what is valuable in a past moral order without accepting an illusory consolation, to acknowledge necessity without falling into cynicism or despair. For such readers George Eliot is both a near-contemporary and an agent of sympathetic understanding of a past age.

Of all great English novelists, certainly of all our nineteenth-century novelists, she was most of an intellectual. Her imaginative achievement was prepared for and accompanied by a passionate and informed interest in the most up-to-date philosophy, theology, sociology and natural science. At the age of twenty-three, at a time when most educated Englishmen dismissed historical criticism of the Bible with the epithet 'German', she translated David Strauss's *Das Leben Jesu,* the most important and influential work of its kind. Between the death of her father in 1849 and her beginnings as a novelist in 1856 she contributed regularly to *The Westminster Review,* perhaps the most distinguished periodical of its time, and was for three years effectively its editor. For some years she lived at the house of John Chapman, the owner of the *Westminster,* where she met most of the important writers and intellectuals in London. She became profoundly interested in the work of Auguste Comte, and for a time her closest friend was Herbert Spencer who, though virtually unread today, was regarded by many of his contemporaries as the most distinguished living English philosopher. She translated Spinoza's *Ethics,* which was never published, and Feuerbach's *Essence of Christianity,* which was published in 1854. George Henry Lewes, with whom she lived from 1854 until his death in 1878, was a distinguished literary critic, natural historian and psychologist who had written a history of philosophy while still in his twenties. George Eliot assisted in the research for his book on natural history, *Seaside Studies,* as well as for his *Life of Goethe,* which was for many years regarded as the standard biography in Germany as well as in England.

What is of particular relevance to the reader of the novels is that there was nothing promiscuous or arbitrary about these experiences and influences. They were absorbed by an intellectually consequent mind at the service of strong moral and spiritual needs. George Eliot was an intellectual in the deepest sense, in that she demanded the assent of her intellect before accepting any proposition about how to live and what to live for. 'There is not a more pernicious fallacy afloat in common parlance, than the wide distinction made between intellect and morality', she wrote in 1855. But it would be misleading to call her a rationalist. 'The truth of feeling'[2] and 'the mystery that lies under the processes'[3] are examples of the phrases that recur throughout her writing, expressing the final impotence of 'reason' to explain the ends of life or, still more important, to understand other people. But these phrases themselves represent propositions which George Eliot accepted *intellectually*: they were not articles of faith at odds with her intellect. Before she ever started writing fiction George Eliot's beliefs were coherent, stable and articulate. Since her main purpose in writing was a moral one, her beliefs are an intrinsic part of her art. The moral *tone* of the novels is evident enough, but it is their structure also which is determined by her beliefs. Although she called herself a realist, she did not practise a neutral surface-naturalism. The reality which she presents is moulded by her beliefs about the nature of moral action. Although she occasionally attempted—in *Silas Marner* entirely successfully —what she called 'romantic and symbolical' modes, the characteristic form of her novels is a complex organisation of the causes and effects of moral action.

It is here that we come to the central critical question of George Eliot's novels. Some readers have dismissed George Eliot's novels just because she is a moral teacher. This is not the place to argue the acceptability of moral teaching in art, but even the reader who does accept it in principle may use the word 'didactic' in a pejorative sense. The power that the novelist has over the reader is that of having invited him into a world over which the novelist has complete control. If the reader feels that the novelist is merely adapting that world to suit his preconceptions he will reject it, or at least consider what he is reading to be something less than a great novel. He will be more persuaded by the work in which the art is not simply the instrument of the preconceived idea, but in which the preconceived idea is put to the test of the art. George Eliot herself believed this. Her essay, 'The Morality of Wilhelm Meister', is an attack on didacticism in this second sense.

'But we question whether the direct exhibition of a moral bias in the writer will make a book really moral in its influence. Try this on the first child that asks you to tell it a story. As long as you keep to an apparently impartial narrative of facts you will have earnest eyes fixed on you in rapt attention, but no sooner do you begin to betray symptoms of an intention to moralise, or to turn the current of facts towards a personal application, than the interest of your hearer will slacken, his eyes will wander, and the moral dose will be doubly distasteful from the very sweet-meat in which you have attempted to insinuate it. One grand reason of this is, that the child is aware you are talking *for it* instead of *from yourself*, so that instead of carrying it along in a stream of sympathy with your own interest in the story, you give it the impression of contriving coldly and talking artificially. Now, the moralising novelist produces the same effect on his mature readers.'[4]

The most obvious kind of didacticism consists of directly addressing or even hectoring the reader. We often find this in the works of Dickens and Lawrence. But this, though often irritating, is not the most damaging kind. It is an intrusion into the organisation of the novel, and it may mean that the writer is wanting to tell us something simpler and cruder than what his art has shown us. In these cases we can, if we wish, simply shut our ears. There is also the didacticism of the simple moral fable, like *Animal Farm,* which does not try to disguise its bias. But there is a more subtle didacticism in which the 'apparently impartial narrative of facts' is not only not impartial (the reader who accepts a moral purpose in art does not expect that) but in which the author is suppressing possibilities that might qualify or contradict his purpose. The morality of great art is that which is most completely honest about the most extensive experience of life; and if the author is hiding something that he knows, or if he does not know something relevant to his concern, he is guilty of didacticism.

In a letter of January, 1876 George Eliot wrote:

'But my writing is simply a set of experiments in life—an endeavour to see what our thought and emotion may be capable of—what stores of motive, actual or hinted as possible, give promise of a better after which we may strive—what gains from past revelations and discipline we must strive to keep hold of as something more sure than shifting theory.'[5]

One of George Eliot's commentators, Bernard J. Paris, has taken the phrase 'experiments in life' as the title of his book, and has made explicit the suggestion in this letter that there is a similarity between the procedures of the novelist and those of the scientist: 'The experimental process employed by the scientist to test his hypotheses is analogous to the novelist's invention of a story.' He supports his argument by quoting from G. H. Lewes's *Principles of Success in Literature:*

'The experiments by which the problems may be solved have to be imagined; and to imagine a good experiment is as difficult as to invent a good fable, for we must have distinctly *present* —in clear mental vision—the known qualities and relations of all the objects, and must *see* what will be the effect of introducing some new qualifying agent. . . . Easy enough, indeed, is the ordinary practice of experiment, which is either a mere repetition or variation of experiments already devised (as ordinary story-tellers re-tell the stories of others), or else a haphazard, blundering way of bringing phenomena together, to see what will happen. To invent is another process. The discoverer and the poet are inventors; and they are so because their mental vision detects the unapparent, unsuspected facts, almost as vividly as ocular vision rests on the apparent and familiar.'[6]

Mr Paris comments, 'This is the best description I know of the process by which George Eliot conceived and developed the action of her novels.' While the comparison is an illuminating comment on the art of the novelist in general and on George Eliot's conscious affinity with natural scientists in particular, it should be obvious that the phrase 'experiments in life' is only a metaphor.[7] While there is probably a very close analogy between the imaginative processes involved in devising an experiment and in constructing a narrative, the actual conduct of the 'experiments' is crucially different. The scientist has no control over the outcome of an experiment, once it has been set in motion. It is completely outside and independent of him, and once it has been devised and conducted it can be reproduced by anyone with the minimum training. The novelist, on the other hand, has the power to distort events at every point, and the experiment cannot be repeated: the only check on the novelist's findings is critical reading, the existence of which depends on the elementary assumption that the medium in which the 'experiment' occurs is not actually life but something that the novelist is inviting us to take for life.

However, although 'experiments in life' is a dangerous phrase for the critic to make use of, one can see that it had a value for George Eliot. Her belief in the moral bearings of the methods of physical science can be seen in the following extract from her review of Lecky's *The Influence of Rationalism*:

'The great conception of universal regular sequence, without partiality and without caprice—the conception which is the most potent force at work in the modification of our faith, and of the practical form given to our sentiments—could only grow out of that patient watching of external fact, and that silencing of preconceived notions, which are urged upon the mind by the problems of physical science.'[8]

This belief was one of the most important links that attached her to Positivism. One of the two fundamental articles of the Positive Philosophy is the Hierarchy of the Sciences, beginning with Mathematics and culminating in Sociology, or the Science of Humanity. Each science is more complex than that which precedes it, and cannot be understood in terms other than its own. Thus, for example, although George Eliot shared the view that all human phenomena have a physiological basis, she did not believe that they could be explained by the laws of Biology. She makes the application herself in her essay on 'The Natural History of German Life':

'It has not been sufficiently insisted on, that in the various branches of Social Science there is an advance from the general to the special, from the simple to the complex, analogous with that which is found in the series of the sciences, from Mathematics to Biology. . . . Chemistry embraces phenomena which are not explicable by Physics; Biology embraces phenomena which are not explicable by Chemistry; and no biological generalization will enable us to predict the infinite specialities produced by the complexity of vital conditions. . . . And just as the most thorough acquaintance with physics, or chemistry, or general physiology will not enable you at once to establish the balance of life in your private vivarium . . . so the most complete equipment of theory will not enable a statesman or a political and social reformer to adjust his measures wisely, in the absence of a special acquaintance with the section of society for which he legislates, with the peculiar characteristics of the nation, the province, the class whose well-being he has to consult. In other words, a wise social policy must be based not simply on abstract social science, but on the Natural History of social bodies.'[9]

An aesthetic equivalent to this is her insistence, in a letter to Frederic Harrison in which she refuses to write a Positivist Utopia, that the artist must not lapse 'from the picture to the diagram'.[10] That is, reality must be treated in its fullest complexity and for the novelist there is no culminating science but an infinitely increasing complexity against which all 'gains from past revelations and discipline' are in danger of appearing over-simple and crude.

There is another important element here. George Eliot was not concerned only to observe humanity but to investigate and enforce values: 'If art does not enlarge men's sympathies, it does nothing morally.'[11] The following quotations from her letters give her formulations of this concern at various stages.

'Speculative truth begins to appear but a shadow of individual minds, agreement between intellects seems unattainable, and we turn to the *truth of feeling* as the only universal bond of union.' [G.E.'s emphasis.][12]

'I can't tell you how much melancholy it causes me that people are, for the most part, so incapable of comprehending the state of mind which cares for that which is essentially human in all forms of belief, and desires to exhibit it under all forms with loving truthfulness.'[13]

'As a fact of mere zoological evolution, woman seems to me to have the worse share in existence. But for that very reason I would the more contend that in the moral evolution we have "an art which does mend nature". It is the function of love in the largest sense, to mitigate the harshness of all fatalities.'[14]

The first passage was written before George Eliot became, in her own way, a Positivist, at a time when she seems to have adhered to a form of Pantheism. Speculative truth is not to be identified with scientific truth, and the Positivists rejected the kind of speculation she seems to be referring to here (the exercise of the reason without reference to objective facts) as completely as Revelation. Her description of it as 'a shadow of individual minds' anticipates this. Nevertheless, 'the truth of feeling' expresses a concern that is permanently present in her work, and there is a continuity of meaning in these passages. The truth of feeling is a part of the highest complexity which the Positivist, while not relaxing his observation of objective reality, must not allow himself to distort.

For the novelist herself then, the 'experiments in life' formula was a way of expressing her sense of an infinitely complex reality whose highest complexity is the human world of values and moral action. Her novelist's art might be described as a kind of sympathetic immersion in this reality, which checks and qualifies the preconceptions that she brings to it. However, it is a little more complex than this. The sense of reality and the preconceptions about it do not exist separately. What a man sees is determined by what he believes, especially if his beliefs take the form of coherent laws. It is impossible in practice to separate the sympathetic immersion from the preconceptions as they appear in the novels. What the critic must do is to testify to the moments when his own sense of reality is affronted by what he reads; for one of the starting points of this book is the contention that George Eliot by no means always succeeds in reconciling reality with her preconceptions, or in qualifying her beliefs in accordance with reality; that in several of her books, (though in markedly different degrees) she *does* distort, both locally and more generally; and that these distortions can be identified in her language, construction and (in Henry James's sense) selection.

The value of a study of George Eliot's ideas then, is not that it explains the novels, but that it helps us to be clear about the nature of her achievement and of her weaknesses. The only true experiment in life is living, and if George Eliot's novels tell us an immense amount about our own lives, we must use our own experiments as a check on what we are told.

I
George Eliot's Moral World

The religion of George Eliot's family was an old-fashioned Churchmanship which set little store by 'doctrines' but was based on the habit of churchgoing and on sound ethical principles not exclusively Christian. It is familiar to the readers of the novels in the religion of the two men modelled on George Eliot's father: Adam Bede and Caleb Garth, whose 'virtual divinities were good practical schemes, accurate work, and the faithful completion of undertakings' but who combined with his 'strong practical intelligence' a 'reverential soul' (*Middlemarch*, Chapter 24). The much more conscious, doctrinal, Evangelical Christianity that dominated Mary Anne Evans's late adolescence was derived from Miss Maria Lewis, the principal governess of the school at Nuneaton to which she was sent at the age of nine, and the Miss Franklins, to whose school at Coventry she went when she was thirteen. The Miss Franklins were Baptists but Miss Evans, like Miss Lewis, was always a communicant of the Church of England, an inheritor of the great reform movement within the Church, begun in the last decades of the eighteenth century and led by William Wilberforce. It was Miss Lewis who was the most important spiritual influence of George Eliot's youth, and to whom the bulk of her early letters were written.[1]

Neither the environment of her home nor that of her school-life deprived her of imaginative and sensuous enjoyment. There was none of the harsh repression that we witness in the upbringing of such characters as Arthur Clennam in *Little Dorrit,* and her teachers appear to have been considerably more humane than the oppressive Mr Brocklehurst in *Jane Eyre.* Mr Brocklehurst may have represented one aspect of Evangelicalism[2]—and a growing one—but the movement did not necessarily exclude gaiety and the life of the imagination. Miss Lewis and the Miss Franklins do not seem to have disapproved of novels or of oratorio, both of which we see George Eliot condemning in her letters. Like Dickens, whose upbringing was by comparison bohemian, George Eliot grew up with full access to the great heritage of English popular literature, as we see in Gordon Haight's biography:

'Her first book—the first present she remembered receiving from her father—was *The Linnet's Life*, which she kept until her death . . . There were then few books for children, in the Evans household, at least, but she had *The Pilgrim's Progress*, *The Vicar of Wakefield*, *Aesop's Fables* with pictures, and less likely favourites in Defoe's *History of the Devil* and *Joe Miller's Jest Book*, from which she sometimes recounted stories that astonished her family. Sir Walter Scott first introduced her to the writing of fiction.'[3]

The more extreme puritanical attitudes expressed in the letters came from within.

In *Janet's Repentance* George Eliot writes, 'Perhaps Milby was one of the last spots to be reached by the wave of a new [Evangelical] movement; and it was only now, when the tide was just on the turn, that the limpets there got a sprinkling' (Chapter 2). The story is based on events that occurred at Nuneaton in the late 1820s, forty years after the movement had begun, and after Wilberforce had retired from his lifetime's work in the service of Evangelicalism. The fact that the movement had only just reached Nuneaton suggests that, despite the late date, the Evangelical atmosphere of George Eliot's youth, like that which the characters in *Janet's Repentance* inhabit, was that of a new and challenging approach to life, not of an already established and complacent orthodoxy. Evangelicalism introduced to Milby the 'idea of duty', the 'recognition of something to be lived for beyond the mere satisfaction of self' (*Janet's Repentance,* Chapter 10); and although the attitudes and language of her Evangelical period are strange and often repugnant, it is the George Eliot we know who responded to that idea, just as when she rejected Christianity she responded to what she thought a higher idea of duty. But when she looked back on her youth it was a more humane, less well-instructed and intellectually consequent Protestantism than her own that she revered. The following anecdote concerns her Methodist aunt Mrs Samuel Evans:

'When my uncle came to fetch her, after she had been with us a fortnight or three weeks, he was speaking of a deceased minister, once greatly respected, who from the action of trouble upon him had taken to small tippling, though otherwise not culpable. "But I hope the good man's in heaven for all that," said my uncle. "O yes," said my aunt, with a deep inward groan of joyful conviction. "Mr. A's in heaven—that's sure." This was at the time an offence to my stern, ascetic hard views—how beautiful it is to me now!'[4]

Miss Evans was a Churchwoman and a Calvinist; her aunt was a dissenter and an Arminian. But tolerence is not a common quality in adolescents whatever their beliefs, and it would be quite wrong to construct upon this a comparison of the Evangelical and Wesleyan movements.

Two cardinal characteristics of Miss Evans's beliefs at this period are illustrated in the following quotations from her letters. The first is on the subject of Oratorio:

'I think nothing can justify the using of an intensely interesting and solemn passage of Scripture, as a rope-dancer user her rope, or as a sculptor the pedestal on which he places the statue, that is alone intended to elicit admiration . . . I ask myself can it be desirable, and would it be consistent with millenial holiness for a human being to devote the time and energies that are barely sufficient for real exigencies on acquiring expertness in trills, cadences, etc.?'[5]

The next passage is about her own feelings for a man:

'Why do we yearn after a fellow mortal but because we do not live and delight in conscious union with Him who condescends to say, "Ye shall no more call me Baali or Lord, but ye shall call me Ishi, my husband".'[6]

We shall see that George Eliot came very rapidly to reverse these attitudes; also that they are perfect texts for Feuerbach's interpretation of Christianity as an alienation of man's reverence from its proper object—his own species. At the same time it must be said that this recoil from earthly pleasures and human relationships is very natural in an adolescent of strong religious instincts and an equally strong spontaneous delight in life and the senses. It might be a protective recoil from emotional complexity and pain; it is certainly an expression of George Eliot's permanent religious need to take her stand by and revere something outside herself.

In 1841 George Eliot moved with her family to Coventry, where she became intimate with Mr and Mrs Charles Bray and Mrs Bray's sister, Sara Hennell. These were life-long friendships, and many of George Eliot's most interesting letters over the next forty years were written to the Brays and Miss Hennell. Bray was a 'free-thinking' ribbon manufacturer, author of *A Philosophy of Necessity* and editor of the *Coventry Herald,* the first journal in which George Eliot was published.[7] Mrs Bray and Miss Hennell were Unitarians. George Eliot's loss of faith was precipitated by reading *An Inquiry into the Origins of Christianity* by C. C. Hennell, Mrs Bray's brother. This book was the result of an investigation begun with the intention of justifying the Gospels as historical records, but whose outcome was the conviction that this basis is unsound. Hennell worked in ignorance of the work of David Strauss, who paid tribute to the *Inquiry,* as a genuine piece of independent Biblical criticism. Like all the heterodox authors whom George Eliot found congenial —Strauss, Feuerbach and Comte—Hennell wrote in a spirit of reverence and tenderness for his subject, quite free from the conceit of enlightenment.[8]

I use the word 'precipitated' advisedly. As Professor Haight has said, 'To attribute the change in her religious view solely to the Brays' influence oversimplifies. It would have come in any case.'[9] George Eliot's friend Mrs Congreve tells us that when asked what had begun the change in her beliefs she replied, 'Walter Scott—he was healthy and historical and it would not fit onto [my] creed'.[10] She must also have felt in the pleasure and extension of sympathies derived from imaginative fiction a good that 'would not fit onto her creed'.

At this point the influence of Wordsworth should be mentioned. On her twentieth birthday George Eliot wrote enthusiastically about Wordsworth to Miss Lewis, with the reservation that 'What I could wish to have added to many of my favourite morceaux is an indication of less satisfaction in terrene objects, a more frequent upturning of the soul's eye.' But she goes on to say immediately, 'I never before met with so many of my own feelings, expressed just as I could [wish] like them.'[11] Those two sentences have the effect of a pivot, expressing the conflict that was not to reach a crisis until two years later. Even the stilted diction of her Evangelical years ceases as she expresses her enthusiasm. The influence of Wordsworth counted for a great deal in the Pantheism that she temporarily espoused after her loss of faith; but Wordsworth's perception of the divine in the love of men for nature and for each other was something that outlasted her Pantheism and became a part of her general belief. The importance of *sympathy*, a crucial word in her moral and aesthetic vocabulary, was first learnt from Wordsworth before she found it confirmed in Comte and Feuerbach. She wrote of *Silas Marner*, 'I should not have believed that anyone would have been interested in it but myself (since William Wordsworth is dead). . . . '[12] In 1858 she and Lewes were reading him 'with fresh admiration for his beauties and tolerance for his faults',[13] and 1877 she wrote to a correspondent, 'I am delighted to see . . . how we are agreed in loving our incomparable Wordsworth.'[14] In Chapter 5 of *Adam Bede*, with reference to Mr Irwine's devotion to his invalid sister, she draws a moral about 'the existence of insignificant people' identical to that of 'The Old Cumberland Beggar'.

Her rejection of Christianity was a positive movement of the spirit, and while one should not discount the pain it must have caused—quite apart from the pain of conflict with her family—there is a feeling of enormous relief in the following passage from a letter written less than a year later:

'I could shed tears of joy to believe that in this lovely world I may lie on the grass and ruminate on possibilities without dreading lest my conclusions should be everlastingly fatal. It seems to me that the awful anticipations entailed by a reception of all the dogmas in the New Testament operate unfavourably on moral beauty by disturbing that spontaneity, that choice of the good for its own sake, that answers my ideal.'[15]

In the years immediately following she appears, by her own account, to have embraced a form of Pantheism. Hennell was a Pantheist, and at this time George Eliot was also reading Spinoza, whose *Tractatus Theologico-Politicus* she began to translate. In a letter to Harriet Beecher Stowe written in 1869 she says, 'For years of my youth I dwelt in dreams of a pantheistic sort, falsely supposing that I was enlarging my sympathy.' Her reasons for rejecting Pantheism are characteristic: 'it is an attempt to look at the universe from the outside of our relations to it (the universe) as human beings. As healthy, sane human beings we must love and hate—love what is good for mankind, hate what is evil for mankind.'[16]

There was no other spiritual revolution like that of 1841, and it is difficult to put dates to the further development of her mind. One can say that in the 1840s the cast of her mind was metaphysical and, in politics, radical—both tendencies which were gradually reversed. Her loss of faith freed her mind from dogmas, but she continued to express her religious feelings in supernaturalistic language:

> 'I fully participate in the belief that the only heaven here or hereafter is to be found in conformity with the will of the Supreme; a continual aiming at the attainment of that perfect ideal, the true logos that dwells in the bosom of the One Father.'[17]

In 1848 she sympathised with the revolutions in France and Italy, warmly admiring Louis Blanc and Mazzini— though even at this time she said, 'I should have no hope of good from any imitative movement at home. Our working classes are eminently inferior to the mass of the French people.'[18] In 1873 she was writing to John Blackwood, 'I wish there were some solid, philosophical Conservative to take the reins.'[19]

Having used the word 'Positivism' several times, I must now give some indication of the sense in which it can properly be used to describe convictions that George Eliot actually held. The word can easily cause confusion, since it has a broad and a narrow meaning, whose implications are quite different, though both are derived from the writings of Auguste Comte. In its broad sense, Positivism is a general intellectual movement which began before Comte and is still very influential, but was perhaps the most marked characteristic of the intellectual life of the mid-nineteenth century, manifested not only in men who were directly influenced by Comte, such as J. S. Mill and G. H. Lewes, but also in men working in such diverse disciplines as Herbert Spencer and Ludwig Feuerbach, whose thought was quite independent of Comte. This movement was a rejection of metaphysical speculation, of inquiry into First Causes, and an extension of the areas of study open to investigation by the methods of natural science. The primary connotation of the word Positive is *real:* the Positivist confines his attention to the world of phenomena; he does not construct theories of the universe on the basis of speculation spun from his own mind. This could result in crudities, even in men of great intellectual distinction—for example, Herbert Spencer's defence of the form of economic conservatism known as 'Social Darwinism' on the grounds that 'if the unworthy are helped to increase, by shielding them from that mortality which their unworthiness would naturally entail, the effect is to produce, generation after generation, a greater unworthiness'[20]—the crude assumption being, that natural selection tends to favour those qualities which, by human evaluation, are regarded as 'worthy'. But I have found only one example of such 'scientific' naivety in the works of George Eliot herself—an attempt to suggest a physiological basis for the differences in temperament of English and French women.[21]

The distinction of Auguste Comte is that he clearly recognised and gave systematic expression to this development. He is an instance of a writer not himself of the greatest, who exerted a strong influence on minds much finer than his own—most notably on George Eliot and John Stuart Mill.

In his *Cours de Philosophie Positive* Comte developed the two fundamental laws of his system. The law of the Hierarchy of Sciences—mathematics, astronomy, physics, chemistry, biology and sociology—was mentioned earlier. The second law, that of the Three Stages, states that the human mind develops from a Theological interpretation of the world (attributing causation to the will of a divine Being or Beings) through the Metaphysical (substituting abstract Forms or Entities for the personal God) to the Positive (recognising the existence of immutable laws in nature). The theological stage itself is divided into fetishism, polytheism and monotheism. He argues that the sciences successively come to be studied in a positive manner (what we would call a scientific manner): the simplest sciences have been positive for centuries; biology became so only recently; only the most complex science, which he variously called Social Physics, Sociology (a word he invented) and the Science of Humanity, remains under the dominion of Theology. In his most primitive state, man attributes volition to everything. Subsequently this Will is transferred from objects to the Deity. As men become acquainted with the laws of nature, the operation of God's will is progressively restricted. Thus few people now think that God directly intervenes to make an apple fall from a tree, but most people believe that he is constantly intervening in human life.

This is the broad basis of Positivism; but there is a great deal more to Comte's system, especially as it was developed in his later work, the *Système de Politique Positive*. Comte conceived of Positivism not only as a theory of knowledge but as a basis for the reform of society and, ultimately, as a new religion. In particular, he proposed it as a way out of the social and moral chaos of which, as a Frenchman whose lifetime had been a period of almost continuous revolution and reaction, he was acutely conscious. His motto was *Ordre et Progrès*—a synthesis of the conservative and revolutionary principles, which is echoed in George Eliot's 'Address to Working Men by Felix Holt'.[22] At the centre of his philosophy is the idea of Humanity: 'Man indeed, as an individual, cannot properly be said to exist, except in the exaggerated abstractions of modern metaphysicians. Existence in the true sense can only be predicated of Humanity.'[23]

This proposition expresses the inter-connection and interdependence of men not merely as a moral duty but as an objective fact. Men are linked by the principles of solidarity and continuity: sympathy between the living, duty to those not yet born and indebtedness to the dead. In the Positive Religion which Comte prescribes in detail in the fourth volume of the *Politique Positive*, Humanity is worshipped as the Great Being. In this part of his work, in which he details a social system and religion in which each class and each nation will, recognising the objective rightness of his proposals, docilely submit to the rôles he prescribes for them, he becomes more and more remote from reality.

To appreciate what George Eliot found of value in all this we must have some general idea of the questions which preoccupied her throughout her mature life, and which are investigated in the novels. What, when faith in a personal God has been lost, can the individual find outside himself to give his life meaning and integrity? Can anything be salvaged from the loss, or is Christianity no more than what Nietzsche saw as 'a transcendence rigged up to slander mortal existence'?[24] What can a man rationally propose to himself as an alternative to unbridled egotism? Why do so many people in fact subdue their egos and live for others, and for such a variety of ostensible reasons? What is the true relation of man, with his overwhelming sense of his own importance, to the impersonal laws of the world in which he lives?

There is no evidence that George Eliot was at any time tempted to agree with Nietzsche that morality, as well as the Christian religion, was a slander on life. On the contrary, one of the most important reasons for her dissatisfaction with Christianity was that it proposed a fundamentally selfish reason for moral action:

'I fear the fatal fact about your story is the absence of God and Hell. "My dear madam, you have not presented *motives* to the children!" It is really hideous to find that those who sit in the scribes' seats have got no farther than the appeal to selfishness which they call God. The old Talmudists were better teachers. They make Rachel remonstrate with God for his hardness, and remind him that she was kinder to her sister Leah than He to his people—thus correcting the traditional God by human sympathy.'[25]

A major attraction of Comte's philosophy was that he explicitly rejected selfish motives for moral action:

'The social sentiment has hitherto been cultivated only in an indirect and even contradictory manner, under the theological philosophy first, which gave a character of exorbitant selfishness to all moral acts; and then under the metaphysical, which bases morality on self-interest. Human faculties, affective as well as intellectual, can be developed only by habitual exercise; and positive morality, which teaches the habitual practice of goodness without any other certain recompense than internal satisfaction, must be much more favourable to the growth of the benevolent affections than any doctrine which attaches devotedness itself to personal considerations.'[26]

The compensations of Christianity are replaced by a more genuine altruism (another word coined by Comte) based on the conception of Humanity.

'If the idea of *Society* still seems to many people to be an abstraction having no existence except in the mind, this is because they are still under the influence of the old philosophy. Really it is the idea of the *Individual* that is an abstraction—at all events in our species. The tendency of the new philosophy as a whole will always be to bring into prominence, in active no less than in speculative life, the tie which unites us each to all, in a multitude of different ways.'[27]

Thus the rejection of God, of theology and the supernatural, and the concentration on the real and 'positive', far from causing a disintegration of morality, in fact reveals its true basis in natural law: in the links which bind men into Humanity, which had been disguised by Christianity's exaltation of the Individual. Both Comte and Feuerbach point out that, whereas their anti-theological universe is governed by immutable laws, the Christian universe is governed by an arbitrary Will, an apotheosis of the human ego, an attempt by the Individual to reverse his relation to Nature by subjecting it to an image of himself.[28] George Eliot's sense of the danger of theological morality is expressed in the characters of Bulstrode in *Middlemarch* and Savonarola in *Romola,* who cannot distinguish between their own wills and that of God.

The conception of Humanity as more real than the Individual, and linked by natural laws, is clearly a basis for a morality of some kind, but it is not sufficient to explain the peculiar attraction of Comte for George Eliot. Humanity as so far defined[29] is compatible with the Utilitarian morality of the greatest happiness of the greatest number. An objective basis for morality was not all that George Eliot needed. Her attachment to her personal and cultural past, her belief that her moral nature was formed by and dependent on the past that she had in many ways rejected, and her conviction that 'precious sentiments and habits of mind' are carried 'in solution'[30] in established forms of society and religion, made her hostile to any philosophy which entailed a sharp break with and contempt for past beliefs and ways of feeling. Also, the value she attached to feeling (and her own deeply emotional nature) prevented her from embracing any system that subordinated feeling to intellect.

Comte's system satisfied both these requirements. He treats all past states of feeling and belief with reverence as necessary and valuable contributions to human development. This is an essential part of the principle of Continuity, which defines Humanity not merely as those people living in the present, but as all who have been and are to be. Comte says:

> 'Being no longer able to believe in the prolongation of his existence except through the continuity of the species, the individual will thus be led to incorporate himself with it as completely as possible by associating himself profoundly with its whole collective existence not only in the present but also in the past and even more in the future.'[31]

Comte satisfies both George Eliot's intellectual and her emotional nature by simultaneously providing (in her view) a more objective basis for morality and showing it to be dependent on the reverence for the past which was part of her own moral nature. That the principle of Continuity issues in a morality very different from the Utilitarian can be seen throughout her works: in Maggie Tulliver's refusal of Stephen Guest; in Romola's refusal to disperse her father's library after his death; in Dorothea's willingness to promise to finish the *Key to All Mythologies;* in Deronda's accept-ance of a racial destiny and the implied condemnation of his mother for trying to thwart her father's will. The reverence for all religions, and above all for Christianity, which the principle of Continuity entails, allows George Eliot to main-tain communication with her own religious past and supports her refusal to be a militant atheist and her respect for any religious belief that fosters human sympathies.[32] That George Eliot had arrived at the principle of Continuity some years before she read Comte can be seen in the following extract from a letter written in 1843:

'We find that the intellectual errors which we once fancied were a mere incrustation have grown into the living body and that we cannot in the majority of causes, wrench them away without destroying vitality. We begin to find that with individuals, as with nations, the only safe revolution is one arising out of the wants which their *own progress* has generated.'[33]

George Eliot's emotional and intellectual needs are also reconciled by the fact that this scientific morality gives feeling predominance over intellect:

'In the treatment of social questions Positive science will be found utterly to discard those proud illusions of the supremacy of reason, to which it had been liable during its preliminary stages. Ratifying, in this respect, the common experience of men even more forcibly than Catholicism, it teaches us that individual happiness and public welfare are far more dependent upon the heart than upon the intellect.'[34]

The function of the intellect is to discern the bonds of dependence and responsibility on which human life depends. The bonds themselves are entirely affective: 'I have had heart-cutting experience that opinions are a poor cement between human souls; and the only effect I ardently long to produce by my writings, is that those who read them should be better able to *imagine* and to *feel* the pains and the joys of those who differ from themselves in everything but the broad fact of being struggling erring human creatures.'[35]

Ludwig Feuerbach, whose *Essence of Christianity* Marian Evans translated in 1853-4 (the only work she published under her own name) set out, like Comte, to establish Humanity as the proper object of man's reverence. He is a much more engaging writer than Comte, and can be more happily recommended to the student of George Eliot. In Feuerbach there is no prescriptive or utopian tendency, though he does look forward to a time when men will recognise the divinity of their own nature. Although George Eliot wrote to Mrs Congreve, wife of the leading English Positivist, 'My gratitude increases continually for the illumination Comte has contributed to my life',[36] it was necessary for her to practise discrimination in her assimilation of his ideas, and she is reported to have tartly remarked, 'I cannot submit my intellect or my soul to the guidance of

Comte,'[37]—clearly a reference to Comte's sacerdotal pretensions. She could never have said of Comte what she said when she was translating *The Essence of Christianity*, 'With the ideas of Feuerbach I everywhere agree'.[38]

While Comte traces the development from the Theological to the Positive in man's understanding of the world, and attempts to place moral law on a positive basis, Feuerbach's central task is an analysis of the idea of God as a projection of man's idea of himself. Because the predicates or attributes of God—Justice, Mercy, Love—are human, it follows that the subject, God himself, is also human. He argues this by saying that whereas the predicates themselves are not dependent for their reality on the idea of God—they are positively perceived to exist—God is dependent on the predicates.

> 'The divine being is nothing else than the human being, or, rather the human nature purified, freed from the limits of the individual man, made objective—*i.e.*, contemplated and revered as another, a distinct being. All the attributes of the divine nature are, therefore, attributes of the human nature.
>
> In relation to the attributes, the predicates, of the Divine Being, this is admitted without hesitation, but by no means in relation to the subject of these predicates. The negation of the subject is held to be irreligion, nay, atheism; though not so the negation of the predicates.'[39]

The last phrase refers to the fact that a man is still considered religious if he declares that 'God cannot be defined', that he is 'unknowable'—an idea perhaps most familiar to English readers in Pope's *Essay on Man:* 'Presume not God to scan'. For Feuerbach, however, this is true atheism; it is robbing God of his qualities and therefore of his reality, and it also denies the divinity of the qualities (Love, Justice, Mercy), by which God is made real. Feuerbach's great strength is his understanding of and sympathy with real, common religious feeling, as distinct from the abstract speculations of theology and metaphysics. This strength is perhaps most apparent in his attack on the notion of an unknowable God:

> 'The alleged religious horror of limiting God by positive predicates, is only the irreligious wish to know nothing more of God, to banish God from the mind. Dread of limitation is dread of

existence. All real existence, *i.e.*, all existence which is truly such, is qualitative, determinate existence. He who earnestly believes in the Divine existence, is not shocked at the attributing even of gross sensuous qualities to God. He who dreads an existence that may give offence, who shrinks from the grossness of a positive predicate, may as well renounce existence altogether.'[40]

Although the divine nature is nothing more than human nature seen as an object, it is of the essence of religion that the believer is unaware of this. In projecting his own attributes on to a being outside himself he alienates himself from his own nature and denies in himself the possession of the qualities that he attributes to God.

For Feuerbach, as for Comte, the proper object of reverence is the species, or Humanity, as distinct from the individual. His specific criticism of Christianity is that Christians, unlike the heathen Greeks and Romans, place too much emphasis on the individual:

'Though (the heathens) thought highly of the race, highly of the excellences of mankind, highly and sublimely of the intelligence, they nevertheless thought slightly of the individual. Christianity, on the contrary, cared nothing for the species, and had only the individual in its eye and mind . . .

To Christianity the individual was the object of an immediate Providence, that is, an immediate object of the Divine Being. The heathens believed in a Providence for the individual, only through his relation to the race, through law, through the order of the world, and thus only in a mediate, natural, and not miraculous Providence; but the Christians left out the intermediate process, and placed themselves in immediate connexion with the prescient, all-embracing, universal being.'[41]

Apart from the invitation to egoism implied in the individual Providence, the identification of the individual with the species is harmful because it disguises the true nature of the Divine Being, i.e. Humanity. Looking into himself, the Christian perceives himself to be infinitely weak and sinful compared with God, and concludes that mankind is worthless; 'the individual does not recognise himself as a part of mankind, but identifies himself with the species, and for this reason makes his own sins, limits and weaknesses, the sins, limits and weaknesses of mankind in general.'[42] Whereas in fact, according to Feuerbach, 'men compensate for each other, so that taken as a whole they are as they should be, they present the perfect man.'[43] He does not discuss the fact that in their vices as well as their virtues men compensate for each other, and that Humanity could with equal logic be described as perfectly wicked. One would like to have seen George Eliot confronted with D. H. Lawrence's argument that 'Humanity is less, far less than the individual, because the individual may sometimes be capable of truth, and humanity is a tree of lies.'[44]

But if the logic of his idealisation of the species is faulty, Feuerbach's strength comes out again in his account of the way in which the idea of the species is made real to the individual through love:

> 'Man and woman are the complement of each other, and thus united they first present the species, the perfect man. Without species, love is inconceivable . . . In love, the reality of the species, which otherwise is only a thing of reason, an object of mere thought becomes a matter of feeling. a truth of feeling;[45] for in love, man declares himself unsatisfied in his individuality taken by itself, he postulates the existence of another as a need of the heart; he reckons another as part of his own being; he declares the life which he has through love to be the truly human life, corresponding to the idea of man, *i.e.*, of the species.'[46]

This confirms Comte's insistence on the primacy of the affections.

Like that of Comte, the influence of Feuerbach on George Eliot is pervasive. Since the objective essence of Christianity is shown to be the moral values which it propounds, the negation of God does not present a threat to morality: rather, it is strengthened. As in Comte, the object of moral action is transferred from the reward of the individual to the benefit of the species, thus supporting altruism. And, again as in Comte, the rational interpretation of an irrational belief is seen to glorify, not depreciate, the life of the feelings. One element in Feuerbach is likely to have had an important personal influence on George Eliot, namely his glorification of love, and especially sexual love, and his insistence that marriage is only truly moral when it is a 'free bond of love'.[47]

George Eliot was working on the translation in the months when she was deciding whether to live with G. H. Lewes, and she left for the Continent with him shortly after seeing it through the press.

By far the strongest influence on the novels, is on the portrayal of religious characters and religious experience. One particular parallel might be noted here:

'Faith in Providence is faith in one's own worth, the faith of man in himself; hence the beneficent consequences of this faith, but hence also false humility, religious arrogance, which, it is true, does not rely on itself, but only because it commits the care of itself to the blessed God. God concerns himself about me; he has in view my happiness, my salvation; he wills that I shall be blest; but that is my will also: thus, my interest is God's interest, my own will is God's will, my own aim is God's aim,— God's love for me nothing else than my self-love deified.'[48]

'In vain he said to himself that, if permitted, it would be a divine visitation, a chastisement, a preparation: he recoiled from the imagined burning; and he judged that it must be more for the Divine glory that he should escape dishonour.'[49]

George Eliot of course had a direct and personal acquaintance with Providence and the Evangelical conscience, but one can see that the sureness of the portrayal of Bulstrode's inability to distinguish between the Divine will and his own in *Middlemarch* owes something to Feuerbach. More generally, George Eliot's ability to dramatise her own principles in such characters as Edgar Tryan, Dinah Morris and Camden Farebrother is dependent on her belief, firmly grounded in Feuerbach, that 'the idea of God, so far as it has been a high spiritual influence, is the ideal of a goodness entirely human'.[50] We shall see apropos of *Daniel Deronda*, however, that the absorption of Feuerbach, like that of Comte, was not entirely beneficial to her art.

George Eliot's beliefs concerning the Individual and the Species are a great deal more complex than a mere amalgam of Comte and Feuerbach, however. The following passage from a letter to Charles Bray is of the utmost significance in considering her relation to any form of species-worship:

'I dislike extremely a passage [in *The Philosophy of Necessity*] in which you appear to consider the disregard of individuals as a lofty condition of mind. My own experience and development deepen every day my conviction that our moral progress may be measured by the degree in which we sympathise with individual suffering and individual joy. The fact that in the scheme of things we see a constant and tremendous sacrifice of individuals is, it seems to me only one of the many proofs that urge upon us our total inability to find in our own natures a key to the Divine Mystery.'[51]

The worship of Humanity runs easily to an afflatus which obscures the fact that the species is meaningless without the individual; and George Eliot would never have said, with Comte, that the individual cannot properly be said to exist —unless as a dialectical antithesis to the fact that the species cannot properly be said to exist. Both statements are equally meaningless unless it is recognised that, as the individual is completed by the species, so the species consists of individuals. The perception of this dialectic is fundamental to the art of her novels—one might say fundamental to the fact of her being a novelist. This will be given further consideration in the section on George Eliot and Tragedy.

Conservatism

It appears that as George Eliot came to adopt a 'positive' attitude to society, she became more conservative. It will be useful to pursue more closely an investigation into the nature of her conservatism, which is very much evident in several of the novels.

We must first recognise that, lying deeper than any theories about society, there is an intensely strong feeling about her personal past, which becomes part and parcel of a sense of the social and national past:

'Life did change for Tom and Maggie; and yet they were not wrong in believing that the thoughts and loves of these first years would always make part of their lives. We could never have loved the earth so well if we had had no childhood in it— if it were not the earth where the same flowers come up again every spring that we used to gather with our tiny fingers as we sat lisping to ourselves on the grass—the same hips and haws on the autumn hedgerows—the same redbreasts that we used to call "God's Birds", because they did no harm to the precious crops. What novelty is worth that sweet montony where everything is known, and *loved* because it is known?'[52]

Here the sense of the past might appear quite simply to be no more than a sense of nature, but it is more than this: it implies a feeling about the social world which the 'autumn hedgerows' represent. I am supported in this contention by George Eliot herself who explicitly acknowledged it in one of her last essays:

'And I often smile at my consciousness that certain conservative prepossessions have mingled themselves for me with the influences of our midland scenery, from the tops of the elms down to the buttercups and the little wayside vetches.'[53]

The nostalgic rhapsody on Leisure at the end of Chapter 52 of *Adam Bede* is a good example of this mingling.

George Eliot espoused no theory which was not confirmed by her own feelings, and the feelings expressed in these passages provided the soil for the Comtean principle of Continuity. We see her using Comte's terminology in her note on 'Historic Guidance':

'The criticism on radical, revolutionary schemes, that they are a breach of continuity, has to be justified by showing that they are made futile by the continuous existence of conditions resulting from the past which either obstinately oppose themselves to the immediate amelioration of things by statute and the high hand and so turn the proposed reform into a fatal condoning and avowal of disregard to the laws and constitution, or else carry in solution precious sentiments and habits of mind which would make it socially pernicious to expunge them. And yet the critic may himself look forward with hope to the gradual disappearance of these inherited conditions, many of them being simply reducible to massive ignorance and low moral tone.'[54]

We see here two considerations. The conditions which are the cause of an imperfect social order *will* persist despite revolutionary attempts to alter their manifestations; and even a faulty social order contains valuable qualities which are in danger of being destroyed along with the faults. The implied assumption in both cases is that society is an organism which expresses the whole moral nature of its human constituents. This assumption is made explicit in George Eliot's review of two works by the conservative German sociologist, W. H. Riehl:

'[Riehl] sees in European society *incarnate history,* and any attempt to disengage it from its historical elements must, he believes, be simply destructive of social vitality. What has grown up historically can only die out historically, by the gradual operation of necessary laws. The external conditions which society has inherited from the past are but the manifestation of inherited internal conditions in the human beings who compose it; the internal conditions and the external are related to each other as the organism and its medium, and development can take place only by the gradual consentaneous development of both.'[55]

The direct application of this is to the lawmaker, politician or revolutionary attempting to change society—a subject not much touched on in George Eliot's novels. But the relation between 'internal and external conditions' is of equal importance in the individual's attempts to live his own life within a society, and this is a central preoccupation of nearly all the novels.

The passage quoted above, although it represents something that George Eliot assented to, is virtually a translation of Riehl himself.[56] It will be profitable to move on from this to a passage in the same essay which is entirely original, and which links George Eliot's social attitudes directly to her artistic preoccupations:

'The historical conditions of society may be compared with those of language . . . Suppose . . . that the effort . . . to construct a universal language on a rational basis has at length succeeded, and that you have a language which has no uncertainty, no whims of idiom, no cumbrous forms, no fitful shimmer of many-hued significance, no hoary archaisms "familiar with forgotten years"—a patently de-odorized and non resonant language, which effects the purpose of communication as perfectly and rapidly as algebraic signs. Your language may be a perfect medium of expression to science, but will never express *life,* which is a great deal more than science. With the anomalies and inconveniences of historical language, you will have parted with its music and its passion, with its vital qualities as an expression of individual character, with its subtle capabilities of wit, with everything that gives it power over the imagination.'[57]

This emphasis on *life* is less common with George Eliot than with many great novelists and the separation of 'life' from 'science', implying a divergence from Comte's Science of Humanity, suggests again that for the novelist there is no culminating science but an infinitely increasing complexity. This essay was written at the time (1856) when George Eliot was preparing herself for her first attempt at fiction, and it is tempting to conclude that the peculiar emphasis on 'life' was prompted by just this sense of the complexity of what she was proposing to represent.

The substance of this comparison is that a social organisation is as much the creation and expression of the individuals whom it encompasses as a language is: 'any attempt to disengage it from its historical elements must . . . be simply destructive of social vitality.' The problem that faces the novelist is to account for the social tensions which are unquestionably present in life, and more particularly in the lives of exceptionally fine and valuable individuals—the Maggies, Dorotheas and Lydgates.

A key phrase in the first quotation from the Riehl review is 'inherited internal conditions'. Societies change, and change can only come as a consequence of changes in the individuals composing them. Yet the societies which George Eliot portrays are dominated by inherited feelings, attitudes and beliefs, customs and prejudices. The majority of the characters who compose the societies—the Poysers, Dodsons, Chettams, Brookes, Vincys and Mallingers—live entirely by these inherited feelings; they originate nothing. It is clear that change, even the gradual organic change favoured by George Eliot, must come through the gradual addition of new elements of practice and belief, in individuals whose natures are not satisfied by inherited feelings. Such are Maggie, Dorothea and Lydgate. They are not necessarily conscious originators, but they are usually made conscious that they are different, and their lives have a tragic potential (though they are not the *only* characters in George Eliot whose lives have this potential). The process of social change is dramatised as conflict between the individual who adds to the stock of inheritance and the mass who live by what they themselves have inherited.

Such conflicts are not unusual in literature. What is peculiar to George Eliot, what makes her essentially un-Romantic and gives the compelling sense of of normativeness which characterises her work, is her comprehensive vision of the process, giving full weight and value to the forces of conservation. The Maggies and Lydgates are her heroes because it is primarily in their lives that the drama occurs, but she is equally concerned for the Dodsons and the Vincys. This important characteristic has been well defined by one of her earliest biographers, Mathilde Blind:

'It may seem singular that having once, in "Armgart", drawn a woman of the highest artistic aims and ambitions, George Eliot should imply that what is most valuable in her is not the exceptional gift, but rather that part of her nature which she shares with ordinary humanity. This is, however, one of her leading beliefs, and strongly contrasts her, as a teacher, with Carlyle. To the author of "Hero Worship" the promiscuous mass—moiling and toiling as factory hands and artisans, as miners and labourers—only represents so much raw material, from which is produced that final result and last triumph of the combination of human forces—the great statesman, great warrior, great poet, and so forth. To George Eliot, on the contrary —and this is the democratic side of her nature—it is this multitude, so charily treated by destiny, which claims deepest sympathy and tenderest compassion; so that all greatness, in her eyes, is not a privilege, but a debt, which entails on its possessor a more strenuous effort, a completer devotion to the service of average humanity.'[58]

It is highly characteristic of George Eliot that her 'democratic' side should also be her conservative side. It is also characteristically a combination of emotional and intellectual forces: her attachment to the period of her youth and the common people among whom she grew up, and her belief (supported by Riehl) that the mass are ruled by custom.

It is part of the purpose of the following chapters to trace the influence of this conservative strain in the novels, and to examine the balances of sympathy in George Eliot's portrayal of the conflict between the innovating individual and the mass.

Determinism

One of the foundations of George Eliot's morality is the belief in the importance of reconciling individual aspirations with impersonal necessity. The scientific, anti-theological, anti-metaphysical movement of thought to which she adhered had a strong determinist bias, which we find her expressing when she advises John Chapman on the appointment of an editor for the *Westminster Review* in 1852:

> 'If you believe in Free Will, in the Theism that looks on manhood as a type of the godhead and on Jesus as the Ideal Man, get one belonging to the Martineau "School of thought" . . .
>
> If not—if you believe, as I do, that the thought which is to mould the Future has for its root a belief in necessity, that a nobler presentation of humanity has yet to be given in resignation to individual nothingness, than could ever be shewn of a being who believes in the phantasmagoria of hope unsustained by reason—why then get a man of another calibre . . . '[59]

One of her habitual ways of dramatizing egoism is to set the egoist's (Hetty Sorrel's, Rosamond Vincy's, Bulstrode's, or Gwendolen Harleth's) will against a clearly inevitable sequence of events, and to show the destructive results. A lack of awareness of reality and necessity is an invariable constituent of egoism in the novels; hence the *mot* which she applied to Rosamond Vincy but deleted in proof, 'the essence of stupidity is egoism'.[60] The awareness of necessity encourages 'resignation to individual nothingness', and a shifting of the self from the centre of one's sense of things. In *Middlemarch* George Eliot created a vivid image for egoism: 'We are all of us born in moral stupidity, taking the world as an udder to feed our supreme selves',[61] an image which reminds us that self-centredness is a natural state. The greatest of George Eliot's egoists is called 'The Spoiled Child'. By contrast, one of her highest forms of praise is that which she bestows on Mrs Garth: 'she had that rare sense which discerns what is unalterable, and submits to it without murmuring'.[62]

From this account it might seem that we must agree with the following statement by Mr George Levine:

'The insistence on unity, harmony, duty, and slow growth, which we have seen in George Eliot's broad social analyses and in her minute psychological investigations of egoism and division within a single human soul, obviously has its roots in a moral bias. But the bias, for George Eliot, has its rational justification in determinism.'[63]

We shall find, however, that both her attitude to determinism and her 'moral bias' are complex matters.

The thinker who is convinced that free-will is objectively an illusion is faced with a paradox: that this conviction does not prevent him from making choices and taking them as seriously as if he believed in free-will. Further, on examining his idea of himself, he may feel that the sense of responsibility for his own actions is an important part of his humanity; he may prefer to be held responsible even for a crime, rather than be excused on the grounds of determining circumstances. In the words of a youth convicted of manslaughter, quoted in a newspaper, 'I blame myself . . . . I don't blame the estate. Some of them are saying there was nothing else to do on the estate. But there was so much to do, only you didn't realise . . . . Parents just don't understand. I wish they would. My mother thinks I'm a little angel . . . I wish they'd realise what I've done'.[64]

No reader of George Eliot's novels could fail to recognise that she regards responsibility and moral choice as realities. She is explicit about the matter on numerous occasions. The following passages are from letters to a lady who confided to her a sense of meaninglessness in a determined universe:

'As to the necessary combinations through which life is manifested, and which seem to present themselves to you as a hideous fatalism, which ought logically to petrify your volition—have they, *in fact*, any such influence on your ordinary course of action in the primary affairs of your existence as a human, social, domestic creature?'

'I shall not be satisfied with your philosophy till you have conciliated necessitarianism—I hate the ugly word—with the practice of willing strongly, willing to will strongly, and so on, that being what you certainly can do and have done about a great many things in life, whence it is clear that there is nothing in truth to hinder you from it—except you will say the absence of a motive. But that absence I don't believe in, in your case—only in the case of empty barren souls.'[65]

We see her discussing the question with herself in her Notebooks:

'Life and action are prior to theorizing, and have a prior logic in the conditions necessary to maintain them. To regard any theory which supplants that logic as having supreme intellectual authority is a contradiction, unless it could be ruled that the human race should commit a slow suicide by the gradual extinction of motive—the poisoning of feeling by inference. When once we have satisfied ourselves that any one point of view is hostile to practice, which means life, it is not the dominance of intellect, but poverty of judgement, that determines us to allow its interference in guiding our conduct . . . *It is rational to accept two apparent irreconcileables, rather than to reject tested processes in favour of reasoning which tends to nullify all processes.*'[66]

On this evidence George Eliot is far from being the hidebound Victorian rationalist suggested by some caricature accounts. (Indeed it is hard to imagine how a novelist could survive without a constantly informing sense of the life that is 'prior to theorizing'.)

Many of the most striking dramatic successes in the novels are accounts of determined sequences of events: the causes and consequences of Arthur Donnithorne's seduction of Hetty Sorrel in *Adam Bede;* Bulstrode's dealings with Raffles and the career of Lydgate in *Middlemarch;* Gwendolen Harleth's acceptance of Grandcourt in *Daniel Deronda.* A discussion of these cases will appear in subsequent chapters, and it will be found that they are extremely complex: that external, social influences combine with inveterate habits of mind and that often the most powerful determinant is a moral choice previously made by the person concerned. I shall be considering one failure in this respect: the career of Tito Melema in *Romola.* With this exception, George Eliot's determinism creates the reverse of the depressing and debilitating effect that I personally experience when reading the novels of Thomas Hardy.

There is a further point to be made here. Having said that George Eliot's 'moral bias' is a complex matter, there is one aspect with which I have not yet dealt which bears an interesting relation to her determinism. This is perhaps best approached by quoting from R. H. Hutton's criticism of George Eliot's moral tone:

'. . . the total effect of her books is altogether ennobling, though the profoundly sceptical reflections with which they are penetrated may counteract, to some extent, the tonic effect of the high moral feeling with which they are coloured. Before or after most of the noblest scenes, we come to thoughts in which it is almost as impossible for the feelings delineated to live any intense or hopeful life, as it is for human beings to breathe in the vacuum of an air-pump.'

Hutton then quotes from the first paragraph of Chapter 24 of *Janet's Repentance:*

'No wonder the sick-room and the lazaretto have so often been a refuge from the tossings of intellectual doubt—a place of repose for the worn and wounded spirit. Here is a duty about which all creeds and all philosophies are at one: here, at least, the conscience will not be dogged by doubt, the benign impulse will not be checked by adverse theory: 'here you may begin to act without settling one preliminary question. To moisten the sufferer's parched lips through the long night-watches, to bear up the drooping head, to lift the helpless limbs, to divine the want that can find no utterance beyond the feeble motion of the hand or beseeching glance of the eye—these are offices that demand no self-questionings, no casuistry, no assent to propositions, no weighing of consequences. . . This blessing of serene freedom from the importunities of opinion lies in all simple direct acts of mercy, and is one source of that sweet calm which is often felt by the watcher in the sick-room, even when the duties there are of a hard and terrible kind.'

Hutton comments:

'There speaks the true George Eliot, and we may clearly say of her that in fiction it is her great aim, while illustrating what she believes to be the true facts and laws of human life, to find a fit stage for ideal feelings nobler than any which seem to her to be legitimately bred by these facts and laws. But she too often finds herself compelled to injure her own finest moral effects by the sceptical atmosphere with which she permeates them.'[67]

Hutton was one of her most intelligent contemporary critics, but he shared with many readers of his time a yearning for ideal fiction which George Eliot very often frustrated. What is important here, however, is the extent to which she shared the feeling. Hutton knew her personally, and his remark about the passage from *Janet's Repentance* is probably justified if we regard 'the true George Eliot' as the woman who was looked to almost as a priestess by those contemporaries who suffered in the Victorian vacuum of religious disillusion. But the 'Great Teacher' was not necessarily synonymous with the great novelist, and in Hutton's comments we have an interesting instance of the difference. The 'ideal feelings' that he admires are certainly present in almost all the novels, and although the modern reader's evaluation of them (or of their expression) is likely to be the opposite of Hutton's, the latter's analysis of George Eliot's intention in passages such as this—'to find a fit stage for ideal feelings nobler than any which seem to her to be legitimately bred by these facts and laws'—is very acute. The passage in question was probably inspired by her experience of nursing her father, and while it is certainly not the critic's business to pry, he may pose the general question: is such a situation *really* so much simpler and open to the expression of exalted feelings than other serious situations in life? His doubts may be reinforced by the language which George Eliot uses—'a refuge', 'a place of repose', 'serene freedom', 'sweet calm', and by the way in which the fact that 'the duties there are of a hard and terrible kind' is almost dismissed in an appendage, and has no qualifying effect on the foregoing exaltation; whereas if it had been presented as a reality it would have placed some difficulty in the way of such words as 'refuge', 'repose', 'serene', and 'sweet'. 'A refuge from the tossings of intellectual doubt' seems strange, coming from the author who little over a year before had affirmed that 'There is not a more pernicious fallacy afloat in common parlance, than the wide distinction made between intellect and morality'.[68] The criticism is given more weight when we remember the very different way in which George Eliot treats two cases of sick-bed attendance in *Middlemarch:* the crises of conscience faced by Lydgate and Bulstrode over Raffles, and by Mary Garth over Featherstone's last wish.

The tendency indicated by this passage appears in a clearer perspective in Chapters 61 and 68 of *Romola* where the heroine tries to abandon self-responsibility by drifting away in a boat, and finds herself in a village stricken by the plague, where she devotes herself to nursing the sick and is apotheosised as the Madonna. We are meant to judge Romola's selfish despair in the light of her subsequent experience of a situation in which she can devote herself to the good of others with 'no self-questionings'.

One is tempted to interpret Hutton's statement of George Eliot's intention in scenes such as the sick-room in *Janet's Repentance* and the plague village in *Romola* as meaning that in her portrayal of 'ideal feelings' she is deliberately escaping from the determined universe which engenders the 'sceptical atmosphere' of her novels. The yearning for such moral situations, one might say, is the yearning for a life not determined by antecedent moral choices and by 'a wider public life'[69]—in which the individual is free to fashion his own circumstances. But the case of Romola, in particular, shows this to be a simplification. Romola's desire to drift away is a desire to have 'freed herself from all claims . . . even from that burden of choice which presses with heavier and heavier weight when claims have loosed their guiding hold'.[70] After her experience in the village she criticises this state of feeling: 'She had felt herself without bonds, without motive; sinking in mere egoistic complaining that life could bring her no content'.[71] And yet the desire to be free from choice, which is intrinsic to the state of feeling criticised, is satisfied by the subsequent event: not only does that event come about without Romola's will—'determined' almost miraculously—but it presents her with a situation in which, as in Janet's, choice is obviated.

> '—she had simply lived, with so energetic an impulse to share the life around her, to answer the call of need and do the work which cried aloud to be done, that the reasons for living, enduring, labouring, never took the form of argument.'[72]

George Eliot described these parts of *Romola* as 'romantic and symbolical elements'.[73] We can, however, certainly describe them as examples of pure determinism—though of a quite different (more 'symbolical') kind from that found elsewhere in her novels. When the character's will is in abeyance, the novel drifts as freely as the boat. More accurately, it drifts in a direction dictated by the *author's* will—her will to fashion circumstances according to desire. The same phenomenon emerges in the other large novel which contains 'romantic and symbolical elements', *Daniel Deronda*. In both cases a form of determinism is used to manipulate events in the interests of a moral and aesthetic bias quite different from that which we admire in George Eliot.

Evolution

I am indebted to Mr Paris for pointing out, in *Experiments in Life*,[74] the fact that George Eliot's conception of evolution included the inheritance of acquired characteristics. Belief in the inheritance of acquired characteristics certainly influenced the conception of *Daniel Deronda,* and since this theory is referred to in the chapter on that novel it will be useful to say something about it here. In particular, it needs to be put into its historical context.

Thought about evolution in the nineteenth century was dominated by two theories. The first, proposed by the Frenchman Lamarck in 1816, is that minute developments taking place in the life of an individual organism are transmitted to its offspring. Thus the giraffe's long neck derives from countless generations of giraffes stretching to reach the foliage on higher branches of trees. Darwin, whose *Origin of Species* appeared in 1859, accepted this as a minor influence, but argued that the main principle of evolution was the effect of natural selection favouring certain spontaneous mutations: a giraffe with a longer neck appears out of the blue, and it and its long-necked offspring find food easier to get. Darwin's theory was first challenged but ultimately confirmed by the science of genetics. G. S. Carter sums up the present state of opinion as follows: 'in the last century, in spite of much effort to prove its truth, no incontrovertible evidence in favour of [the inheritance of acquired characteristics] has been put forward, and it is very difficult to bring its truth into line with our present knowledge of genetics. It is now generally discredited, but . . . argument about it played a large part in post-Darwinian discussion, and may be revived in the future'.[75] I think it is safe to say, however, that no geneticist would countenance the use George Eliot makes of it in *Daniel Deronda*, stated thus by Mr Paris:

'After Deronda discovered his parentage and learned that his grandfather, like Mordecai, was an ardent advocate of Jewish separateness, he had "a quivering imaginative sense of close relation to the grandfather who had been animated by strong impulses and beloved thoughts, which were now perhaps being roused from their slumber within himself" (Chap. LVI). He was thus organically predisposed to assume for himself the aspirations of Mordecai and of his grandfather to establish a Jewish homeland in Palestine.'[76]

The currency of the theory in George Eliot's lifetime, however, was considerable. Comte, it is true, denied altogether the development of species out of other species in the Biology section of his *Positive Philosophy*, although he says:

'As for . . . the gradual and slow improvement of human nature, within narrow limits, it seems to me impossible to reject altogether the principle proposed (with great exaggeration, however) by Lamarck, of the necessary influence of a homogeneous and continuous excercise in producing, in every animal organism, and especially in Man, an organic improvement, susceptible of being established in the race, after a sufficient persistence.'[77]

This, as we shall see, was enough for George Eliot's purposes. She was interested in evolution only *within* humanity.

Lamarckism was much more strongly championed by Herbert Spencer. Section 82 of his *Principles of Biology* (1864) presents a sustained argument, with numerous supporting instances, in favour of the inheritance of acquired characteristics, and the following is the most succinct expression of the idea illustrated in *Daniel Deronda:* 'The forms of thought, or the accumulated and transmitted modifications of structure produced by experience, lie latent in each newly-born individual. . . .'[78]

Darwin did in fact accept the inheritance of acquired characteristics as a small element in evolution, but in *The*

Descent of Man he argues that moral qualities, if inherited at all, must be inherited in this manner, 'and in a quite subordinate degree, or not at all, by the individuals possessing such virtues having succeeded best in the struggle for life'.[79]

Darwinism and Lamarckism have, or seemed to have, very different implications for the moral life. Darwin quotes a reaction to his theory from a writer in the *Theological Review:* 'I cannot but believe that in the hour of [the evolutionists'] triumph would be sounded the knell of the virtue of mankind!'[80] The inheritance of acquired characteristics, on the other hand, is a source of moral optimism. By exerting ourselves for the good, we contribute biologically to the moral development of the race. I think that this is partly what George Eliot means when she talks about 'the moral evolution'.

> 'As a fact of mere zoological evolution, woman seems to me to have the worse share in existence. But for that very reason I would the more contend that in the moral evolution we have "an art which does mend nature". It is the function of love in the largest sense, to mitigate the harshness of all fatalities.'[81]

'Mere zoological evolution' is amoral. George Eliot, in this same letter, rejects what she calls 'the "intention of Nature" argument' as 'a pitiable fallacy'. But 'the moral evolution' is not a mere metaphor. We have seen that Comte, Spencer and (more cautiously) Darwin believed in it as an objective reality. George Eliot also believed that 'precious sentiments and habits of mind' are carried 'in solution' in social forms and traditions'[82] (a belief discussed in the section on her conservatism) and this is much more important in relation to the novels. But societies can be overthrown, and the biological inheritance is a more stable basis for that optimism which is now perhaps more alien to us than any of the qualities that come under the heading, 'Victorian':

> 'Is it not cheering to think of the youthfulness of this little planet, and the immensely greater youthfulness of our race upon it?—to think that the higher moral tendencies of human nature are yet only in their germ?'[83]

George Eliot described herself not as an optimist but as a 'meliorist',[84] meliorism being defined by the *Shorter Oxford English Dictionary* as 'the doctrine, intermediate between optimism and pessimism, which affirms that the world may be made better by human effort.' This doctrine is clearly very strongly supported by the Lamarckian theory of inheritance.

But the theory's most important contribution was to George Eliot's belief in the necessity of living by something outside the self—her continuing religious sentiment—and in particular its most prominent form, the sanctity of the past. We owe our own innate moral qualities to the efforts of our ancestors, and we have a duty to our descendants to continue the development. It is a particularly vivid and dynamic illustration of the Comtean doctrine of Continuity.

In fact the theory is almost certainly untrue in the form in which George Eliot understood it; and the sanctity of the past is the most frequent and damaging source of didacticism in the novels, above all in *The Mill on the Floss* and *Daniel Deronda*. I have given the theory this much consideration because it casts an interesting light on the relation of belief to art, especially in relation to *Daniel Deronda*.

Didacticism and Tragedy

George Eliot had a lifelong interest in tragedy and in several of her works made a conscious effort to achieve it. The conclusion of *The Mill on the Floss* is intended to be tragic, and the Transome plot in *Felix Holt* is strongly influenced by Greek tragedy. In her dramatic poem *The Spanish Gypsy*, begun before and finished after *Felix Holt*, she made her most deliberate attempt at a formally tragic work of art. When she had finished it she wrote in her Journal some 'Notes on the Spanish Gypsy and Tragedy in general':

'Suppose for a moment that our conduct at great epochs was determined entirely by reflection, without the immediate intervention of feeling which supersedes reflection, our determination as to the right would consist in an adjustment of our individual needs to the dire necessities of our lot, partly as to our natural constitution, partly as sharers of life with our fellow-beings. Tragedy consists in the terrible difficulty of this adjustment . . .

49

A good tragic subject must represent a possible, sufficiently probable, not a common action; and to be really tragic, it must represent irreparable collision between the individual and the general (in differing degrees of generality). It is the individual with whom we sympathise, and the general of which we recognise the irresistible power.'[85]

The 'possible, sufficiently probable' etc. seems merely conventional, but the rest is quite clearly of a piece with George Eliot's most persistent beliefs about life: she is thinking about tragedy as a part of life and not as a literary form to be academically defined. Most readers will I think acknowledge that the 'collision between the individual and the general' is a source of tragedy, and that it is so because the individual matters. One cannot imagine Charles Bray or Auguste Comte having a strong tragic sense. The weakness of Positivism, its limitation in relation to the full scope of George Eliot's art, is that by denying the reality of the individual it attempts to circumvent tragedy.

It has often been remarked that tragedy is essentially pagan, and irreconcilable with the Christian substitution of a man-centred Providence for impersonal Fate. Since Positivism, while rejecting Providence, withdraws from a tragic expression of life, George Eliot needed another inspiration, and this she got from Greek tragedy, in which she was immersed throughout her writing life, and particularly in the years 1856-58.[86] Her fundamental belief in the irrevocableness of deeds, while obviously not incompatible with the Christian doctrine of repentance and forgiveness, places a significantly different emphasis, and finds one form of expression in the tragic concept of Nemesis, for which modern civilisation has no word. Nemesis plays a part in the lives of many of George Eliot's characters, notably Arthur Donnithorne, Mrs. Transome, Bulstrode and Gwendolen Harleth.

The Spanish Gypsy, however, is not a tragedy. The love of Don Silva, a Spanish hidalgo, and Fedalma, a Gypsy foundling, is threatened when Fedalma's father Zarca reveals himself to her as the leader of his tribe, and persuades her that it is her hereditary duty to join him and serve her people. Don Silva responds by joining the Gypsies, renouncing his people and faith for the sake of his love; but when

Zarca attacks the town which it had been Silva's duty to defend, Silva's own hereditary loyalties determine him, and he kills Zarca, thus depriving the Gypsies of their leader. Fedalma is left as the Queen of a doomed people (Zarca had been 'one That ages watch for vainly') and Silva withdraws to lonely repentance. The result of the individual's attempt to defy the general has been the destruction of the communities to which both Silva and Fedalma owed allegiance, and the thwarting of their individual destinies. Those who have read the poem will agree that, despite George Eliot's assertion that 'A tragedy has not to expound why the individual must give way to the general: it has to show that it is compelled to give way,'[87] the upshot is as didactic as this brief summary makes it sound. A tragic experience, or tragic meaning, cannot so easily be reduced to a moral law as that in *The Spanish Gypsy*.

With George Eliot didacticism is very often closely related to the question of the individual and the general, to the necessity of living for something outside the self. In the case of *The Spanish Gypsy* the didacticism is part and parcel of the inability to believe that the protagonists matter as individuals. And yet George Eliot clearly believed in her sympathy for them. My earlier phrase 'sympathetic immersion' for the invocation of reality by which the author tests his preconceptions, is relevant here. The sympathy essential for tragedy, for the sense of reality without which tragedy cannot exist, is more than a personal warmth of feeling in the author, and has nothing to do with partisanship. I am speaking of the kind of sympathy that Shakespeare has for Macbeth. In these terms the attempt to give a tragic ending to *The Mill on the Floss* is a failure. A more authentically tragic experience is communicated by the lives of Hetty Sorrel, Mrs. Transome, Lydgate and Gwendolen Harleth. These are characters in whose lives the 'terrible difficulty' is most fully expressed and the three women are egoists whose manner of life George Eliot despises. Their stories are told concurrently with those of characters who embody the author's own values and whose lives have an exemplary quality, but they are the creations into which has gone an imaginative sympathy more intense and profound than has gone into the exemplary characters. This sympathy is so fine, and is so strongly communicated to the reader, that the characters refuse to be contained within the moral schemes that they were intended to be a part of. Because they are more fully realised than the exemplary characters (who are in some cases, notably Adam Bede and Dinah Morris, themselves fine achievements) they cannot be measured against them. This is above all what makes George Eliot a great novelist, but it does create conflict and disproportion within the pattern of at least three of the novels: *Adam Bede, Felix Holt* and *Daniel Deronda*. Furthermore, in at least the first and last of the novels George Eliot's commitment to a didactic purpose causes her to dishonour her finest creations, to try to suppress their unruly reality in the interests of the moral scheme. This is surely why many critics have failed to do justice to the creation of Hetty Sorrel, and some even to that of Gwendolen Harleth.

This conflict between moral purpose and imaginative sympathy, didacticism and tragedy, is one of the major fascinations of George Eliot's art.

2
Scenes of Clerical Life

Throughout the year 1856 George Eliot was preparing herself to begin writing fiction. Her preparation can be seen in the detailed accounts of what she saw on holiday with Lewes at Ilfracombe[1] and in her articles of that year, particularly 'The Natural History of German Life' and 'Silly Novels by Lady Novelists'. *Scenes of Clerical Life*, which she began in September 1856, are the creative product of the thought about realism, attention to common (particularly lower middle-class) life and the power of fiction as an agent of sympathy, that we find in the essays. As the central figures of all three stories are clergymen, and two of them gentlemen, their subject is not what we might at first understand by common life. They are, however, concerned with obscure, unfashionable provincial lives, not placed out of the ordinary either by wealth or by extreme hardship. Particularly in the first two, *Amos Barton* and *Mr Gilfil's Love-story*, George Eliot attempts to base her drama on the fact of human experience, on what the reader has in common with the characters, rather than relying for her effects on the unusual or the factitiously exciting. In the third story, *Janet's Repentance*, the setting remains provincial and obscure, but the subject is a remarkable man's influence on a community in general and on one woman in particular. This is distinctly the most successful of the stories and sets a pattern for George Eliot's subsequent work. She never again attempted to take as her central figure a person so unexceptional as Amos Barton or Mr Gilfil.

It was in this avoidance of the unexceptional that George Eliot was, when writing these stories, most conscious of being an originator. In the first of them, *Amos Barton*, this consciousness is insistently outspoken:

'The Rev. Amos Barton, whose sad fortunes I have undertaken to relate, was, you perceive, in no respect an ideal or exceptional character; and perhaps I am doing a bold thing to bespeak your sympathy on behalf of a man who was so very far from remarkable,—a man whose virtues were not heroic, and who had no undetected crime within his breast; who had not the slightest mystery hanging about him, but was palpably and unmistakeably commonplace; who was not even in love, but had had that complaint favourably many years ago. "An utterly uninteresting character!" I think I hear a lady reader exclaim—Mrs. Farthingale, for example, who prefers the ideal in fiction; to whom tragedy means ermine tippets, adultery, and murder; and comedy, the adventures of some personage who is quite a "character".

But, my dear madam, it is so very large a majority of your fellow-countrymen that are of this insignificant stamp. At least eighty out of a hundred of your adult male fellow-Britons returned in the last census are neither extraordinarily silly, nor extraordinarily wicked, nor extraordinarily wise . . .

Depend upon it, you would gain unspeakably if you would learn with me to see some of the poetry and the pathos, the tragedy and the comedy, lying in the experience of a human soul that looks out through dull grey eyes, and that speaks in a voice of quite ordinary tones.'   (Chapter 5)

The tone of this is badly misjudged. The readers of *Amos Barton* had for some years had the opportunity of reading *David Copperfield*, *Vanity Fair*, *Villette* and *North and South*, all of which could make some claim to the qualities which George Eliot is commending; and the readers were surely more likely to have one of those works as their tacit standard of fiction, than *The Enigma* or *Rank and Beauty*.[2] One feels that George Eliot is still working off her irritation at the silly novels by lady novelists, and gratuitously insulting her own readers in the process. She was to develop the authorial commentary into a subtle and effective device for adjusting the reader's response, but in *Amos Barton* it too often seems to express self-righteousness. There is also too much of it—a far larger proportion of the story is a direct address to the reader than of any later work.

The figure of Amos is, however, convincing. His self-satisfaction, insensitiveness and tactlessness are effectively rendered, especially when George Eliot has enough self-confidence to be wholly dramatic, as in the exchange between Amos and a workhouse boy:

> ' "Do you like being beaten?"
> "No-a".
> "Then what a silly boy you are to be naughty. If you were not naughty, you wouldn't be beaten. But if you are naughty, God will be angry, as well as Mr. Spratt; and God can burn you for ever. That will be worse than being beaten".
> Master Fodge's countenance was neither affirmative nor negative of this proposition.
> "But", continued Mr. Barton, "If you will be a good boy, God will love you, and you will grow up to be a good man. Now, let me hear next Thursday that you have been a good boy".'
> (Chapter 2)

The farce of the vain and egotistical Countess Czerlaski's prolonged visit to the Bartons, and the absurdly incongruous scandal that it causes is successful, and enough to inspire in the reader some fellow-feeling with poor Amos. However, George Eliot is more ambitious than this. Her design is to show the failure of a mediocre curate to win the love of his flock, his further isolation due to malicious slander, and finally his union with them in a bond of sympathy on account of a serious misfortune: 'Amos failed to touch the spring of goodness by his sermons, but he touched it effectually by his sorrows; and there was now a real bond between him and his flock.' (Chapter 10) The sorrows which touch the spring of goodness are caused by the death of Amos's wife, Milly. Milly is worn out by overwork, aggravated by Amos's failure to see what is happening, and by the demands of the Countess, which Amos is too foolish to put an end to. To that extent the death is in keeping with George Eliot's intentions. However, she also felt it necessary to include a formal death-bed scene. This was regarded by herself and Lewes as a test of her powers. When Lewes read it he congratulated her, 'Your pathos is better than your fun'.[3] The use of the word 'pathos' is ominous, for the idea of pathos as an isolated literary effect belongs to a convention alien to George Eliot's intentions. Milly's death is not by any means grossly sentimental; it is 'literary': it has origins in other works of literature rather than in life. In a story which owes its strengths to the author's freedom from received ideas about fiction, this failure over such a crucial incident is a serious weakness.

Amos Barton is the most extreme of George Eliot's stories. She never again made mediocrity her central theme. The hero of her second story, the worldly and humane clergyman Mr Gilfil, is unexceptional, but he is a 'brave, faithful, tender nature', and there is no resistance to be overcome in the reader. The story of his devotion to the passionate, timid Italian girl Tina; her love for the worthless Captain Wybrow; and the contrast between the romantic young Gilfil and the 'whimsical' old Vicar to whom we are introduced at the beginning of the tale, are graceful and touching. In the treatment of Wybrow there is some of the intelligent sharpness that is applied to George Eliot's later egoists:

> 'He was a young man of calm passions, who was rarely led into any conduct of which he could not give a plausible account to himself. . . . He really felt very kindly towards her, and would very likely have loved her—if he had been able to love anyone. But nature had not endowed him with that capability . . . ; as if to save such a delicate piece of work from any risk of being shattered, she had guarded him from the liability to a strong emotion.'
> (Chapter 4)

But there is a sense that, even so early in her career, George Eliot is working within her capacities. Mr Gilfil is a precursor of Mr Irwine in *Adam Bede* and Mr Farebrother in *Middlemarch,* and the effect of his 'love-story' is as if such fine minor incidents as Mr Irwine's devotion to his mother and sisters, and Mr Farebrother's renunciation of Mary Garth in favour of Fred Vincy, had been the central episodes of independent stories. *Mr. Gilfil's Love-story* also shares a weakness with *Amos Barton.* Tina's decision to kill Wybrow, and her discovery of his dead body just when she intended to murder him is, like Milly Barton's death, 'literary'. George Eliot believed in it enough to defend it against her publisher's criticism, and one can agree to the extent of admitting that the episode might have occurred; but it reads like a formal contribution to a melodramatic genre.

The success of these first two stories is limited to the conception and effective dramatisation of characters less exceptional than was usual in fiction. George Eliot had yet to escape from convention in her crucial dramatic incidents, and create a narrative which would carry a developing, rather than a static, conception. In this respect, particularly, *Janet's Repentance* is an important advance. It is the best of the *Scenes,* and has most of the characteristics of her later novels. Perhaps its most enduring quality is the creation of a community. In contrast to the leisurely, reminiscing introductions of the earlier stories, we are plunged straight into the 'medium' of the town of Milby. We gather from historical sources that Milby is Nuneaton, while Middlemarch is Coventry, but the two are closely akin. The attempts of Lawyer Dempster and his cronies to put a stop to Mr Tryan's Sunday evening lectures are identical in spirit to the hounding of Bulstrode by Lawyer Hawley and his allies. A casual remark about the Milby medical practitioners, Pilgrim and Pratt, foreshadows the fate of Lydgate:

'They had both been long established in Milby, and as each had a sufficient practice, there was no very malignant rivalry between them; on the contrary, they had that sort of friendly contempt for each other which is always conducive to a good understanding between professional men; and when any new surgeon attempted, in an ill-advised hour, to settle himself in the town, it was strikingly demonstrated how slight and trivial are theoretic differences compared with the broad basis of common human feeling. There was the most perfect unanimity between Pratt and Pilgrim in the determination to drive away the obnoxious and too probably unqualified intruder as soon as possible. Whether the first wonderful cure he effected was on a patient of Pratt's or of Pilgrim's, one was as ready as the other to pull the interloper by the nose, and both alike directed their remarkable powers of conversation towards making the town too hot for him.'   (Chapter 2)

The leading characteristic of Milby, as of Middlemarch, is a tenacious and poisonous hatred of any call to a higher conception of life, or superior practical efficiency.

The method by which the community is presented is also similar to that of *Middlemarch.* Different groups are seen pursuing and discussing their private affairs and those of the town; but the smaller scale of the story makes it necessary that, while in *Middlemarch* the activities of these various groups bear on one or more of four central interests, in *Janet's Repentance* everything centres round one major drama: the entry of Mr Tryan and Evangelicalism into the life of Milby, and their influence on the destiny of Dempster's wife.

The advance in dramatic power can be seen in the opening scene at the Red Lion:

"The Presbyterians," said Mr. Dempster, in rather a louder often said his father had given him "no eddication, and he didn't care who knowed it; he could buy up most o' th' eddicated men he'd ever come across."

"The Presbyterians," said Mr. Dempster, in rather a louder tone than before, holding that every appeal for information must naturally be addressed to him, "are a sect founded in the reign of Charles I, by a man named John Presbyter, who hatched all the brood of Dissenting vermin that crawl about in dirty alleys, and circumvent the lord of the manor in order to get a few yards of ground for their pigeon-house conventicles."

"No, no, Dempster," said Mr. Luke Byles, "you're out there. Presbyterianism is derived from the word presbyter, meaning an elder."

"Don't contradict *me*, sir!" stormed Dempster. "I say the word presbyterian is derived from John Presbyter, a miserable fanatic who wore a suit of leather, and went about from town to village, and from village to hamlet inoculating the vulgar with the asinine virus of Dissent."

"Come, Byles, that seems a deal more likely," said Mr. Tomlinson, in a conciliatory tone, apparently of opinion that history was a process of ingenious guessing.

"It's not a question of likelihood; it's a known fact. I could fetch you my Encyclopaedia, and show it you this moment."

"I don't care a straw, sir, either for you or your Encyclopaedia," said Mr. Dempster; "a farrago of false information, of which you picked up an imperfect copy in a cargo of waste paper. Will you tell *me*, sir, that I don't know the origin of Presbyterianism? I, sir, a man known through the county, intrusted with the affairs of half a score parishes; while you, sir, are ignored by the very fleas that infest the miserable alley in which you were bred."

A loud and general laugh, with "You'd better let him alone, Byles;" "You'll not get the better of Dempster in a hurry," drowned the retort of the too well-informed Mr. Byles, who, white with rage, rose and walked out of the bar.

"A meddlesome, upstart, Jacobinical fellow, gentlemen," continued Mr. Dempster. "I was determined to be rid of him. What does he mean by thrusting himself into our company? A man with about as much principle as he has property, which, to my knowledge, is considerably less than none. An insolvent atheist, gentlemen. A deistical prater, fit to sit in the chimney-corner of a pot-house, and make blasphemous comments on the one greasy newspaper fingered by beer-swilling tinkers. I will not suffer in my company a man who speaks lightly of religion. The signature of a fellow like Byles would be a blot on our protest."

(Chapter 1)

There is nothing in the previous stories as good as this. It is as good as the Rainbow Inn in *Silas Marner*. Dempster is a completely successful portrayal of a decaying, violent egoist. The episode which indirectly causes his death—an irrational assault on his servant—is thoroughly convincing. As a result he has to drive himself when drunk, and has a fatal accident. More remarkable, George Eliot convincingly and economically suggests the better self from which he has decayed, in his relation to his mother: 'a nucleus of healthy life in an organ hardening by disease' (Chapter 7).

Janet's Repentance is the work in which George Eliot pays tribute to the religion of her youth. Elsewhere in her fiction the treatment of Evangelicalism is akin in spirit to her essay on the teaching of Dr Cumming,[4] but here she regards the movement as, on balance, an instrument of moral improvement and Mr Tryan as a representative of the true, human essence of Christianity. In her other novels the Christianity George Eliot most admires is the old-fashioned Churchmanship of her father, which did not inquire deeply into spiritual experience and upheld a more or less pagan morality: the 'short moral sermons' of Mr Irwine and Mr Gilfil. But in Milby good Churchmanship means a complete moral and spiritual lethargy. The curate, Mr Crewe's, sermons are inaudible, and the young ladies pass the time during the services by tittering at the angle of his wig. The Churchmen who present the petition against Mr Tryan's lectures are the drunken bully Dempster, Mr Budd a notorious libertine, and Mr Tomlinson a mercenary miller.

George Eliot's estimate of the Evangelical influence on Milby is temperate but decided:

'The movement, like all other religious "revivals," had a mixed effect. Religious ideas have the fate of melodies, which, once set afloat in the world, are taken up by all sorts of instruments, some of them woefully coarse, feeble, or out of tune, until people are in danger of crying out that the melody itself is detestable. It may be that some of Mr Tryan's hearers had gained a religious vocabulary rather than religious experience; that here and there a weaver's wife, who, a few months before, had been simply a silly slattern, was converted into that more complex nuisance, a silly and sanctimonious slattern. . . .

Nevertheless, Evangelicalism had brought into palpable existence and operation in Milby society that idea of duty, that recognition of something to be lived for beyond the mere satisfaction of self, which is to the moral life what the addition of a great central ganglion is to animal life. . . . Miss Rebecca Linnett, in quiet attire, with a somewhat excessive solemnity of countenance, teaching at the Sunday-school, visiting the poor, and striving after a standard of purity and goodness, had surely more moral loveliness than in those flaunting peony-days, when she had no other model than the costumes of the heroines in the circulating library. Miss Eliza Pratt, listening in rapt attention to Mr Tryan's evening lecture, no doubt found evangelical channels for vanity and egoism; but she was clearly in moral advance of Miss Phipps giggling under her feathers at old Mr Crewe's peculiarities of enunciation.'   (Chapter 10)

It will be noted that in George Eliot's analysis a religious movement is a shaping influence, encouraging the finer qualities latent in the individual character and curbing excesses of egoism. No one's character is completely transformed by it, though Janet Dempster's *life* is transformed. However, we are to see in *Middlemarch* the influence of Evangelicalism on an egoism more powerful and sinister than Miss Eliza Pratt's.

The true nature of Evangelical virtue, as George Eliot understands it, can be seen in the influence of Mr Tryan on Janet. The brutal treatment by her husband has led her to drink also, and when one night Dempster turns her out of the house in her nightdress she goes to an old 'Tryanite' friend and asks to see Mr Tryan, despite having concurred in her husband's hostility to him. The reason for this request is a superficially slight incident characteristic of Eliot's portrayal of moral influence. Once when she visited a sick girl Janet heard Tryan talking to the girl and asking her to pray for him 'that I may have strength too when the hour of great suffering comes. It is one of my worst weaknesses to shrink from bodily pain. . . . '

'The most brilliant deed of virtue could not have inclined Janet's good-will towards Mr Tryan so much as this fellowship in suffering, and the softening thought was in her eyes when he appeared in the doorway, pale, weary, and depressed. The sight of Janet standing there with the entire absence of self-consciousness which belongs to a new and vivid impression, made him start and pause a little. Their eyes met, and they looked at each other gravely for a few moments. Then they bowed, and Mr Tryan passed out.

There is a power in the direct glance of a sincere and loving human soul, which will do more to dissipate prejudice and kindle charity than the most elaborate arguments. The fullest exposition of Mr Tryan's doctrine might not have sufficed to convince Janet that he had not an odious self-complacency in believing himself a peculiar child of God; but one direct, pathetic look of his had dissociated him with that conception for ever.'

(Chapter 12)

When he becomes her spiritual adviser their intercourse is an expansion of this meeting. She confesses to him her addiction to drink and he responds by making a confession himself: that when he was an undergraduate he seduced a girl whom he later saw dead on the streets; that he suffered the same despair that Janet's temptation causes her, until a friend persuaded him that conviction of sin is the prelude to the reception of grace. Thus the bond of sympathy is strengthened by common experience of suffering.

George Eliot persuades the reader that Mr Tryan, like his successor Dinah Morris, is a true believing Christian. He speaks the language of Christianity and thinks of God as an active, immanent personality. All but the most theologically informed of its first readers would have had every reason to accept *Janet's Repentance* as a Christian work. To the reader acquainted with the ideas which George Eliot absorbed from Feuerbach, however, the story's fundamentally non-Christian basis is clear. When Janet was shut out of the house by her husband, 'if there was any Divine Pity, she could not feel it; it kept aloof from her, it poured no balm into her wounds, it stretched out no hand to bear up her weak resolve, to fortify her fainting courage' (Chapter 15). No one in George Eliot's novels undergoes an orthodox Christian experience of Divine Love: a direct, personal revelation of Christ without the intervention of another person. 'The tale of the Divine Pity was never yet believed from lips that were not felt to be moved by human pity' (Chapter 18). In reality George Eliot believes that Divine pity and human pity are identical, but she succeeds in establishing this reality through a drama in which the characters are fully convinced of the opposite. She does not, however, deny a real value in the Christian belief, for it fortifies Janet against the loss of Tryan by death.

The fundamental weakness of the sick-bed scene in this story mentioned on pp. 43–44 is not isolated, and there are general shortcomings in the later part of the story, including Janet's relation to Tryan. Its unassailable strengths are in the portrayal of Milby society and of Dempster in particular, but it cannot as a whole be placed among George Eliot's satisfactory works. I shall not labour these weaknesses, however, since unlike those of the other two *Scenes,* which she outgrew, they look forward to her later work. In Janet's relations with Tryan there is a certain sanctimony which persists in the last novels, in the relations of Dorothea and Ladislaw, and Gwendolen and Deronda. Accompanying this (and supported by the language of refuge in the sick-bed scene) is a sense, which comes out more fully in relation to characters in *Adam Bede* and *Daniel Deronda,* that Janet's experience is exemplary: it never offers a threat to the values which the story is affirming; Janet never lives outside the rôle that her author's moral purpose dictates for her. It is a telling symptom of George Eliot's didacticism. In both strength and weakness, in everything but scope, *Janet's Repentance* is her first fully characteristic work.

3
Adam Bede

If most of George Eliot's novels dramatise social development as a conflict between the exceptional individual and the social norm, it must be recognised that *Adam Bede* is the major exception.[1] Two characteristic elements which have already become apparent in *Janet's Repentance* are absent from *Adam Bede*. The medium in which the hero of that story, Mr Tryan, moves—the town of Milby—is presented as narrow and hostile to a fuller, finer conception of human life. This relation between Mr Tryan and his world is repeated in different ways, and with different degrees of complexity in *The Mill on the Floss, Romola, Felix Holt, Middlemarch* and *Daniel Deronda*. With the exception of *The Mill*, these later novels also present the conflict at a time of notable social change (actual or imminent) or as part of a particular historical development—the Evangelical movement, the expulsion of the Medici and dominance of Savonarola, political and medical reform, Zionism.

In *Adam Bede* by contrast George Eliot creates the illusion of a stable and immemorial rural world. Despite the manifesto on realism in Chapter 17, and despite the abundantly observed detail, it is only equivocally a 'realistic' novel. It is realistic in that it charts as minutely as *Middlemarch* the consequences of moral action. It differs from *Middlemarch* in the absence of social and historical analysis. The world of *Adam Bede* does not appear to contain within it the seeds of its own dissolution and transformation. It is, as I have said, immemorial. It is true that a village community would seem less subject to change than a provincial centre, and that many of the conditions of change would come from outside. But much of the sense of history in *Middlemarch* is provided by the fact that although the action does not (apart from Dorothea's wedding journey and a few retrospects) stray more than a few miles from the town, the *world* of the novel is very much more extensive. The wider experience of several of the protagonists, and the numerous references to events in the public world, thoroughly persuade the reader that the community is not self-sufficient, that it is subject to the influence of events of which it is unaware.

But the world of *Adam Bede* is self-sufficient. The fertile county of Loamshire is a kind of Eden, to which it is explicitly compared.[2] The changes which threaten it are the consequences not of historical necessity but of sin. Furthermore, although social relations are described and dramatised, they are of secondary importance in influencing events. The nice distinctions between tenant-farmer and artisan, and even between the artisan with good prospects, Adam, and his 'wool-gathering' brother Seth, are convincingly conveyed. But it is worth noting that although for most of the novel the inhabitants of Hayslope are under the domination of a mean and malicious Squire, social relations enjoy a harmony and order more appropriate to the millenial era looked forward to on Arthur's accession. This pervading sense of harmony is not even disrupted by the bad grace with which the tenants drink to the Squire's health on Arthur's birthday, or the brilliant scene in which Mrs Poyser 'has her say out'. The consequence of that scene—the Poysers' threatened eviction—is merged into and subordinated to their determination to move because of Hetty's disgrace. The poignancy of their uprooting is withheld from the effects of squirearchical acquisitiveness and reserved for the consequences of Arthur's sexual immorality.

This illusion of an immemorial society is appropriate to the values represented by the hero and heroine. In her next novel George Eliot was to present a world of 'oppressive narrowness', so that we should understand 'how it has acted on young natures in many generations, that in the onward tendency of human things have risen above the mental level of the generation before them'.[3] The world of Hayslope is no less narrow than that of St. Ogg's, but it is not felt to be oppressive simply because George Eliot is explicitly not concerned here with 'the onward tendency of human things'.

'[Adam] was not an average man. Yet such men as he are reared here and there in every generation of our peasant artisans —with an inheritance of affections nurtured by a simple family life of common need and common industry, and an inheritance of faculties trained in skilful courageous labour.' (Chapter 19)

For Maggie Tulliver 'inheritance' is in conflict with a striving beyond to a form of life not comprehended by her world. Adam's task is simply to maintain his inheritance. He will improve his world by his practical endeavours and his moral example, but he will not try to create new forms: his inheritance provides him with all that he needs for personal fulfilment and for the exercise of his creative gifts. His practical genius and moral rectitude are themselves immemorial and are honoured in his world. So too are the altruism and Christian sympathy of Dinah Morris. Although she belongs to a movement that was making historically significant changes in the spiritual lives of the common people of England, she is no more shown to be struggling in an oppressive and hostile medium than Adam is. It is true that in Hayslope she is working on rather inert material, and that the dramatic conversion of Bessie Cranage is subject to backsliding; but despite her example of a foreign and challenging conception of the spiritual life she meets with no hostility and is honoured as much as Adam is. Her career is in marked contrast to that of Mr Tryan. There may be good historical reasons for this—as a Methodist she is not such a threat to good Churchmanship as an Evangelical clergyman[4]—but one suspects that a more important reason for the difference is that *Adam Bede* is a different kind of drama from *Janet's Repentance*.

Dr Raymond Williams, in *The Country and the City,* makes some perceptive and challenging remarks about these aspects of *Adam Bede,* ascribing its pastoral mellowness to the operation of a selective memory and a representation of what he calls the 'knowable' rather than the 'known' community.[5] He points out George Eliot's awkward addresses to the reader, such as her assertion that she is 'not ashamed of commemorating' the old labourer Kester Bale—seeing them as symptomatic of the difficulties of writing in a language and a form which expressed a sensibility in common with her readers but not with Kester. One feels that in the very act of writing novels George Eliot was aware of entering into an uneasy 'compact' (Dr Williams's word) with a class of people whom she despised—a compact which she occasionally breaks away from by means of almost violent and distasteful addresses to the reader whom she unaccountably (in view of the respect implicit in most of the writing) figures as an exceptionally stupid and frivolous lady of fashion.

In her essay 'The Natural History of German Life', George Eliot made a plea for realism in art, particularly in the portrayal of the common people which, for her, as for Riehl, meant the peasantry and the agricultural poor. In her opinion the conventional, sentimental view of the rustic was positively vicious because it distracted sympathy from its proper place—the actual countryman who is likely to be stupid, boorish, dirty and coarse.

> 'Observe a company of haymakers. When you see them at a distance, tossing up the forkfuls of hay in the golden light, while the wagon creeps slowly with its increasing burthen over the meadow, and the bright green space which tells of work done gets larger and larger, you pronounce the scene "smiling," and you think these companions in labour must be as bright and cheerful as the picture to which they give animation. Approach nearer, and you will certainly find that haymaking time is a time for joking, especially if there are women among the labourers; but the coarse laugh that bursts out every now and then, and expresses the triumphant taunt, is as far as possible from your conception of idyllic merriment.'[6]

This passage from the essay is paraphrased in the nineteenth chapter of *Adam Bede:*

> 'The jocose talk of haymakers is best at a distance; like those clumsy bells round the cows' necks, it has rather a coarse sound when it comes close, and may even grate on your ears painfully; but heard from far off, it mingles very prettily with the other joyous sounds of nature.'

The dominant theme in George Eliot's argument for realism is sympathy: 'We want to be taught to feel, not for the heroic artisan or the sentimental peasant, but for the peasant in all his coarse apathy, and the artisan in all his suspicious selfishness'.[7] 'The greatest benefit we owe to the artist, whether painter, poet, or novelist, is the extension of our sympathies'.[8] It seems extraordinary that in her first full-length novel, the first of all her works to take common rural life for its subject, these difficult objects of sympathy should recede altogether into the background. The novelist's creative sympathy—that which consists in having thoroughly imagined an individual's life—is not extended beyond (among the common people) the Bedes and the Poysers, Hetty Sorrel and Dinah Morris. Lisbeth Bede is certainly a triumph, but this clean, respectable, affectionate and not totally foolish woman is far removed from the coarse peasant of the essay. Hetty Sorrel is indeed a difficult object of sympathy, but not because of any class characteristics. The characters in subsequent novels who resemble her belong to a wide range of classes. For the ploughmen, shepherds and haymakers George Eliot can only achieve a *stated* sympathy in the language which, by identifying with the cultivated reader at a distance from the character, excites Dr Williams's criticism: 'I am not ashamed of commemorating old Kester: you and I are indebted to the hard hands of such men' (Chapter 53). In her essay George Eliot criticises Dickens for the 'false psychology' of his common people, yet in Jo the crossing-sweeper in *Bleak House,* Dickens achieved an imaginative sympathy that is lacking in any of George Eliot's portrayals of really poor people.

Adam Bede is not really a sociological novel. It is a schematic moral drama in which sociological interest is subordinate and for the most part fragmentary. As indicated earlier, the social order of Hayslope is threatened not by historical necessity but by sin, and the consequences of the Squire's acquisitiveness are subordinated to those of Arthur's seduction of Hetty. Whereas the communities of Milby, St. Ogg's and Middlemarch actively determine crucial events in the lives of the characters, and are subject to historical change, the unchanging nature of Hayslope makes it a sensitive register of the consequences of a sin which is indeed influenced by class assumptions and class differences, but which is mainly considered as a matter of private morality. It is in relation to this that suggestions of Hayslope as a kind of Eden are relevant. Arthur and Hetty's sin drives them out of Hayslope, and threatens also to drive out Adam and the Poysers. These consequences are much more striking, and carry the moral burden more vigorously, than if the community had been shown as of necessity subject to change. Apart from the principals, the threatened loss of Eden is not the exchange of a physically easier for a harder life. Its importance is largely due to the characters' feeling of rooted-ness and attachment to custom. In this respect George Eliot's art is thoroughly true to a perception which she quoted from Riehl:

> 'When our writers of village stories transferred their own emotional life to the peasant, they obliterated what is precisely his most predominant characteristic, namely, that with him general custom holds the place of individual feeling.'[9]

George Eliot does not in this novel, as she does in her next, systematically set out the rule of custom as a quasi-religious code. Nevertheless, the elements of the code—the sense of what is fitting, the attachment of meaning to external signs, the consciousness of place both physically and socially—are of the utmost importance in the lives of the characters. It is these feelings, together with their closely-linked pride, which render the Poysers' sense of disgrace so poignant, and give poetry to that commonplace old man, Martin Poyser, senior:

> ' "Pity?" said the grandfather, sharply. "I ne'er wanted folks's pity i' *my* life afore . . . an' I mun begin to be looked down on now, an' me turned seventy-two last St. Thomas's, an' all th' under-bearers and pall-bearers as I'n picked for my funeral are i' this parish and the next to 't ... It's o' no use now ... I mun be ta'en to the grave by strangers." '   (Chapter 40)

On the occasion of the earlier threat, caused by Mrs Poyser's abuse of the Squire, the younger Martin expresses sentiments which are closely echoed by Maggie Tulliver and her father: 'I should be loath to leave th' old place, and the parish where I was bred and born, and father afore me. We should leave our roots behind us, I doubt, and niver thrive again' (Chapter 32). The same popular civilisation expresses itself in Lisbeth Bede's feelings when her husband has died:

> 'it was right that things should look strange and disordered and

wretched, now the old man had come to his end in that sad
way: the kitchen ought not to look as if nothing had happened.'

(Chapter 10)

Such things as this make it impossible for the sensitive
reader to feel superior to Lisbeth. George Eliot's anthropological interest in the peasants is an interest in what gives
value, meaning and dignity to their lives. It is the meaning
of the Poysers' lives—the sense of not being accidentally
dropped on a spot of earth, but a necessary and contributory
part of it—and not a narrow class-pride and insularity,
which is threatened by Hetty's disgrace. But there are
distinctions. The code of custom and fitness is not something
that automatically confers strength on the individual—as will
be seen in another complaining woman, Mrs Tulliver in
The Mill on the Floss. Lisbeth's strength is partly strength
of character (she says some very shrewd things to Adam about
his father, and about Hetty Sorrel, in Chapter 4, and it is she
who perceives that Dinah is in love with Adam) and her
sense of fitness is seen to be superior to Mrs Tulliver's
because it expresses human affections.

The moral scheme of the novel can be discerned by
examining the four central characters. Adam and Dinah
represent complementary virtues: in Adam's case practical
intelligence and moral rectitude linked by a strong awareness
of consequences; in Dinah's an intuitive sympathy, genuine
humility, and altruism. These characters have corresponding
limitations, and the scheme dictates that experience shall
make them each more complete. The convergence of complementary virtues is finally symbolised by their marriage.
Arthur and Hetty are conceived as opposites to Adam and
Dinah: Arthur is good-natured but has a fatal belief in his
power to make amends and in a personal Providence that will
fit consequences to his intentions rather than his actions;
Hetty is a complete egotist.

However, George Eliot's greatness is not that of a deviser
of 'moral schemes', and a great part of her fascination is the
complex relationship, and frequent conflict, between her
didacticism and her creative sympathy. Her creative sympathy is beyond schematic morality, and it is finer and rarer
than the conscious partisanship towards the characters she

admires. These two contrasted qualities are most strikingly seen in her last novel, *Daniel Deronda,* one part of which is completely controlled by didacticism and partisanship, while the other is centred on her subtlest analysis of a human soul, Gwendolen Harleth, whom she does *not* admire, and whose experience she renders with a poignancy that approaches the tragic. *Adam Bede* is a much less extreme case. Adam and Dinah, unlike Deronda, Mirah and Mordecai, are convincing presences. But they are like these characters, and also like the heroine of *Janet's Repentance,* in being under the author's protection: their experience is dictated by the moral scheme, and the reader feels that it will never be too extreme or too terrible for the moral scheme to deal with. But Hetty's experience is as terrible as that, and she is consequently left outside the novel's dispensation, uncared for once she has repented and been reprieved. It is for this reason that many readers are most alienated by what is really the novel's greatest achievement.

Adam's story is that of a hard man who learns, first through the death of his father and then through the suffering of an inferior being whom he loves, sympathy towards weakness. But what the idea of Adam represents in one's mind is not such a development, but something much more static. What we remember about him are the qualities that he has from the first, summed up in his words to Arthur, 'I've seen pretty clear, ever since I could cast up a sum, as you can never do what's wrong without breeding sin and trouble more than you can ever see' (Chapter 16). Adam is a massive representation of this central Eliotic belief, but his dramatic existence, his learning through suffering, even his suffering itself, are by comparison notional.

'Deep, unspeakable suffering may well be called a baptism, a regeneration, the initiation into a new state. The yearning memories, the bitter regret, the agonised sympathy, the struggling appeals to the Invisible Right—all the intense emotions which had filled the days and nights of the past week, and were compressing themselves again like an eager crowd into the hours of this single morning, made Adam look back on all the previous years as if they had been a dim sleepy existence, and he had only now awaked to full consciousness. It seemed to him as if he had always before thought it a light thing that men should suffer; as if all that he had himself endured and called sorrow before, was only a moment's stroke that had never left a bruise. Doubtless a great anguish may do the work of years, and we may come out from that baptism of fire with a soul full of new awe and new pity.'   (Chapter 42)

But how much do we remember of Adam's 'deep, unspeakable suffering'? It does not possess and haunt the reader's imagination as Hetty's does. By comparison with that, we have only George Eliot's word that Adam suffers. Part of the reason is that in passages such as this the reader is constantly being encouraged to look beyond the suffering to its beneficent consequences. It is too tractable, too much contained by, and subservient to, the moral scheme to really pain the reader. The reader feels that 'Adam learns through suffering' more strongly than that 'Adam suffers'. And because the process does not possess the reader's imagination, the learning seems like something added to the character, rather than a growth of the character. I do not mean to imply that suffering with beneficent consequences is always less moving than such suffering as Hetty's. Prince André in *War and Peace* grows through suffering, but the process is painful and moreover dangerous: we do not know how it will end. George Eliot's commentary prevents the reader from thinking that there are any other possible consequences for Adam —such as cynicism or despair.

Dinah, like Adam, is more convincing as a static than as a developing character. She is a convincing portrayal of a Christian faith that is recognisably rooted in human love, but which is nevertheless dependent on a conception of the supernatural. In other words, despite the evident Feuerbachian intention, Dinah is a real Christian. The influence of her preaching on the vain and foolish Bessy Cranage is beautifully portrayed:

'She had a terrified sense that God, whom she had always thought of as very far off, was very near to her, and that Jesus was close by looking at her, though she could not see him. For Dinah had that belief in visible manifestations of Jesus, which is common among the Methodists, and she communicated it irresistibly to her hearers; she made them feel that he was among them bodily, and might at any moment show himself to them in some way that would strike anguish and penitence into their hearts.'   (Chapter 2)

One cause of this effect is her way of addressing Jesus 'in the same moderate tone [that she uses to her audience], as if speaking to someone quite near her'. In the account of the preaching the reader is given a double awareness—of the real effect of the 'divine' qualities manifested in Dinah herself, and of the fact that for all concerned the experience is one of the supernatural. Dinah's nearest approach to a conscious humanising of Christianity is her interpretation of Christ's words, 'If any man love me, let him take up my cross': 'I have heard this enlarged on as if it meant the troubles and persecutions we bring on ourselves by confessing Jesus. But surely that is a narrow thought. The true cross of the Redeemer was the sin and sorrow of this world—*that* was what lay heavy on his heart—and that is the cross we shall share with him, that is the cup we must drink of with him, if we would have any part in that Divine Love which is one with his sorrow'. (Chapter 30).

Dinah's more superstitious beliefs are handled in the same way. This is how she accounts for her decision to leave Hayslope for Snowfield:

'"I'm called there. It was borne in upon my mind while I was meditating on Sunday night, as sister Allen, who's in a decline, is in need of me. I saw her as plain as we see that bit of thin white cloud, lifting up her poor thin hand and beckoning to me. And this morning when I opened the Bible for direction, the first words my eyes fell on were, 'And after we had seen the vision, immediately we endeavoured to go into Macedonia.' If it wasn't for that clear showing of the Lord's will I should be loth to go, for my heart yearns over my aunt and her little ones, and that poor wandering lamb Hetty Sorrel."'   (Chapter 3)

The balancing of the subtle claims of her relatives and the obvious needs of the suffering people of Snowfield is a hard task—not, one might think, to be performed by such arbitrary use of the Bible. And yet—is such a choice likely to be satisfactorily made with the use of reason? Dinah's superstition at least shows a purity of intention (the most

72

difficult of things to maintain when reasoning about one's own moral conduct) and it expresses an awareness of dependence on forces outside the self. The use a Bulstrode, a William Dane or even a Savonarola might make of such 'showings' would quite likely be tainted by egotistical desires; but in Dinah's case it is certainly not intended to encourage a sense of superiority in the reader. And Dinah's 'leadings' do not always or usually take a superstitious form. They commonly mean the abeyance of the egotistic will and obedience to the delicate sense of right which she calls God: 'We mustn't be in a hurry to fix and choose our own lot; we must wait to be guided. . . It isn't for you and me to lay plans; we've nothing to do but to obey and to trust' (Chapter 3).

The real limitation of Dinah is in her very lack of egotism. 'I seem to have no room in my soul for wants and fears of my own, it has pleased God to fill my heart so full with the wants and sufferings of his poor people' (Chapter 3). George Eliot did not regard this as an ideal condition. There is a passage which bears on this in her last book, *Theophrastus Such*:

> 'I am really at the point of finding that this world would be worth living in without any lot of one's own. Is it not possible for me to enjoy the scenery of the earth without saying to myself, I have a cabbage-garden in it? But this sounds like the lunacy of fancying oneself everybody else and being unable to play one's own part decently—another form of the disloyal attempt to be independent of the common lot, and to live without a sharing of pain.'[10]

In fact the most admirable character in the early chapters is not Dinah but Seth, who maintains a spirit of Christian acceptance, meekness and love *despite* having 'wants and sufferings' of his own: despite his unreturned love for Dinah and his mother's constant belittling of him in comparison with Adam. In reply to Dinah's words Seth says, 'I feel now how weak my faith is. It seems as if, when you are gone, I could never joy in anything any more. . . . Perhaps I feel more for you than I ought to feel for any creature. . . . That may be wrong, and I am to be taught better.'

In fact it is Dinah who is to be taught better, and Seth is confirmed by the author in the rightness of his feelings: 'Love of this sort is hardly distinguishable from religious feeling.' But when I come to consider Dinah's being 'taught better', I find the same difficulties as with Adam. Even less than with Adam does the idea of growth form part of my conception of her. The last part of the novel, Dinah's love for Adam and their marriage, is gracefully done, but I find it hard to share the response that Dickens conveyed to the author: 'that part of the book which follows Hetty's trial (and which I have observed to be not as widely understood as the rest), affected me far more than any other, and exalted my sympathy with the writer to its utmost height.' When she and Adam have confessed their love for each other in Chapter 52, Dinah says:

> ' "Adam, it's hard to me to turn a deaf ear . . . you know it's hard; but a great fear is upon me. It seems to me as if you were stretching out your arms to me, and beckoning me to come and take my ease, and live for my own delight, and Jesus, the Man of Sorrows, was standing looking towards me, and pointing to the sinful, and suffering, and afflicted. I have seen that again and again when I have been sitting in stillness and darkness, and a great terror has come upon me lest I should become hard, and a lover of self, and no more bear willingly the Redeemer's cross." '

Adam's reply is:

> ' "I don't believe your loving me could shut up your heart; it's only adding to what you've been before, not taking away from it; for it seems to me it's the same with love and happiness as with sorrow—the more we know of it the better we can feel what other people's lives are or might be, and so we shall only be more tender to 'em, and wishful to help 'em." '

We know from the passage quoted earlier from *Theophrastus Such* that Adam is expressing George Eliot's belief. However, this argument concerns a fundamental life-choice for Dinah, who as a Christian has striven to imitate Christ and the Apostles. For her to accept Adam's view is to move from a purely Christian way of life towards a religion of humanity in which all values are based on personal love.[11] We do not, however, see this choice being made; we are given nothing of the struggles by which Dinah emerges into the acceptance of a new way of life. All we have are her words to Adam on the hill outside Snowfield.

' "Adam," she said, "it is the Divine Will. My soul is so knit to yours that it is but a divided life I live without you. And this moment, now you are with me, and I feel sure that our hearts are filled with the same love, I have a fulness of strength to bear and do our heavenly Father's Will, that I had lost before." '

(Chapter 54)

The marriage of Adam and Dinah is the culmination of the moral scheme, the synthesis of the complementary virtues. But because Dinah's development has not been imagined, the effect is not that she has grown more completely human but that an impressively pure and uncompromising representation of the Christian life has been sacrificed for something more accommodating, comfortable, and even sentimental. It is sadly appropriate that the ensuing chapter is tritely headed 'Marriage Bells'.

One reason for dissatisfaction with the last part of the novel, then, is the belief that both Adam and Dinah are more impressive as static figures than as developing characters. Another reason is a feeling (common to many readers) that something has gone wrong with the distribution of concern; and consideration of this involves a close look at other elements in the novel.

Arthur Donnithorne and Hetty Sorrel are two recognisable types of George Eliot's egotists. Arthur's type reappears (with sufficient variations to make them positively distinct characters) in Godfrey Cass, Tito Melema and Fred Vincy. His is the egotism of the warm hearted, thoughtless young man who means no harm but nevertheless causes it. In him as in Godfrey and Fred (but not in Tito) conscience is too strong to allow the deliberate pursuit of vicious courses, and his experience embodies two of the fundamental principles of George Eliot's moral outlook: 'Our deeds determine us, as much as we determine our deeds', and 'consequences are determined not by excuses but by actions.' Hetty, the self-regarding egotist with no conception of reality outside her own pleasures and discomforts, bears a resemblance to Rosamond Vincy and Gwendolen Harleth; but, being more comprehensively ignorant than Rosamond, she is more vulnerable, and being less intelligent than Gwendolen she is (it seems) less capable of growth.

Arthur's seduction of Hetty is presented as a determined

sequence of events, the main determining influences being Arthur's conception of himself, and the false picture of reality imposed on him by his social position. But, as I have argued above, George Eliot's determinism does not exclude moral responsibility, and throughout the drama Arthur is presented as a fully responsible being: he is responsible because the main determining causes are in himself. The elements of Arthur's 'case' are set out at the beginning of Chapter 12, which describes his first assignation with Hetty:

'No young man could confess his faults more candidly; candour was one of his favourite virtues; and how can a man's candour be seen in all its lustre unless he has a few failings to talk of? But he had an agreeable confidence that his faults were all of a generous kind—impetuous, warm-blooded, leonine; never crawling, crafty, reptilian. It was not possible for Arthur Donnithorne to do anything mean, dastardly, or cruel. "No! I'm a devil of a fellow for getting myself into a hobble, but I always take care the load shall fall on my own shoulders." Unhappily there is no inherent poetical justice in hobbles, and they will sometimes obstinately refuse to inflict their worst consequences on the prime offender, in spite of his loudly-expressed wish. It was entirely owing to this deficiency in the scheme of things that Arthur had ever brought any one into trouble besides himself. He was nothing, if not good-natured; and all his pictures of the future, when he should come into the estate, were made up of a prosperous, contented tenantry, adoring their landlord, who would be the model of an English gentleman. . . . '

(Chapter 12)

A man with this moral complacency, George Eliot argues, is more likely to fall a victim to determining circumstances because he cannot perceive the real bearings of his own actions. We see Arthur becoming more and more dangerously involved, and allowing it to happen precisely because of the purity of his intentions. He is one of a line of characters, culminating in Gwendolen Harleth, in whom a blindness to reality entails a disastrous overestimation of the power of will. His very 'good nature' prevents him from causing Hetty the necessary pain of breaking with her before it is too late, and his desire to be well thought of prevents him from carrying out his intention of confessing his infatuation to Mr Irwine. At the same time his social position encourages in him the dangerous illusion of 'making amends'.

It is because he is confronted with the impossiblity of making amends that Arthur behaves so ungraciously towards Adam both before and after their fight. When the affair with Hetty is still at an early stage Arthur and Adam have a talk about temptation and it is then that Adam (who does not of course know the situation with Hetty) says 'you can never do what's wrong without breeding sin and trouble more than you can ever see' (Chapter 16): that principle is what Adam most impressively represents, and it is diametrically opposed to Arthur's reliance on good intentions and belief in making amends. After the fight, when Arthur has learned that Adam loves Hetty and has promised to write to her and break off their affair, we are told:

'if deeds of gift, or any other deeds, could have restored Adam's contentment and regard for him as a benefactor, Arthur would not only have executed them without hesitation, but would have felt bound all the more closely to Adam, and would never have been weary of making retribution. But Adam could receive no amends; his suffering could not be cancelled; his respect and affection could not be recovered by any prompt deeds of atonement. He stood like an immovable obstacle against which no pressure could avail; an embodiment of what Arthur most shrank from believing in—the irrevocableness of his own wrong-doing.'
(Chapter 29)

In the previous chapter Adam 'stood like a terrible fate before Arthur'. Adam figures thus primarily because he is Arthur's victim, also because he lives by the truth that Arthur is unwilling to learn; but the vividness with which he makes this figure ('an immovable obstacle') owes a great deal to his physical size and strength, and to the fact that he has knocked Arthur down.

The re-statement of this principle is the very last note of the novel when Arthur, having returned to Hayslope and learned that Hetty has died without his having been able to do anything for her, recalls Adam's words: 'There's a sort of wrong that can never be made up for'. It is not until this very last moment that he recognises the truth. Even after his confrontation with Adam he slips into his old habit: 'And perhaps hereafter he might be able to do a great deal for her, and make up to her for all the tears she would shed about him. She would owe the advantage of his care for her in future years to the sorrow she had incurred now. *So* good comes out of evil. Such is the beautiful arrangement of things!' (Chapter 29). We see that Arthur's downfall owes something to class, wealth and paternalistic traditions (of which George Eliot also acknowledged the good side). In a way this truth of irrevocableness is more accessible to the poor man, who is more directly aware of his inability to control events.[12]

It is easy enough to say of Arthur Donnithorne that, despite the determining influences on his actions, he is morally responsible. But George Eliot's determinism turned a sharper edge when she was forced in her honesty to contemplate beings who seemed to be incompletely human. One senses a chill horror in her writing when she is dealing with people in whom she can find no signs of sympathy or conscience. The three most important characters of this kind are Hetty Sorrel, Rosamond Vincy and Henleigh Grandcourt. But the horror they excite is of different kinds. The mere existence of such a man as Grandcourt is frightening—the thoughts he prompts about what it *can* mean to be human. In addition to this there is the suffering that he can cause to others. The feelings excited by Hetty are quite different from this. There is no animus in her portrayal,[13] and George Eliot is quite capable of conveying sheer joy in the existence of such a beautiful young girl:

> 'Hetty's was a spring-tide beauty; it was the beauty of young frisking things, round-limbed, gambolling, circumventing you with a false air of innocence—the innocence of a young star-browed calf, for example, that, being inclined for a promenade out of bounds, leads you a severe steeple-chase over hedge and ditch, and only comes to a stand in the middle of a bog.
>
> And they are the prettiest attitudes and movements into which a pretty girl is thrown in making up butter—tossing movements that give a charming curve to the arm, and a sideward inclination of the round white neck; little patting and rolling movements with the palm of the hand, and nice adaptations and finishings which cannot at all be effected without a great play of the pouting mouth and the dark eyes.'[14]
>
> (Chapter 7)

The irony here is minimal. When it is more severe it is directed less against Hetty than against men's expectations of women and a facile conception of Nature's 'intentions':

> 'Ah, what a prize the man gets who wins a sweet bride like Hetty! How the men envy him who come to the wedding breakfast, and see her hanging on his arm in her white lace and orange blossoms. The dear, young, round, soft, flexible thing! Her heart must be just as soft, her temper just as free from angles, her character just as pliant. If anything ever goes wrong, it must be the husband's fault there: he can make her what he likes—that is plain. And the lover himself thinks so too: the little darling is so fond of him, her little vanities are so bewitching, he wouldn't consent to her being a bit wiser; those kitten-like glances and movements are just what one wants to make one's hearth a paradise. Every man under such circumstances is conscious of being a great physiognomist. Nature, he knows, has a language of her own, which she uses with strict veracity, and he considers himself an adept in the language.'
>
> (Chapter 15)

George Eliot subjects Hetty to several characteristic tests. Her first appearance for example is symbolic: 'Hetty Sorrel often took the opportunity, when her aunt's back was turned, of looking at the pleasing reflection of herself in those polished surfaces . . . and she could see herself sometimes in the great round pewter dishes that were ranged on the shelves above the long deal dinner-table, or in the hobs of the grate, which always shone like jasper' (Chapter 6). In the formal contrast with Dinah in Chapter 15, 'The Two Bedchambers', Hetty is seen looking at herself in the mirror whereas Dinah 'delighted in her bedroom window'. Unlike Adam and the Poysers, Hetty has no tender feelings about the past, and no special love for the place where she has grown up. 'Hetty could have cast all her past life behind her, and never cared to be reminded of it again. I think she had no feeling at all towards the old house, and did not like the Jacob's Ladder and the long row of Holly-hocks in the garden better than other flowers—perhaps not so well' (Chapter 15).

Hetty appears to lack all the elements of the moral life as George Eliot conceives it, but animus and irony against her would be inappropriate. George Eliot's response in fact is the same as that which she attributes to Dinah: 'this blank in

Hetty's nature, instead of exciting Dinah's dislike, only touched her with a deeper pity: the lovely face and form affected her as beauty always affects a pure and tender mind, free from selfish jealousies: it was an excellent divine gift, that gave a deeper pathos to the need, the sin, the sorrow with which it was mingled, as the canker in a lily-white bud is more grievous to behold than in a common pot-herb' (Chapter 15). One wonders, however, whether this sympathy is enough for the novelist.

The painful feelings aroused by the contemplation of Hetty are, as I have said, quite different from those inspired by Grandcourt. They are stated here:

'it is too painful to think that she is a woman, with a woman's destiny before her—a woman spinning in young ignorance a light web of folly and vain hopes which may one day close round her and press upon her, a rancorous poisoned garment, changing all at once her fluttering, trivial butterfly sensations into a life of deep human anguish.' (Chapter 22)

Dorothea Brooke thinks that her sister Celia is no more in need of salvation than a squirrel. George Eliot cannot allow herself such an evasion when she contemplates Hetty, since for her salvation and damnation are not matters of faith but facts observable in this life. That Hetty's being incompletely human does not absolve her from a human destiny is a harsh fact; hers is the one case in which George Eliot's belief in moral responsibility appears to break down. Nevertheless, her story is not emptied of moral significance.

George Eliot's conviction that all human life is a serious concern, and her communication of that conviction in the telling of Hetty's story, makes it impossible for the reader to regard the character with either contempt or condescension. This is true above all of the magnificent chapters entitled 'The Journey in Hope' and 'The Journey in Despair', which describe Hetty's journeys to Windsor in search of Arthur and back again when she has failed to find him. Here, in the most sustained inward study of a consciousness without conscience that George Eliot was ever to attempt, we have pre-eminently what Mathilde Blind called her 'democratic side', which is a matter not of egalitarianism but a perception of continuity and relatedness in human life, so that Hetty's experience becomes more general and representative than one could ever have predicted. The following necessarily long quotation is from Chapter 37 ('The Journey in Despair') and concerns Hetty's failure to carry out her intention of drowning herself:

'The horror of this cold, and darkness, and solitude—out of all human reach—became greater every long minute: it was almost as if if she were dead already, and knew that she was dead, and longed to get back to life again. But no: she was alive still; she had not taken the dreadful leap. She felt a strange contradictory wretchedness and exultation: wretchedness, that she did not dare to face death; exultation, that she was still in life—that she might yet know light and warmth again. She walked backwards and forwards to warm herself, beginning to discern something of the objects around her, as her eyes became accustomed to the night: the darker line of the hedge, the rapid motion of some living creature—perhaps a field-mouse—rushing across the grass. She no longer felt as if the darkness hedged her in: she thought she could walk back across the field, and get over the stile; and then, in the very next field, she thought she remembered there was a hovel of furze near a sheepfold. If she could get into that hovel, she would be warmer; she could pass the night there, for that was what Alick did at Hayslope in lambing-time. The thought of this hovel brought the energy of a new hope: she took up her basket and walked across the field, but it was some time before she got in the right direction for the stile. The exercise and the occupation of finding the stile were a stimulus to her, however, and lightened the horror of the darkness and solitude. There were sheep in the next field, and she startled a group as she set down her basket and got over the stile; and the sound of their movement comforted her, for it assured her that her impression was right: this *was* the field where she had seen the hovel, for it was the field where the sheep were. Right on along the path, and she would get to it. She reached the opposite gate, and felt her way along its rails, and the rails of the sheepfold, till her hand encountered the pricking of the gorsy wall. Delicious sensation! She had found the shelter: she groped her way, touching the prickly gorse, to the door, and pushed it open. It was an ill-smelling close place, but warm, and there was straw on the ground: Hetty sank down on the straw with a sense of escape. Tears came—she had never shed tears before since she left Windsor—tears and sobs of hysterical joy that she had still hold of life, that she was still on the familiar earth, with the sheep near her. The very consciousness of her own limbs was a delight to her: she turned up her sleeves, and kissed her arms with the passionate love of life. Soon warmth and weariness lulled her in the midst of her sobs, and she fell continually into dozing, fancying herself at the brink of the pool again—fancying that she had jumped into the water, and then awaking with a start, and wondering where she was. But at last deep dreamless sleep came; her head, guarded by her bonnet, found a pillow against the gorsy wall; and the poor soul, driven to and fro between two equal terrors, found the one relief that was possible to it—the relief of unconsciousness.'   (Chapter 37)

After such writing as that, what room can there be for criticism of Hetty's treatment? Yet almost all the novel's readers do feel dissatisfied; they feel that by the end of the book the problem of Hetty has been somehow put aside. This issue might be clarified by considering two questions: Why is Hetty reprieved? And why is the account of the reprieve written in such a bunglingly melodramatic manner?

The fact of Hetty is one of the harshest that George Eliot confronted herself with in her novels. In addition to this, by the time we have followed Hetty to and from Windsor, she has become the most thoroughly imagined human centre of the novel. But George Eliot had other interests to work out—those, centred on Adam and Dinah, which I have argued are less effectively imagined than she would have hoped. These interests are more closely related to the didactic elements in her work than anything that she could have gone on to do with Hetty would be. We might posit, in opposition to the human centre, a thematic or notional centre which is defined by the author's didactic intentions rather than by the discovered human reality. When these centres come into conflict we have the division alluded to in my Introduction, between preconceived ideas and imaginative sympathy. In some cases it is also the conflict between didacticism and tragedy.

The dissatisfaction is not just a matter of the novel's going on after Hetty's story has finished. Tolstoy goes on after Anna Karenina's death to devote a final book to Levin, and this modifies the effect of Anna's tragedy, but her story nevertheless is tragic and is treated as such. The problem of Hetty—the fact that someone so incompletely human has nevertheless to face a human destiny—would appear to be a subject for tragedy. But George Eliot fails to commit herself to it. It is here that the reprieve comes in. What reason can there have been for it but that the author wishes to reduce the intensity of the reader's interest in Hetty—to remove from herself the pressure of an expectation that she cannot or will not fulfil? As for the melodrama, which is presumably unintentional, it strongly suggests, by its extreme incongruity with the rest of the novel, that the author has no conviction in what she is doing.

A similar conflict to this occurs in *Daniel Deronda*. Gwendolen Harleth comes closer to achieved tragedy than Hetty (and, being intelligent and capable of moral growth, can be more comfortably encompassed by our ideas of the tragic hero) but at the end of the novel George Eliot makes a revealing reference to Gwendolen's 'small life'. The standard of comparison is the thematic hero, Daniel, who is devoting himself to a national cause. Despite her championing of the individual, George Eliot was unwilling to attach a supreme value to an intense and profound experience which did not have beneficial repercussions in the wider life of humanity. And, while the type of the tragic hero is certainly not the Romantic egoist on the Childe Harold model, an acknowledgement of some such value is a necessary part of tragic art. If this is so, then the reason for the reprieve, the silence about Hetty's years of transportation, and the casual treatment of her death, is that George Eliot wanted to direct the reader's sympathy and attention to those lives she considerd valuable: in other words, the shape of the novel and the distribution of concern are deliberately directed from its didactic rather than its human centre.

4
The Mill on the Floss

A useful way to approach *The Mill on the Floss* is to compare the central relationship, that of Tom and Maggie, with a brother-sister relationship in Dickens: that of Charley and Lizzie Hexam in *Our Mutual Friend*. The Hexams belong to a much lower social stratum than the Tullivers (their father lives by what he dredges from the river). But Charley has social aspirations which his sister does not share, and the conflict between them reaches a climax when she refuses to marry Charley's friend and mentor, the schoolteacher Bradley Headstone. There are several points of similarity between the two relationships. In both cases the brother is unimaginative, conventional and censorious, the sister passionate, affectionate and morally disorientated. (In her recoil from Headstone, whose struggle for respectability has entailed a denial and perversion of his passions, Lizzie's only apparent resource is the attentions of the morally dubious gentleman Eugene Wrayburn, whom she loves.) The differences, at first sight, point to a superiority in George Eliot's treatment: the issues are far more complex, and Tom is more sympathetically portrayed than Charley; George Eliot is much bolder than Dickens in the representation of her heroine's sensuousness. Lizzie, when she is rejected by Charley, has some of the simple emotional appeal of a Cinderella:

> 'But then, with the breaking up of her immobility came the breaking up of the waters that the cold heart of the selfish boy had frozen. And "Oh, that I were lying here with the dead!" and "Oh, Charley, Charley, that this should be the end of our pictures in the fire!" were all the words she said, as she laid her face in her hands on the stone coping.'[1]

The appeal is of a general kind; the reader responds—if he responds at all—to the idea, dramatised by Lizzie's pose on the stone coping, of the girl rejected by her loved but unloving brother. The situation has been created only by the 'cold heart of the selfish boy', and Lizzie is simply a victim.

Tom Tulliver is neither cold-hearted nor selfish, and the scene in which he reproves Maggie for her association with Philip Wakem provides a striking contrast with Dickens's scene: 'Tom had his terrible clutch on her conscience and her deepest dread: she writhed under the demonstrable truth of the character he had given to her conduct, and yet her whole soul rebelled against it as unfair from its incompleteness.'[2] The reader's response to this is determined by the specific terms of Maggie's relation to Tom, and her own ambivalent attitude to the conduct which he condemns. Tom appears at his least attractive in this chapter; the spirit of revenge which motivates his disapproval is primitive and brutal, and his threat to tell his father if Maggie does not promise to stop seeing Philip is a form of blackmail. Nevertheless, he is able to touch Maggie's conscience even here, and if his crude rectitude is inferior to Maggie's moral complexity, George Eliot intimates that he is, after all, right: that his judgement of her conduct is that of Maggie's own conscience.

For all this difference, there is an important point of similarity between the two scenes. It occurs in the language used by the two young men:

'"Upon my soul, you are a pretty piece of disinterestedness! And so all my endeavours to cancel the past and to raise myself in the world, and to raise you with me, are to be beaten down by *your* low whims; are they?"'[3]

'"But," he added, his voice trembling with indignation, "while I have been contriving and working that my father may have some peace of mind before he dies—working for the respectability of our family—you have done all you can to destroy both."'[4]

'Respectability' is a word often used by both brothers, and both Maggie and Lizzie offend against their brothers' social values in their personal lives. The similarities and differences having been thus stated, it would appear that there is a straightforward distinction of quality between the two novels.

Such a conclusion, however, would be inexact; for the differences between the two relationships express a more fundamental difference in the writers' understanding of social processes. The higher valuation which George Eliot accords to Tom is not merely a matter of personal sympathy and understanding, but of a greater sympathy for what he represents. The main theme of *Our Mutual Friend* is the conflict of class-values (though not necessarily those of a particular class) and primary human values. The 'social' is seen not as an extension of the personal but as a denial of it; not as an expression of the complex relations between individuals, but as a self-justifying code which provides, for a character like Mr Podsnap, a complete alternative to individual life. It is above all something imposed on individual life by fear and prejudice. Charley Hexam's desire to become respectable initially compels our sympathy. That sympathy is lost when his aspiration comes into conflict with Lizzie's determination to vindicate her father's memory (he is believed to have committed murder), which involves adherence to the hated and admittedly evil social circumstances in which she was born. Charley's social aspirations are judged, partly, by their incompatibility with the primary personal duty by which Lizzie acts. When he rejects her because of her refusal to marry Bradley Headstone, the incompatibility becomes direct conflict; and in that refusal there is the further relevant factor of the repugnance Lizzie feels towards the condition which Bradley's own struggle for respectability has brought him to.

Mr Grahame Smith has remarked of George Eliot that, in contrast to Dickens: 'it is not the *specific* quality of nineteenth-century life that compels her attention so much as the complexities of attempting a personal and public life in *any* social setting.'[5] Beneath this difference lies the difference in her understanding of 'society' itself. Dickens's interest is directly in the society of his own time, and its influence on the possibilities of individual life. This is true even of his novels which are set in the past. The date of *Little Dorrit* allows him to use the Marshalsea Prison, and in *Great*

Expectations we are reminded that prisoners are better treated now than then; but we do not need to make a positive effort of imagination to understand the social criticism. In *The Mill on the Floss* such an effort is intrinsic to the method. Our attention is constantly being drawn, almost always ironically, to the fact that society is different now:

> 'Why should an auctioneer and appraiser thirty years ago, who had as good as forgotten his free-school Latin, be expected to manifest a delicate scrupulosity which is not always exhibited by gentlemen of the learned professions, even in our present advanced stage of morality?' (Book 1, Chapter 3)

> 'It was a time when ignorance was much more comfortable than at present, and was received with all the honours in very good society, without being obliged to dress itself in an elaborate costume of knowledge.' (Book 1, Chapter 12)

The irony is a defence against complacency: George Eliot does not allow her meliorism to degenerate into self-congratulation at the expense of the past. But the belief in progress is not compromised:

> 'I share with you this sense of oppressive narrowness; but it is necessary that we should feel it, if we are to understand how it acted on the lives of Tom and Maggie—how it has acted on young natures in many generations, that in the onward tendency of human things have risen above the mental level of the generation before them, to which they have been nevertheless tied by the strongest fibres of their hearts.'

> (Book 4, Chapter 1)

This, though it is in one respect misleading, is a statement of the novel's central concern, and it points to the reason why the historical perspective is so important. George Eliot set so many of her novels in this period not only because of the potency of her youthful impressions, but also because it was an age which she had experienced and understood in detail, but which was dominated by assumptions which seemed quite foreign thirty or forty years later. The historical perspective enabled her to be analytic, to be concerned with the social process as a historical development, in a way which did not interest Dickens. It also meant—and this is the most important difference—that she saw the forces of social repression as part of a natural process, in which the repressive assumptions express the stage of development of the average of humanity, and change only as the average itself changes. It is partly this intellectual attitude to social change that enables George Eliot to deal so sympathetically with the forces that are hostile to Maggie's individuality. Her sympathy, moreover, is even greater than the intellectual argument might suggest: it issues in a moral imperative that runs counter to what the reader might expect, and certainly counter to anything that we find in Dickens: George Eliot's doctrine of continuity in one of its most extreme forms.

'Custom,' says Riehl of the peasant, 'with him holds the place of sentiment, of theory, and in many cases of affection.'[6] The 'Dodson code' is substantially the rule of custom, but the Dodsons are not peasants, and the power of custom varies according to the strength of the individual character. Jerome Thale has put the case well:

> 'In Mrs. Tulliver, the "weakest vessel", the code is pathetic and absurd. When the family has been sold up she is unable to sleep nights thinking of her linen scattered all over England. Because she lacks her sisters' rigidity and clear-sightedness, one part of the code, the domestic, comes into conflict with another, the acceptance of fact. In the other sisters the strength of the code enables them to order their lives successfully. For them domestic rites and duties operate within larger sets of moral stringencies.'[7]

Mrs Tulliver's grief at the catastrophe is more for her 'treasures' than for her desperately-ill husband. The force of custom operates so powerfully on her that the loss of her domestic objects—each of them associated with a particular time and event—is a radical disorientation. It is not that she does not love her husband, but that she lives most immediately through the environment which she has built up around herself, through the objects which have given continuity to her life. She is so subject to the potency of the past that she does not think of her marriage as something that has given her a new inner direction, but as an accident that has remained outside her: ' "And I'm not to be answerable for my bad luck i' marrying out o' my own family into one where the goings-on was different." ' (Book 3, Chapter 7).

The moulding-force of the past operates also on Mr Tulliver, in a way which does not seem at all absurd:

> ' "But it's forty good year since they finished the malt-house, and it isn't many days out of 'em all, as I haven't looked out into the yard there, the first thing in the morning—all weathers, from year's end to year's end. I should go off my head in a new place. I should be like as if I'd lost my way." '
>
> (Book 3, Chapter 9)

Maggie, too, as we shall see later, is influenced by yet another, more highly-developed form of the same feeling. In this way George Eliot shows us how Mrs Tulliver's attachment to her treasures is not an aberration, but an extreme form of a quite natural feeling. There is a still closer parallel in Maggie's grief over the loss of the 'dear old *Pilgrim's Progress*': ' " I thought we should never part with that while we lived—everything is going away from us—the end of our lives will have nothing in it like the beginning." ' (Book 3, Chapter 6).

Mrs Tulliver's emotions are inadequate not because they are controlled by custom but because—unlike for example her husband's attachment to the Mill—they do not nourish strong personal affections and, as Mr Thale says, because they inhibit the acceptance of fact. Mrs Glegg is admirable when, at the family council, she bursts out:

> ' "It drives me past patience to hear you all talking o' best things, and buying in this, that, and the other, such as silver and chany. You must bring your mind to your circumstances, Bessy, and not be thinking o' silver and chany; but whether you shall get so much as a flock bed to lie on, and a blanket to cover you, and a stool to sit on." '
>
> (Book 3, Chapter 3)

She is admirable, because for all her Pharisaism we do not hesitate to believe that she would act on her own advice if she were in the same situation—only, like Tom when he chastises Maggie, she would never be in the same situation. She is the spokesman for the Dodson code, and she is also the most individual and—though the most insistent on custom—the least blindly conservative of the sisters. In her the code comes closest to meeting the demands of real life.

She is scathing about Mrs Pullet's excessive locking-up and polishing of stairs, and there is a real moral strength in her championing of Maggie in the face of public opinion: the cult of 'kin' is seen to involve a strong moral commitment.

Mr Thale has stressed the prominence of death in the Dodson code: 'it has its last triumph at death'.[8] In the second chapter Mrs Tulliver expresses her pride in the state of her sheets: 'An' if you was to die tomorrow, Mr. Tulliver, they're mangled beautiful'; Mrs Pullet makes her first appearance in tears over the death of 'Mrs. Sutton o' the Twentylands'—'there isn't another such a dropsy in the parish'—and Mrs Glegg, 'who always cried just as much as was proper when anything happened to her own "kin", but not on other occasions', reproves her (Book 1, Chapter 7); Mrs Glegg is brought out of a bad temper by her husband's hint of 'testamentary tenderness': 'To survive Mr Glegg, and talk eulogistically of him as a man who might have his weaknesses, but who had done the right thing by her, notwithstanding his numerous poor relations—to have sums of interest coming in more frequently, and secrete it in various corners, baffling to the most ingenious of thieves (for, to Mrs Glegg's mind, banks and strong-boxes would have nullified the pleasure of property—she might as well have taken her food in capsules)—finally, to be looked up to by her own family and the neighbourhood, so as no woman can ever hope to be who has not the praeterite and present dignity comprised in being a "widow well left",—all this made a flattering and conciliatory view of the future,' (Book 1, Chapter 12); and of her own will, 'No one must be able to say of her when she was dead that she had not divided her money with perfect fairness among her own kin' (Book 1, Chapter 13).

The manner of death—the clean linen and 'unimpeachable will'—is the justification of life. The chapter (Book 4, Chapter 1) in which George Eliot gives an extensive account of the Dodson theory of life, is entitled 'A Variation of Protestantism Unknown to Bossuet'; and the title is not merely facetious. That theory is a kind of parody of the Protestantism so well known to Mary Ann Evans:

'. . . and still I must believe that those are happiest who are not fermenting themselves by engaging in projects for earthly bliss, who are considering this life merely a pilgrimage, a scene calling for diligence and watchfulness, not for repose and amusement.'[9]

To Mrs Glegg, too, life is 'a scene calling for diligence and watchfulness', but her religion has 'the very slightest tincture of theology':

'The religion of the Dodsons consisted in revering whatever was customary and respectable: it was necessary to be baptised, else one could not be buried in the church-yard, and to take the sacrament before death as a security against more dimly understood perils; but it was of equal necessity to have the proper pall-bearers and well-cured hams at one's funeral, and to leave an unimpeachable will.' (Book 4, Chapter 1)

This attitude towards death gives a peculiar quality to the Dodsons' materialism. Their reverence and sense of mystery is transferred entirely to the material objects associated with death, and is absorbed into the idea of 'respectability'; it is a parallel to the way in which the sanctity of the past is represented for Mrs Tulliver entirely by the objects which she has gathered around her. A corrupt form of this attitude is seen in Peter Featherstone in *Middlemarch*: 'In writing the programme for his burial he certainly did not make clear to himself that his pleasure in the little drama of which it formed a part was confined to anticipation.' (Chapter 34). This *is* a corruption, however, and when Dr Leavis says that 'the Gleggs and the Pullets and the Dodson clan associate, not with the frequenters of Mrs Poyser's kitchen, but with the tribe that foregathers at Stone Court waiting for Peter Featherstone to die',[10] he ignores the tribute that George Eliot pays not only directly—'society owes some worthy qualities in many of her members to mothers of the Dodson class'—but in the very structure of the book. There is a clear continuity between the code of custom and the doctrine of the sanctity of the past which determines Maggie's behaviour in her relations first with Philip Wakem and then with Stephen Guest. (Stephen's late appearance in the novel, and the authorial bias against him, help to foist upon the reader the suggestion that any life which involves a breach of continuity will be morally bankrupt.)

The Dodson spirit at its best is represented not by any of

the sisters, but by Tom. In quoting George Eliot's account of her theme I remarked that it is in one sense misleading. Tom has, like Maggie, risen above the mental level of his elders, but his moral world is still that of the Dodsons. He does not share the totemistic habits of his mother and his aunts, but as the theme is expressed in the drama it is Tom who represents the level of development beyond which Maggie has progressed, and with which she comes into conflict.

Dr Leavis, among others, has criticised the expression of this conflict, singling out the passage from Book 3, Chapter 5, in which Maggie is described as 'a creature full of eager, passionate longings for all that was beautiful and glad . . . with an ear straining after dreamy music that died away and would not come near to her; with a blind, unconscious yearning for something that would link together the wonderful impressions of this mysterious life, and give her soul a sense of home in it.' Leavis says that this represents an 'immaturity' in George Eliot herself: 'This "blind, unconscious yearning" never . . . learns to understand itself: Maggie remains . . . incapable of analysing it into the varied potentialities it associates.'[11] He does not, however, quote the sentence immediately following the above passage, which should alert the reader to George Eliot's attitude: 'No wonder, when there is this contrast between the outward and the inward, that painful collisions come of it.' One possible attitude towards the painful collision between the inward and the outward is that the outward should be despised. This was not George Eliot's view. What Maggie moves towards (and continually falls back from) is not (in Leavis's words) 'emotional exaltation', but a spirit of renunciation which will fit the inward to the outward, and which will renounce that exaltation itself. The book is governed by a moral imperative which, if it hampers Maggie's moral development, does not do so by conniving at the perpetuation of the stage of immaturity represented by 'emotional exaltations'.

'[She was] unhappily quite without that knowledge of the irreversible laws within and without her, which, governing the habits, becomes morality, and, developing the feelings of submission and dependence, becomes religion.'

(Book 4, Chapter 3)

The point is made with similar clarity in relation to Thomas à Kempis:

> 'She had not perceived—how could she until she had lived longer?—the inmost truth of the old monk's outpourings, that renunciation remains sorrow, though a sorrow borne willingly. Maggie was still panting for happiness, and was in ecstasy because she had found the key to it.' (ibid.)

Maggie's yearning is not analysed 'into the varied potentialities it associates', not because it is indulged but because the moral imperative does not allow it to run its course. The weakness of the book is not self-idealisation but didacticism: a didacticism which, in the last third of the novel, is disastrously damaging.

The moral imperative is that which ultimately persuades Maggie to renounce Stephen, and it is Maggie herself who articulates it: 'If the past is not to bind us, where can duty lie? We should have no law but the inclination of the moment.' (Book 6, Chapter 14). This is a development out of the statement of the theme previously quoted: that Maggie and Tom are tied to the previous generation 'by the strongest fibres of their hearts'. In the final crisis the past is represented by the tacit engagements with Philip and Lucy; when Maggie resolved to renounce Philip, it was for the sake of her father. Throughout the novel, the major moral agent is the sense of the past's action on the present and future: Mr Tulliver is lenient with his sister because he hopes that Tom will be kind to Maggie; Wakem is reconciled to Philip's marrying Maggie by the memory of his wife; Bob Jakin offers Tom his little fortune because of the gift of a pocket-knife when they were boys.

Maggie's conscientious doubts about her relation to Philip are the first major example of the moral imperative working against her finer perceptions. Her doubts are prompted not merely by the fear of discovery and of the possible effect of it on her father, but by the fact of concealment. The relationship represents a development out of the moral world of the Dodsons and Tullivers; yet Maggie must not merely conform outwardly to the inferior standards—by concealing the relationship—she must modify her behaviour absolutely in accordance with them. (Tulliver's spirit of revenge is not a Dodson feeling, but it receives the stamp of Dodson rectitude when championed by Tom in the name of respectability.)

One is conscious here of arguing on strictly moral grounds; that is, from outside the novel. Much as one may protest against the didactic intention, it works within an acceptable drama: it is not strictly identifiable as an aesthetic weakness. Argument has developed along similar lines about Maggie's renunciation of Stephen, and perhaps the most impressive case against George Eliot has been made by Joan Bennett in *George Eliot*:

'A part of what is wrong with the close of the novel is that the problem facing Maggie and Stephen at the crisis is not a satisfactory vehicle for the conception the author intended to symbolize by it. . . .

When we apply the moral standards that the author herself invites us to apply (to cause as little unhappiness as the circumstances would allow) we feel that Maggie and Stephen should have shown more courage and honesty when they first discovered that they were in love. Their intention to marry Philip and Lucy in spite of that discovery seems the reverse of noble. That intended deception shocks the reader more than does the failure to carry it out. The qualities needed in their difficult situation were not self-sacrificing heroism, but patience and tact and delicacy of feeling.'[12]

The manoeuvring of Maggie into an impossible situation can be attributed, by this argument, to George Eliot's ignoring a prior set of moral criteria. The argument is a very strong one, but it is open to the objection made by Mr Paris, that Mrs Bennett has misunderstood George Eliot's 'theory of morality': the criteria that we are invited to apply are not those that she names:

'Maggie's choice is not between kindness and unkindness, or between degrees of pleasure and pain for those involved; it is between a life which is motivated and sanctified by the recognition of a moral law which is independent of personal desire and a meaningless life guided by nothing but random impulse. . . .

The sanctification of her life lies, for Maggie, in obedience to that which she feels to be her duty, in faithfulness to the ties of love, trust, and dependence which have grown out of her past life.'[13]

Mr Paris is paraphrasing Maggie's own arguments, and he is obviously right. But for him, a correct interpretation of George Eliot's intentions is a vindication of the novel. His argument does not help the reader who follows his interpretation but remains dissatisfied with the novel. For the moralist, the argument is open to a number of attacks: George Eliot might be accused of falsely denying the validity of 'impulse' in the formation of moral choice (is Maggie most herself when drifting on the river or when battling with Stephen the following morning?); or it may be objected that the 'past' which is to 'bind us' is arbitrarily defined—at what point does the relation with Stephen become sufficiently past to have a binding power? Maggie renounced Philip because of prior attachments, but now he himself has come to represent the sanctity of the past. But such objections do not advance criticism of the novel: the moralist is simply left with the choice between Mrs Bennett's criteria and those of George Eliot as interpreted by Mr Paris.

The difficulties experienced by readers are caused by a didacticism which falsifies the drama and makes genuine moral choice impossible. One key passage in Maggie's inner struggle is the following:

'There were moments in which a cruel selfishness seemed to be getting possession of her: why should not Lucy—why should not Philip suffer? *She* had had to suffer through many years of her life; and who had renounced anything for her? And when something like that fulness of existence—love, wealth, ease, refinement, all that her nature craved—was brought within her reach, why was she to forego it, that another might have it— another, who perhaps needed it less? But amidst all this new passionate tumult there were the old voices making themselves heard with rising power, till, from time to time, the tumult seemed quelled. *Was* that existence which tempted her the full existence she dreamed? Where, then, would be all the memories of early striving—all the deep pity for another's pain, which had been nurtured in her through years of affection and hardship— all the divine presentiment of something higher than mere personal enjoyment, which had made the sacredness of life?'

(Book 6, Chapter 13)

The didactic purpose shows through very clearly here, and

the moralist again has his answer. George Eliot identifies the capacity for goodness so absolutely with reverence for the past that she almost forces the objection: such a relation as marriage, no matter how materially comfortable, is continually providing new occasions for 'deep pity for another's pain', and a nature like Maggie's would be qualified to meet the perpetually renewed demands on her capacity for self-sacrifice. To assert that by once choosing her own happiness at the expense (dubiously) of others she would lose that capacity, is simply perverse. The moralist's voice has its relevance here, because George Eliot is appealing directly to the reader's moral sense. The didacticism is present not only in the explicit moral imperative but also—and this is where it is damaging—in the assumption that life with Stephen will be a life of ease, with no duties. This assumption is dishonest because at the moments when Maggie's struggle is most poignant, Stephen is seen as having his own claim on her conscience: 'He had called up a state of feeling in which the reasons which had acted on her conscience seemed to be transmuted into mere self-regard.' (Book 6, Chapter 13). The picture wavers: in the final struggle, after the receipt of Stephen's letter, the decision to marry him is again represented as a choice of ease rather than hardship: 'And here—close within her reach—urging itself upon her even as a claim—was another future, in which hard endurance and effort were to be exchanged for easy delicious leaning on another's loving strength!' (Book 7, Chapter 5). The last phrase recalls the George Eliot we know from biographical sources, who was 'always requiring some one to lean upon . . . not fitted to stand alone'.[14] The point here is that with what we know of Maggie, and what we know of Stephen, we cannot imagine the marriage being like that at all. The stronger cannot lean on the weaker.

What we know of Stephen: that is the crux. It is the presentation of Stephen's character, above all, that falsifies the moral issues. The moralist objects that marriage with Stephen would impose new duties and be a perpetually renewing force upon Maggie's moral nature. The spontaneous reader (who is very elusive, but who for my purpose is the reader who follows—as we are likely to at least on a first reading—where the author leads him) is unlikely to make this objection. There is a strong pressure on the reader, which is very hard to resist except by distancing oneself as in making a critical analysis, to acquiesce in the suggestion that life with Stephen would be both easy and mediocre. The pressure is the portrayal of Stephen himself, particularly on his first appearance:

> ' . . . the fine young man who is leaning down from his chair to snap the scissors in the extremely abbreviated face of the "King Charles" lying on the young lady's feet, is no other than Mr. Stephen Guest, whose diamond ring, attar of roses, and air of nonchalant leisure, at twelve o'clock in the day, are the graceful and odoriferous result of the largest oil-mill and the most extensive wharf in St. Ogg's.'   (Book 6, Chapter 1)

There have been some very unappealing characters in the first two-thirds of the book, but there is a new kind of distance and irony in the description of Stephen that registers almost as animus. He immediately stands apart from all the other characters in the novel. This effect is partly the result of the abrupt change of tone, as if we are moving into a new world and even a new novel, that every reader notices at this point. The world that we have come out of is that of Maggie's childhood and early youth, the world from which the sanctities which sway her have been derived. We ourselves have vicariously experienced that childhood, and the part of ourselves which temporarily lives inside the novel has been modified by the world of the Dodsons and Tullivers. Stephen is immediately placed as an outsider; he has no antecedents; he does not share the experience and values of the novel. George Eliot tells us as much in that brief description. Moreover, the description may recall, and certainly echoes, a passage in which George Eliot makes her nearest approach to the kind of social criticism we expect from Dickens:

> 'In writing the history of unfashionable families, one is apt to fall into a tone of emphasis which is very far from being the tone of good society, where principles and beliefs are not only of an extremely moderate kind, but are always presupposed, no subject being eligible but such as can be touched with a light and graceful irony. But then, good society has its claret and its

velvet carpets, its dinner-engagements six weeks deep, its opera and its faëry ballrooms; rides off its ennui on thoroughbred horses, lounges at the club, has to keep clear of crinoline vortices, gets its science done by Faraday, and its religion by the superior clergy who are to be met in the best houses: how should it have time or need for belief and emphasis? But good society, floated on gossamer wings of light irony, is of very expensive production; requiring nothing less than a wide and arduous national life condensed in unfragrant deafening factories, cramping itself in mines, sweating at furnaces, grinding, hammering, weaving under more or less oppression of carbonic acid—or else, spread over sheepwalks, and scattered in lonely houses and huts on the clayey or chalkey corn-lands, where the rainy days look dreary. This wide national life is based entirely on emphasis—the emphasis of want, which urges it into all the activities necessary for the maintenance of good society and light irony: it spends its heavy years often in a chill, uncarpeted fashion, amidst family discord unsoftened by long corridors. Under such circumstances, there are many among its myriads of souls who have absolutely needed an emphatic belief: life in this unpleasurable shape demanding some solution even to unspeculative minds; just as you inquire into the stuffing of your couch when anything galls you there, whereas eider-down and perfect French springs excite no question.'   (Book 4, Chapter 3)

Read in context, this passage seems an intrusion. We are not reading about the lives of miners, factory-hands or even agricultural labourers; there is no 'want' in the sense which George Eliot gives the word here. The world of Maggie's childhood is one of comfortable lower middle-class respectability, which has its own idea of 'good society'. Even when a catastrophe occurs, poverty does not extend beyond the loss of furniture. This outburst reads very much like a dishonest attempt to arouse emotions that are not relevant to the actual situation. It does, however, present a contrast between those who work to provide the world's goods and those who enjoy them: between the Dodsons and Tullivers, and Stephen Guest. Stephen is fond of light irony, goes on long rides when he wants to forget his troubles, and introduces contemporary science (not Faraday but the Bridgewater Treatises) into drawing-room conversation. Most important, he is the useless product of other men's labour: 'You've had a sort of learning that's all very well for a young fellow like our Mr. Stephen Guest, who'll have nothing to do but sign cheques all his life, and may as well have Latin inside his head as any other sort of stuffing', says Mr Deane to Tom (Book 3, Chapter 5), making the only mention of Stephen before he appears in Book 6. The contrast with Tom, implied here, is an important part of Stephen's portrayal. Our admiration for Tom grows as we see him 'opening the oyster', and applying himself with all the strength of an iron nature to the recovery of the family's fortunes. In the course of the same visit to Mr Deane (the beginning of Tom's efforts) we are told, 'There were no impulses in Tom that led him to expect what did not present itself to him as a right to be demanded.' There are few qualities that George Eliot admired more than this; it is the finest expression of the Dodson spirit, the firm and uncomplaining acceptance of reality. Four pages after Stephen's first appearance, this contrast with Tom is made again, and George Eliot leaves us in no doubt about her own attitude, though she allows Stephen to condemn himself out of his own mouth:

> ' "Oh, ah; I've heard about that [Tom's restoration of the family fortunes]. I heard your father and mine talking about it a little while ago, after dinner, in one of their interminable discussions about business. They think of doing something for young Tulliver: he saved them from a considerable loss by riding home in some marvellous way, like Turpin, to bring them news about the stoppage of a bank, or something of that sort. But I was rather drowsy at the time." '   (Book 6, Chapter 1)

Stephen's 'odoriferous' cultivation then, is built upon, not merely the efforts of the toiling masses generally, but those of Tom Tulliver in particular; efforts which he is too languid to take an interest in. The early prejudice against Stephen which is so forcibly rooted in the reader in this chapter remains with him, despite the process of moral education that he sees Stephen undergoing in his relationship with Maggie. Moreover, he is again shown in an unfavourable moral light at the final crisis, in his letter to Maggie which was, we are told, 'From beginning to end . . . a passionate cry of reproach', ' "Maggie! whose pain can have been like mine? whose injury is like mine?" ' (Book 7,

Chapter 5). Again Stephen damns himself out of his own mouth, and George Eliot enforces the contention that the alternative to renunciation for Maggie, is mediocrity. If Maggie feels that that alternative is 'urging itself upon her even as a claim', the reader is made to feel that the claim is a selfish one, of inferior power to those of Philip and Lucy (whose unselfishness has been carefully re-asserted in the previous two chapter). Stephen remains, to the last, a pariah in the moral world of the novel, and it is this which gives critical rather than simply moral support to Mrs Bennett's contention that 'the problem facing Maggie and Stephen at the end of the novel is not a satisfactory vehicle for the conception the author intended to symbolize by it'—even if we accept Mr Paris's definition of that conception. The conception is—to redefine—that a choice based on the desire for personal happiness will, by rupturing the past ties which embody moral law, inhibit the capacity for moral action and desecrate the future. The inadequacy of the 'vehicle' consists in the refusal to take into account—or to allow the reader to take into account—the counter-argument that the moral nature grows in response to new claims, and that law is not so completely embodied in the past as George Eliot asserts. This argument is not allowed to exist in the novel, because the emphasis on Stephen's mediocrity and egotism —and even more so his position as an outsider—persuades the reader to believe that such a future *would* be desecrated. He cannot protest—as he might well do if Stephen were more admirable—that Maggie should have married him. It is reasonable to consider the case of a more worthy Stephen, because then the moral issue would be very much clearer. The moral burden of the book is the same *whatever* Stephen might be, but if the issue were clearer so, one suspects, would be the protests.[15]

The means—particularly the structural means—by which the prejudice against Stephen is created, have a significance in relation to George Eliot's social concerns. One of Sir Edward Lytton's criticisms which she recognised as just was that 'the tragedy is not adequately prepared'. She explains: 'The *"epische Breite"* into which I was beguiled by love of my subject in the two first volumes, caused a want of proportionate fulness in the treatment of the third, which

I shall always regret.'[16] But this very disproportion creates the feeling that Stephen is an outsider: a feeling that is essential to the didactic purpose. The *epische Breite* has been bestowed upon the 'emmet-like Dodsons and Tullivers' (Book 4, Chapter 1), and it is against that life that Stephen is measured and found wanting—both implicitly in the abrupt change of tone and explicitly in the emphasis on Stephen's idleness and the contrast with Tom. It is out of the 'emmet' life that Maggie's moral nature has grown, and if she has developed far beyond her mother's pagan reverence for domestic trivia, there is an inescapable link between her belief in the binding power of the past and her elders' worship of 'custom'. In one manifestation, Maggie's feelings are identical to those of her father:

'I have no heart to begin a strange life again. I should have no stay. I should feel like a lonely wanderer—cut off from the past.'
(Book 7, Chapter 2)

'I should go off my head in a new place. I should be like as if I'd lost my way.'   (Book 3, Chapter 9)

Even Tulliver's employee Luke has the same feeling, 'I can't abide new places mysen. . . . It's poor work, changing your country-side.' (ibid.)

The worship of the past is thus seen on several levels. If it appears absurd and even immoral in Mrs Tulliver's concern for her household goods, it is moving in Mr Tulliver's attachment to the Mill, and eminently respectable in Mrs Glegg's loyalty to 'kin'. In Maggie's assertion, 'If the past is not to bind us, where can duty lie?' it achieves the status of doctrine. The emphasis is on continuity, and we are shown that Maggie and Tom are 'tied by the strongest fibres of their hearts' to the previous generation—not just emotionally, but intrinsically.

The doctrine of continuity comes close to being identified with an adherence to the customary values when Maggie, after her escapade with Stephen, comes back to Tom. With masterly art, George Eliot places immediately after the scene at Mudport this description of Tom:

'Between four and five o'clock on the afternoon of the fifth day from that on which Stephen and Maggie had left St Ogg's, Tom Tulliver was standing on the gravel-walk outside the old house at Dorlcote Mill. He was master there now: he had half-fulfilled his father's dying wish, and by years of steady self-government and energetic work he had brought himself near to the attainment of more than the old respectability which had been the proud inheritance of the Dodsons and Tullivers.

But Tom's face, as he stood in the hot still sunshine of that summer afternoon, had no gladness, no triumph in it.'

(Book 7, Chapter 1)

This is of a different quality from the shift of tone at the beginning of the previous book. We move outside Maggie's experience and see it from a new centre, in the perspective of the self-denying struggle that has made Tom, for all his Pharisaical narrowness, so admirable. All the strands of suggestion that have influenced the reader in favour of the life of custom are gathered together in sympathy for Tom's bitterness and disappointment. He becomes, temporarily, the moral centre:

'In her deep humiliation under the retrospect of her own weakness—in her anguish at the injury she had inflicted—she almost desired to endure the severity of Tom's reproof, to submit in patient silence to that harsh disapproving judgement against which she had so often rebelled: it seemed no more than just to her now—who was weaker than she was?' (ibid.)

There is no answering sense of injustice now, as there was in the case of Philip. Maggie has erred by straining the bonds of the past, and she submits to the judgement of the person who most powerfully—in consciousness and in action—embodies those bonds. The reader is, of course, immediately made aware once again of Tom's limitations; he is repelled by the violence of the rejection. Tom lacks charity. Yet when charity comes, it comes not from a source outside the circle of customary values—from a representative of progress beyond the Dodson code—but from the 'weakest vessel' of the Dodson clan, the most undeveloped consciousness in the novel:

'But the poor frightened mother's love leapt out now, stronger than all dread.

"My child! I'll go with you. You've got a mother." ' (ibid.)

It is an irresistibly moving moment, and the reader is forced to recognise that judgement and sympathy are both contained, albeit separately, in the inherited feelings. The vindication of the past is complete: there is no appeal to progress.

But this is not the end. There remains the final reconciliation with Tom in death, in which it is suggested that Tom comes at last to a recognition of elements in life that he had previously been unaware of:

> 'It was not until Tom had pushed off and they were on the wide water—he face to face with Maggie—that the full meaning of what had happened rushed upon his mind. It came with so overpowering a force—it was such a new revelation to his spirit, of the depths in life, that had lain beyond his vision which he had fancied so keen and clear—that he was unable to ask a question. They sat mutely gazing at each other: Maggie with eyes of intense life looking out from a weary, beaten face—Tom pale with a certain awe and humiliation. Thought was busy though the lips were silent: and though he could ask no question, he guessed a story of almost miraculous divinely-protected effort.'
>
> (Book 7, Chapter 5)

It is easy to dismiss this as fantasy wish-fulfilment, and this must surely be the final judgement. In *George Eliot: her life and books* Mr Gerald Bullett cogently asks, referring to Tom and Maggie's death 'in an embrace never to be parted':

> 'Coming from the agnostic George Eliot, what does "never to be parted" [which comes at the end of the book] mean? Heaven being not among the possibilities she envisaged, one is tempted to retort with the gravedigger in *Hamlet* that "your water is a sore decayer of your whoreson dead body" and will dissolve all embraces.'[17]

It is a cruel retort, but such reflections are prompted by resentment against the overloaded emotional response that George Eliot calls for. However, before dismissing the scene, it will be useful to analyse it into its constituent parts. There is, of course, the element of personal involvement, which is present here more certainly than in the earlier portrayals of Maggie's 'yearning'. There is a pathetic irony in the contrast between this fiction and Isaac Evans's stilted letter of reconciliation that so thrilled George Eliot in the last year of her life.[18] The tremor of self-involvement, however, is accompanied by the suggestion that Tom at last sees beyond his hitherto limited horizons and understands the 'depths in life' that account for Maggie's previously unaccountable behaviour. Here, perhaps, is George Eliot's token for the 'progress' in which she devoutly believed, and whose operation she has been so resolutely determined to qualify. But how does this enlightenment come to Tom? In what way is Maggie's 'divinely-protected effort' related to those elements in her character which had previously alienated him? The answer, surely, is not at all. Maggie's effort has nothing to do with the finer perception of things that drew her to Philip Wakem and persuaded her to return from Mudport to face undeserved shame rather than marry Stephen Guest. It seems, in fact, to have more in common with the best of the traditional Dodson virtues: resolute, fearless practical action. Is it not easier to imagine that Tom was reconciled to Maggie because she did *precisely what he would have done*, rather than because, in that action, he recognised the quality of her difference from him?

5
Silas Marner

At the centre of *Silas Marner* there is a single dominant perception: that most men inevitably attach themselves to some object outside them, and that their selves are determined by the objects which they choose.

Of all George Eliot's characters, Silas is most like Everyman. This might seem a strange observation to make about a novel with so much sociological interest, and a character whom readers are likely to feel very remote from themselves. What can be large and general enough in the life of this cataleptic Baptist weaver to make such a contention plausible? The answer lies in the fact that the heart of Silas's experience is less that of a particular kind of man, than is that of any other major character in George Eliot's novels.

Such a generality of intention is hinted at in the suggestions of *The Pilgrim's Progress*[1] at the beginning of the novel: the 'mysterious burden' that the wandering weavers always carried on their backs and the situation of Silas's cottage 'not far from the edge of a deserted stone-pit'. These hints are supported by an explicit reference at the end of Chapter 14:

> 'In the old days there were angels who came and took men by the hand and led them away from the city of destruction. We see no white-winged angels now. But yet men are led away from threatening destruction: a hand is put into theirs, which leads them forth gently towards a calm and bright land, so that they look no more backward; and the hand may be a little child's.'

These are small contributions to the feeling that the imaginative life of the novel is substantially a matter (in the words

George Eliot used of *Romola*) of 'romantic and symbolical elements'. Together with this goes a sense of freedom and ease in the handling. What has been said of all George Eliot's early work, that it comes spontaneously from the central fount of the author's genius, with the assurance and naturalness of the thoroughly known and confidently believed, is in fact true only of *Silas Marner*. In both *Adam Bede* and *The Mill on the Floss* didacticism, theory, and the distorting authorial will are very much more in evidence than in *Middlemarch*.

But *Silas Marner*, it is generally agreed, possesses a quality lacking in any of these novels, and equally lacking in the 'romantic and symbolical elements' of *Romola* and *Daniel Deronda*. Romola drifting away and beaching at the plague-village, Daniel drifting (again!) and discovering Mirah or rowing out of the sunset to meet Mordecai, are plainly not inhabiting the 'working-day world'[2] of George Eliot's less privileged characters; and the worlds they do inhabit are similar. The world of Silas when he sees Eppie and mistakes her hair for his gold is also 'unreal'. But it is not at all the same as the other two.

The word 'romantic' means many things. When George Eliot applied it to elements in *Romola* she associated it with 'ideal': 'The various *strands* of thought I had to work out forced me into a more ideal treatment of Romola than I had foreseen at the outset.'[3] In these episodes in *Romola* and *Deronda* the real and the ideal are one. 'Obstacles, incongruities, all melted into the sense of completion with which his soul was flooded by this outward satisfaction of his longing'.[4] That description of Mordecai's feelings when he sees Daniel coming 'from the golden background' is a fair indication of what George Eliot meant by 'ideal'—and, I think, of how seriously it can be taken. The symbolism which carries these idealisations suggests vagueness, arbitrariness, and a laziness of thought overcome by wish-fulfilment.

It may be argued that 'thought' is not a notable characteristic of *Silas Marner*, and that here too George Eliot is relaxing her standards of causation in the interests of her theme. But one thing referred to by the word 'romantic' is a changing sense of what can be meant by 'thought'—at least if we think of 'romanticism' as the romanticism of Blake.

Here are some comments by F. R. Leavis on Blake's 'The Sick Rose':

> 'The seeing elements of our inner experience as clearly defined objects involves, of itself, something we naturally call "thought". . . .
> There is, then, much more solid ground for attributing "thought" to this wholly non-ratiocinative and apparently slight poem than to that ostensibly syllogistic, metaphysical piece of Shelley's ["Music, when soft voices die"].'[5]

'Seeing elements of our inner experience as clearly defined objects' is not how most readers would describe those elements in *Romola* and *Daniel Deronda*. Is it not, on the other hand, what is happening in the following passages?

> 'Strangely Marner's face and figure shrank and bent themselves into a constant mechanical relation to the objects of his life, so that he produced the same sort of impression as a handle or a crooked tube, which has no meaning standing apart.'
> (Chapter 2)

> 'The light of his faith quite put out, and his affections made desolate, he had clung with all the force of his nature to his work and his money; and like all objects to which a man devotes himself, they had fashioned him into correspondence with themselves. His loom, as he wrought in it without ceasing, had in its turn wrought on him, and confirmed more and more the monotonous craving for its monotonous response. His gold, as he hung over it and saw it grow, gathered his power of loving into a hard isolation like its own.'
> (Chapter 5)

> 'They had to knock loudly before Silas heard them; but when he did come to the door he showed no impatience, as he would once have done, at a visit that had been unasked for and unexpected. Formerly, his heart had been as a locked casket with its treasure inside; but now the casket was empty, and the lock was broken.'
> (Chapter 10)

> 'Instead of the hard coin with the familiar resisting outline, his fingers encountered soft warm curls.'
> (Chapter 12)

The gold above all is used in a varied and extended way as a metaphor or symbol for Silas's inner experience. The symbol is neither arbitrary nor esoteric. To take a similar instance, the metaphors in the following lines from Chaucer's account of the Friar are much more than lightly ironical:

'For many a man so hard is of his herte,
He may nat wepe, althogh hym soore smerte.
Therfore in stede of wepynge and preyeres
Men moote yeve silver to the povre freres.'[6]

Silver and tears, gold coins and golden hair, spark off meanings in each other in a way that is very similar to the imagery of Blake's 'Sick Rose'; and when the meanings are controlled and exploited as they are in that poem and in *Silas Marner,* it is obviously a mode of *thought.*

The gold provides a continuity in Silas's life. His inner experience during his fifteen-year withdrawal from human life is compared to that of a man in prison for whom the marking-up of days on the wall becomes an obsession; but the quality and meaning of the experience is very much bound up with the fact that what Silas is piling up is *gold.* The passages quoted earlier show just how George Eliot uses the image of gold. Its appearance of warmth as against its real coldness; the isolation necessitated by his worship of it; the repetitiveness and lack of growth in his relation to it (in contrast to the accumulation of the coins themselves)—these are not accidents of Silas's life but facts which determine it both inwardly and outwardly.

It is to its source in a perception of this kind of reality (akin to Blake's) that the novel owes its comparative freedom and ease, and also its 'romance' quality, which has nothing to do with evasion or softening of reality. The meaning of Silas's regeneration is not that misers in rural communities are likely to be saved by little girls, but that such must be the orientation of all men's hearts if they are to achieve spiritual health. There is nothing sentimental about the portrayal of the community itself. George Eliot's general comments on it are in the spirit of a sociological or anthropological observer, and the particularities are in keeping with her scorn of the idealised peasant of conventional art (expressed in the Riehl review). Eppie's mind has been kept 'in that freshness which is sometimes falsely supposed to be an invariable attribute of rusticity' (Chapter 16). If Eppie herself is somewhat idealised (can we really believe that her undisciplined upbringing would have had no bad effects?) the idealisation belongs to the non-realistic mode of the scene in which Silas discovers her, and we are deliberately prevented from drawing the wrong conclusions.[7]

Although the symbolism of the gold is of central importance to the treatment of Silas's inner life, it is only a part of that treatment, and a complete view necessarily involves the subject of religion. Silas's religious experience is entirely founded on his experience of men. His life among the brethren of Lantern Yard was a life of community, and at the centre of it was his love for his friend, William Dane. It is William's vile act, supported by the drawing of lots, and the loss of his betrothed, that drives Silas away from community and from God. It is true that there is an interval, before the drawing of lots, in which faith in God survives the loss of faith in man—

> 'Silas knelt with his brethren, relying on his own innocence being certified by immediate divine interference, but feeling that there was sorrow and mourning behind for him even then—that his trust in man had been cruelly bruised.' (Chapter 1)

—and if the decision had favoured him (assuming William had not cheated) Silas's future would probably have been different. The truth is obviously more complex than a simple equation of God and man would suggest. In any case (since there are grounds for detecting the influence of Feuerbach here) the conception of God is based not upon any individual man but upon Humanity—and it is Humanity (or the community that for him represents Humanity) that casts Silas out.

Silas's reaction to the drawing of the lots is a blasphemy: ' "there is no just God that governs the earth righteously, but a God of lies, that bears witness against the innocent." ' (Chapter 1). Silas has no capacity to abstract the idea of God from the practices of the community to which he belongs:

> 'To people accustomed to reason about the forms in which their religious feeling has incorporated itself, it is difficult to enter into that simple, untaught state of mind in which the form and

111

the feeling have never been severed by an act of reflection. We are apt to think it inevitable that a man in Marner's position should have begun to question the validity of an appeal to the divine judgement by drawing lots; but to him this would have been an effort of independent thought such as he had never known.'   (Chapter 1)

It is part of the portrayal of Silas's early religious experience that we are invited to criticise the particular 'form' that it took and, subsequently, to compare it unfavourably with the loose, pagan, worldly-superstitious religion of Raveloe. When the robbery of Silas's gold is investigated, a tinder-box is produced as evidence. Mr Macey, the parish-clerk,

'pooh-poohed the tinder box; indeed, repudiated it as a rather impious suggestion, tending to imply that everything must be done by human hands, and that there was no power which could make away with the guineas without moving the bricks. Nevertheless, he turned round rather sharply on Mr. Tookey, when the zealous deputy, feeling that this was a view of the case peculiarly suited to a parish-clerk, carried it still further, and doubted whether it was right to inquire into a robbery at all when the circumstances were so mysterious.
"As if," concluded Mr. Tookey—"as if there was nothing but what could be made out by justices and constables."
"Now, don't you be for overshooting the mark, Tookey," said Mr. Macey, nodding his head aside admonishingly. "That's what you're allays at; if I throw a stone and hit, you think there's summat better than hitting, and you try to throw a stone beyond. What I said was against the tinder-box: I said nothing against justices and constables, for they're o' King George's making, and it 'ud be ill-becoming a man in a parish office to fly out again' King George." '   (Chapter 8)

It is Mr Macey who represents Raveloe opinion: Tookey is the universal butt. While George Eliot is clearly amused by this woolliness of distinction between the mysterious and the investigable, she regards it as healthier and more realistic than the Lantern Yard brethren's rigid reference of matters of fact to the lottery (which is not to be confused with Dinah Morris's reference of highly complex spiritual choices to such external 'leadings' as the arbitrary opening of the Bible). Vagueness as to where mystery begins is itself a part of the sense of mystery, and so is the awareness that some things are not mysterious; the brethren's mystification of all things makes one wonder whether they are truly aware of mystery at all. George Eliot's own belief in the importance of such awareness is beyond doubt: 'But to me the Development theory and all other explanations of processes by which things come to be, produce a feeble impression compared with the mystery that lies under the processes.'[8]

Another respect in which the Raveloe religion is seen to be superior to that of Lantern Yard (pointed out by Mrs Leavis) is the belief that 'to go to church every Sunday in the calendar would have shown a greedy desire to stand well with Heaven, and get an undue advantage over their neighbours' (Chapter 10). The spiritual pride of William Dane, his confidence in his own 'calling and election', makes an unpleasant contrast to this and Silas's humility. Silas's inability to 'arrive at anything higher than hope mingled with fear' (Chapter 1), is closer to the spirit of Dolly Winthrop, whose reference to the Deity as 'Them' signifies unwillingness to express a presumptuous familiarity. But Raveloe is no more idealised in this respect than in any other. The people's superstition thwarts an early occasion for fellowship with Silas, when his cure of Sally Oates (with the aid of his inherited herbal lore) makes them believe that he is in league with the Devil.

Silas's life between his departure from Lantern Yard and his discovery of Eppie is godless. The only sign of positive spiritual life is the little incident of the brown pot which, when he has broken it, Silas puts together and keeps 'for a memorial' (Chapter 2). This, in contrast to the accumulation of the gold, is a substitute for human affections. It is worth noting that when George Eliot uses the word 'fetishism', she applies it not to the gold but to the old brick hearth which he loved 'as he had loved his brown pot. . . . The gods of the hearth exist for us still; and let all new faith be tolerant of that fetishism, lest it bruise its own roots' (Chapter 16). The idea that fetishism is the historical root of all religion derives from Comte, who proposed that this original form should be incorporated into the Religion of Humanity.[9] But a knowledge of Comte is not necessary to understand what George Eliot means here. The gods of the hearth represent

G.E.—H

the human love on which all true religion is founded, and this is why she distinguishes Silas's attachment to the hearth and to the pot from his feeling about the gold.

The effect of Eppie on Silas's life can best be indicated by quotation:

'Unlike the gold which needed nothing, and must be worshipped in close-locked solitude—which was hidden away from the daylight, was deaf to the song of birds, and started to no human tones—Eppie was a creature of endless claims and ever-growing desires, seeking and loving sunshine, and living sounds, and living movements; making trial of everything, with trust in new joy, and stirring the human kindness in all eyes that looked on her. The gold had kept his thoughts in an ever-repeated circle, leading to nothing beyond itself; but Eppie was an object compacted of changes and hopes that forced his thoughts onward, and carried them far away from their old eager pacing towards the same blank limit—carried them away to the new things that would come with the coming years, when Eppie would have learned to understand how her father Silas cared for her; and made him look for images of that time in the ties and charities that bound together the families of his neighbours. The gold had asked that he should sit weaving longer and longer, deafened and blinded more and more to all things except the monotony of his loom and the repetition of his web; but Eppie called him away from his weaving, and made him think all its pauses a holiday, re-awakening his senses with her fresh life, even to the old winter-flies that came crawling forth in the early spring sunshine, and warming him into joy because *she* had joy.'   (Chapter 14)

While this magnificent passage is 'ideal', it is by no means sentimental. It is a celebration of growth and vitality, recalling the imagery of uninhibited joy in Blake's *Songs of Innocence*—its ideal quality is of that kind. It is enough to dispose for ever of the life-and-beauty-hating Puritan that W. B. Yeats was taught to see George Eliot as by his father. Eppie retains the animal spirits that give life to this description when she is grown up:

' "O daddy!" she began, when they were in privacy, clasping and squeezing Silas's arm, and skipping round to give him an energetic kiss. "My little old daddy! I'm so glad. I don't think

I shall want anything else when we've got a little garden; and I knew Aaron would dig it for us," she went on with roguish triumph—"I knew that very well."

"You're a deep little puss, you are," said Silas, with the mild passive happiness of love-crowned age in his face; "but you'll make yourself fine and beholden to Aaron."

"O no, I shan't," said Eppie, laughing and frisking; "he likes it." '　　　　　　　　　　　　　　　　　　　　　　　　(Chapter 16)

Where else in George Eliot does one find this beautiful effect of 'the mild passive happiness of love-crowned age' being clasped and squeezed by the skipping, laughing and frisking adolescent girl? It is one token of the superior ease and freedom of the novel when compared particularly with the latter stages of *The Mill on the Floss*. The forward-looking celebration of life is in sharp contrast to the dominance of the past in that novel.

Emphasis is given to this point when we consider the scene in which Silas returns to Lantern Yard and finds that it has disappeared. The scene shows that Silas, alone among George Eliot's characters, survives and benefits from a complete uprooting. One of the reasons for his return is that he wants at last to have the drawing of the lots explained to him; but he has to remain in the dark. When he comes back to Raveloe Dolly Winthrop says:

' "You were hard done by that once, Master Marner, and it seems as you'll never know the rights of it; but that doesn't hinder there *being* a rights, Master Marner, for all it's dark to you and me.'

"No," said Silas, "no; that doesn't hinder. Since the time the child was sent to me and I've come to love her as myself, I've had light enough to trusten by; and now she says she'll never leave me, I think I shall trusten till I die." '　　　　(Chapter 21)

This trust in life, born of new, developing experience, is just what is lacking in Maggie Tulliver when she refuses to marry Stephen Guest on the grounds that 'If the past is not to bind us, where can duty lie? We should have no law but the inclination of the moment.'

And yet it would be absurd to suppose that George Eliot had abandoned her belief in continuity only to reaffirm it, as we shall see, in her next two novels. In fact one of the things we are told about Silas in his period of alienation is that he has lost continuity:

> 'He hated the thought of the past; there was nothing that called out his love and fellowship toward the strangers he had come amongst; and the future was all dark, for there was no Unseen Love that cared for him.' (Chapter 2)

In Silas's consciousness the Unseen Love that he has lost is the God of his religion, but we are invited to see it as being Humanity whose two aspects, Continuity and Solidarity,[10] are summarised in this passage. Living from moment to moment, which is what Silas does when he first comes to Raveloe, is not an acceptable alternative to being rigidly bound by the past. But these alternatives are not exclusive. Although Silas is in most senses irretrievably cut-off from his past, it is *old* quiverings of tenderness' that he feels when he finds Eppie:

> ' . . . there was a vision of the old home and the old streets leading to Lantern Yard—and within that vision another, of the thoughts which had been present with him in those far-off scenes. The thoughts were strange to him now, like old friendships impossible to revive; and yet he had a dreamy feeling that this child was somehow a message come to him from that far-off life: it stirred fibres that had never been moved in Raveloe—old quiverings of tenderness—old impressions of awe at the presentiment of some Power presiding over his life.' (Chapter 12)

His very first impression is, 'Could this be his little sister come back to him in a dream—his little sister whom he had carried about in his arms for a year before she died, when he was a small boy without shoes or stockings?' and this link with past feeling has an obvious practical value in his attempts to look after Eppie.

As Silas becomes (as far as he can be) integrated into Raveloe life and culture, a fuller measure of continuity asserts itself:

> 'By seeking what was needful for Eppie, by sharing the effect that everything produced on her, he had himself come to appropriate the forms of custom and belief which were the

mould of Raveloe life; and as, with reawakening sensibilities, memory also reawakened, he had begun to ponder over the elements of his old faith, and blend them with his new impressions, till he recovered a consciousness of unity between his past and present.' (Chapter 16)

One readily concedes that early memories of family love are necessary for an old bachelor miser to be awakened to life by a little girl; and that a blending of old faith with new impressions is needful for a harmonious life. This is a conception of continuity which falls far short of Maggie Tulliver's rigid life-denying doctrine, and one which is compatible with 'trusting' openness to new life and altered circumstances. One is tempted to believe that the unique nature of the conception[11] and form of *Silas Marner* made this freedom possible.

The other centre of interest in the novel, the story of Godfrey Cass, is in no way inferior, but it calls for less comment since it is more of a piece with other elements in George Eliot's work. Godfrey is another Arthur Donnithorne whose moral life is dominated by 'the old disposition to rely on chances which might be favourable to him' (Chapter 8). Chances are favourable to him insofar as his clandestine wife dies, leaving him free to marry Nancy Lammeter, but he is nevertheless made to learn the hard reality of consequences. Perhaps the most terrible moment in the novel is when his wife's body is found and Godfrey finds himself hoping that she is dead:

'Godfrey felt a great throb: there was one terror in his mind at that moment: it was, that the woman might *not* be dead. That was an evil terror—an ugly inmate to have found a nestling-place in Godfrey's kindly disposition; but no disposition is a security from evil wishes to a man whose happiness hangs on duplicity.' (Chapter 13)

When, after sixteen years, the daughter he did not acknowledge as a child refuses to leave her adopted father for him, Godfrey learns the truth that Adam Bede and Mr Irwine try to teach Arthur: 'there's debts we can't pay like money debts, by paying extra for the years that have slipped by' (Chapter 20). His career reminds us that we are in the familiar George Eliot world of moral responsibility, in which intentions count for nothing in comparison with acts, and the evil-doer cannot comfort himself with the thought that he meant no harm. But a comparison of Godfrey and Silas does not create in one the feeling that one has when comparing, for example, Gwendolen Harleth and Daniel Deronda: that the character whose world contains 'romantic and symbolical elements' is privileged. My earlier phrase for the art by which George Eliot tests her preconceptions—'sympathetic immersion in the actual'—clearly will not do for the art of *Silas Marner*. But the basis of the story is nevertheless something other than her didacticism, something which, like the sense of the actual in her other great works, controls that didacticism, and which entails a grasp of something real. Among her attempts at non-realistic modes, *Silas Marner* is uniquely successful.

6
Romola

Romola is the one novel of George Eliot's in which didacticism triumphs completely over imagination. Whether it is because she chose a foreign setting, or because she approached the work in a too scholarly manner (the only other work for which she did so much research—with the same results— was the Jewish part of *Daniel Deronda*) the novel refuses to come alive and the didactic will is all-powerful. For that reason it has an interest of its own.

Not that it is entirely devoid of less equivocal interest. It is full of information about the politics, culture and everyday life of fifteenth-century Florence. The figure of Savonarola is an intelligent and scrupulous portrayal of an historical figure, and being an historical figure he has a reality lacking to, for example, Mordecai. He has not, however (and here one might compare Solzhenitsyn's portrayal of Stalin) the reality of a dramatic creation. Only two important figures in the novel have this reality: Bardo Bardi, Romola's father, the honest, distinguished scholar embittered by his blindness, his son's defection to the religious life, and his lack of recognition, who makes an interesting comparison with Casaubon (he has Casaubon's dissatisfaction but with more genuine grounds); and Baldassarre Calvo, the adoptive father of the traitor Tito, who is an impressive study of a mind enfeebled by suffering and obsession. The central figures, however, Tito and Romola, are not of this order, and the interest of the mass of minor characters who make up the world of the novel is severely limited by their tendency to talk like this:

> ' "that pitiable tailor's work of thine makes thy noddle so overhang thy legs, that thy eyeballs can see nought above the stitching-board but the roof of thy own skull." '   (Chapter 1)

—which is a sad contrast to Mrs Poyser and the Rainbow Inn.

Since the novel is so little read it is worth giving a brief summary of the story.

The novel opens on the 9th of April 1492, the day of Lorenzo the Magnificent's death, and also of the arrival in Florence of the shipwrecked Greek Tito Melema, with nothing but a small collection of precious gems. Tito is a brilliant scholar and a winning personality, and rapidly makes his way in Florence. He wins the confidence of Bardo Bardi, takes the place of his son in helping him with his work, and marries his daughter Romola. In the meantime we learn that his adoptive father, who took him from the streets and made a scholar of him, and to whom the gems rightfully belong, was shipwrecked with him and may have been captured as a slave. Tito's first crisis of conscience is to choose between using the money from the jewels to search for Baldassarre, and remaining in Florence. He chooses the latter, arguing that he is uncertain whether Baldassarre is even alive. Subsequently he learns, from a Dominican monk who turns out to be Bardo's estranged son, that Baldassarre *is* alive and in slavery. He still takes no action. When, shortly before their betrothal, Romola is called to her brother's death-bed, Tito believes that the truth will be revealed and Romola's faith in him destroyed. In this state he renews the acquaintance of a peasant girl, Tessa, and goes through a mock-marriage with her, conducted by a street magician. But the brother had only a vision to impart, and Romola and Tito are married; Tito never, however, detaches himself from Tessa and throughout his married life maintains her as a second wife, having two children by her.

Romola's discovery of Tito's true character occurs after her father's death, when Tito sells Bardo's library, which it had been the old man's greatest wish to have preserved intact and named after him. In her anger and disillusionment she attempts to leave Florence, but is intercepted on the road by Savonarola, who had been present at her brother's death, and who tells her that she is trying to evade her responsibilities.

Shortly before this, Baldassarre has turned up in Florence in rags and accosted Tito, who refuses to recognise him.

From this time Tito wears a chain shirt, fearing that Baldassarre will try to murder him. He also begins to take an opportunistic part in the political strife which has followed the death of Lorenzo—acting simultaneously as an agent for all three parties: the Mediceans, the *Arrabbiati* or old aristocratic party, and Savonarola's Popular party. Romola has become attached to Savonarola as a result of their encounter on the road. Through his influence she, who had been brought up by her father to disdain religion, enters into communion with the Church without exactly becoming a believing Christian, and takes a leading part in the efforts of Savonarola's supporters to help those suffering from famine and plague.

Tito has two further encounters with Baldassarre. On one occasion the old man finds shelter in an outbuilding of the house where Tito has established Tessa, and Tito makes his one attempt to win his forgiveness—which is repelled. Subsequently Baldassarre accuses Tito publicly at an important dinner-party. He is nerved to this by the temporary recovery of his memory for scholarship, but on being challenged to prove his identity by reading a passage of Greek, his memory fails again and he is put in prison.

Whereas Tito has no commitment to any party, Romola has strong emotional connections with both Savonarola's party and, through her godfather Bernardo del Nero, the Mediceans. Tito is instrumental in the betrayal and execution first of Bernardo and then of Savonarola himself. The death of Bernardo also strains Romola's relations with Savonarola who, for political reasons, refuses to intervene. Romola is unable to support the inevitable lapses of integrity imposed on Savonarola by his reputation as a prophet and his position as a political leader. It is after the death of Bernardo, her second father, and disillusionment with the man she most admired, that Romola leaves Florence a second time. (This leads to the events discussed in the section on Determinism in Chapter One: Romola drifts away in a boat and discovers a village stricken with the plague, where she is forced to help the sufferers.)

Tito's career comes to an end when the leader of the third party suspects that he is betraying him too, and sets the mob on to Tito. To escape, he jumps into the Arno and after swimming for some time is thrown exhausted on to the bank, two yards from Baldasarre, who strangles him, and dies.

When Romola returns to Florence—after Tito's death—she witnesses the execution of Savonarola, to whom she has become more sympathetic, and seeks out and gives a home to Tessa and her family.

Although the character of Romola is not static, it is Tito's career which carries the main burden of the novel's subject, which is a familiar one: the moral disorientation of the man who, not wishing harm to anyone, seeks his own pleasure; who cuts himself off from the past; who has no commitment to the corporate life of society; who is unwilling to own fellowship with pain and grief. Above all there is the great law that 'we prepare ourselves for sudden deeds by the reiterated choice of good or evil which gradually determines character' (Chapter 23). Many of the incidents which demonstrate these laws are symbolic. When he thinks that Romola is going to learn the truth about his foster-father, Tito sells a ring which Baldassarre has given him.

'It was true that it had been taken from Baldassarre's finger and put on his own as soon as his young hand had grown to the needful size; but there was really no valid good to anybody in those superstitious scruples about inanimate objects. The ring had helped towards the recognition of him [by Romola's brother]. Tito had begun to dislike recognition, which was a claim from the past.'
(Chapter 14)

Both the symbolic value of inanimate objects and the claims of the past will be recognised as motifs for the conditions of the moral life by readers of *The Mill on the Floss*. The selling of the ring also causes one of the novel's many Hardyesque coincidences, for Baldassarre in his wanderings meets the man to whom it is sold. Tito's rejection of the past is constantly reiterated. It is the cause of the first breach with Romola, whose determination to preserve her father's library is entirely founded on her feelings for the past. The contrast between husband and wife is emphasised when Romola tries to take off her betrothal ring:

'But that force of outward symbols by which our active life is knit together so as to make an inexorable external identity for us, not to be shaken by our wavering consciousness, gave a strange effect to this simple movement towards taking off her ring. . . . It brought a vague but arresting sense that she was somehow violently rending her life in two.'   (Chapter 36)

Another symbolic incident of this kind is Tito's present to Romola of a box or tabernacle painted with a representation of the two of them as Bacchus and Ariadne. He persuades her to lock up in it the crucifix that her brother gave her on his death-bed. 'My Ariadne must never look backward now—only forward to Easter, when she will triumph with her Care-dispeller' (Chapter 20). The cross symbolises the fellowship with suffering that Tito despises and Romola espouses through the influence of Savonarola. The incident is a felicitous combination of themes, but this very description indicates that, unlike the symbolism of *Silas Marner* or *Daniel Deronda,* it is didactically conscious rather than imaginatively perceptive.

Another interesting aspect of the novel is that it contains George Eliot's most explicit rejection of utilitarian morality. When Tito knows for certain that Baldassarre is alive, he is forced to make a more bald assessment of his motives, and he argues thus:

'What, looked at closely, was the end of all life, but to extract the utmost sum of pleasure? And was not his own blooming life a promise of incomparably more pleasure, not for himself only, but for others, than the withered wintry life of a man who was past the time of keen enjoyment, and whose ideas had stiffened into barren rigidity?'   (Chapter 11)

Again the point is underlined by comparison with Romola: her unselfish love for her father and her response to the first sight of Baldassarre, long before she knows who he is: 'for grey hairs made a peculiar appeal to her, and the stamp of some unwonted suffering in the face, confirmed by the cord round his neck, stirred in her those sensibilities towards the sorrows of age, which her whole life had tended to develop' (Chapter 24). And once more a link is made with the influence of the past: 'The feelings that gather fervour from novelty will be of little help towards making the world a home for dimmed and faded human beings; and if there is any love of which they are not widowed, it must be the love that is rooted in memories and distils perpetually the sweet balms of fidelity and forbearing tenderness' (Chapter 9).

One indication of the novel's fundamental weakness is given by Romola's first attempt to desert Tito. Her only reason, apart from a vague sense of disappointment in her married life and a very faint suspicion about Baldassarre, is that Tito has sold her father's library. When this happens, she immediately ceases to love him, and yet at the same time we are told, 'That tenderness and keen fellow-feeling for the near and the loved which are the main outgrowth of the affections, had made the religion of her life' (Chapter 36). In fact Romola must appear to the reader at this moment as a woman who places rigid principle before affection. It is true that she is rebuked for her attempt to leave, but George Eliot cannot have intended the attempt to be the complete dereliction that it in fact is. Its true nature is disguised from the reader by the fact that he knows far more of Tito's true nature than Romola does. One must believe that this is the case with George Eliot as well, and that she is excessively influenced by the symbolic significance of Tito's behaviour. In other words, what she has before her most vividly is her general theme rather than the detailed dramatic embodiment.

The same is true extensively of the treatment of Tito. He is an automaton who, faced with a series of moral choices, predictably makes the choice which edges him further into callousness and dissimulation. The novel gives the impression of being excessively analytic, but in fact there is no more analysis than in *Middlemarch*. The difference is in the kind of analysis, illustrated by these passages on Tito and Bulstrode:

' "*Some madman, surely*," said Tito. [He has just been accosted by Baldassarre.]

He hardly knew how the words had come to his lips: there are moments when our passions speak and decide for us, and we seem to stand by and wonder. They carry in them an inspiration of crime, that in one instant does the work of long premeditation....

There was still one resource open to Tito. He might have turned back, sought Baldassarre again, confessed everything to him—to Romola—to all the world. But he never thought of that. The repentance which cuts off all moorings to evil, demands something more than selfish fear. He had no sense that there was strength and safety in truth; the only strength he trusted to lay in his ingenuity and his dissimulation. Now that the first shock, which had called up the traitorous signs of fear, was well past, he hoped to be prepared for all emergencies by cool deceit —and defensive armour.' (Chapters 22 & 23)

'Whatever prayers he might lift up, whatever statements he might inwardly make of this man's wretched spiritual condition, and the duty he himself was under to submit to the punishment divinely appointed for him rather than to wish for evil to another—through all this effort to condense words into a solid mental state, there pierced and spread with irresistible vividness the images of the events he desired. And in the train of those images came their apology. He could not but see the death of Raffles, and see in it his own deliverance. What was the removal of this wretched creature? He was impenitent—but were not public criminals impenitent?—yet the law decided on their fate. Should Providence in this case award death, there was no sin in contemplating death as the desirable issue—if he kept his hands from hastening it—if he scrupulously did what was pre-scribed. Even here there might be a mistake: human prescriptions were fallible things: Lydgate had said that treat-ment had hastened death,—why not his own method of treatment? But of course intention was everything in the question of right and wrong.' (*Middlemarch*, Chapter 70)

Bulstrode's case is an illustration of a general law, and George Eliot is no more averse to stating her laws in *Middle-march* than in *Romola*. But the analysis of Bulstrode's conscience substantially consists of internal events, which constitute a drama as real as that of actions. The author is inhabiting her character. The account of Tito's motives, by contrast, is perpetually falling back on general reflections. Instead of 'through all this effort to condense words into a solid mental state, there pierced and spread with irresistible vividness the images of the events he desired', we have, 'The repentance which cuts off all moorings to evil, demands something more than selfish fear.'

One consequence of this inattention to the particular case can be seen at the opening of Chapter 14 when Tito, thinking that Romola's brother is going to reveal the truth, is wandering through the town: 'his thought had even glanced towards going in search of Baldassarre after all.' This is rather surprising here. Tito has not yet been presented as utterly without conscience, and his future in Florence seems hopeless. Wouldn't the impulse to search for Baldassarre be quite strong at this moment, since among other motives, it is the only thing that could restore Romola's favour? But we are given no more than this passing statement, and the actual consequences of Tito's fear are the sale of the ring and the involvement with Tessa: all events move inexorably in one direction.

As early as the ninth chapter, when Tito has done nothing worse than invest the money that he should have used to find Baldassarre, we are told, 'He had made it impossible that he should not from henceforth desire it to be the truth that his father was dead; impossible that he should not be tempted to baseness rather than that the precise facts of his conduct should not remain for ever concealed.' Impossible? Only in a world governed by a very crude kind of determinism, unless Tito is conceived as utterly depraved from the start, in which case his development, which is offered as a descent from 'a mere mild insufficiency of positive unselfishness into a positive and lethal viciousness,'[1] is emptied of all moral substance.

Romola remains a curiously impressive work, full of force-fully stated moral propositions (one's notes on the novel tend to be predominantly quotations of this kind). Yet its artistic deficiency entails a moral deficiency too. In Chapter 39 we are told, 'Our lives make a moral tradition for our individual selves, as the life of mankind at large makes a moral tradition for the race; and to have once acted nobly seems a reason why we should always be noble.' Tito's career is a remorseless demonstration of the complete opposite. In *Daniel Deronda*, Gwendolen has her first experience of real sympathy towards her mother just before she receives Grandcourt's proposal; but this contribution to her 'moral tradition', far from acting beneficently, encourages her to make the wrong choice. Gwendolen is a creation of the consummate George Eliot, who in subjecting her beliefs to the test of her creative imagination offers a much more challenging vision than the 'good makes better, bad makes worse' of *Romola*.

7
Felix Holt

Felix Holt is the one novel in which George Eliot attempted to deal with the problems of industrialism, and there is general agreement among readers and critics that she failed: that while the part of the novel centred upon the gentry and the middle classes—the Transome-Jermyn drama—can be placed among her greatest achievements, Felix himself and all that concerns him is flat and unimagined.

The failure, however—like all George Eliot's failures—is an interesting one, and there tends to be some confusion and misconception concerning its causes. Mr C. T. Bissell, in an article on 'Social Analysis in the Novels of George Eliot',[1] argues that whereas her 'imagination is kindled by the spectacle of man in society', 'any exclusive concern with a particular programme is bound to be narrowing and stultifying'. Now there is clearly something wrong with George Eliot's treatment of social problems in *Felix Holt*, but it is hard to believe that 'an exclusive concern with a particular programme' can be ascribed to the author who said:

> 'My function is that of the *aesthetic*, not the doctrinal teacher—the rousing of the nobler emotions, which make mankind desire the social right, not the prescribing of special measures, concerning which the artistic mind, however strongly moved by social sympathy, is often not the best judge.'[2]

This was written in 1878, twelve years after the novel, but it was only three months after *Felix Holt* was finished that she wrote her letter to Frederic Harrison refusing to write a novel illustrating the 'particular programme' of Positivism on the grounds that 'aesthetic teaching' must not lapse 'from the picture to the diagram'.[3] In fact when we look at the novel we see that she did not take 'particular programmes'—and more important the social needs that they sought to meet—seriously enough. Her hero is aloof from the practical problems of Radicalism and from the working-men themselves.

Raymond Williams in *Culture and Society* makes a different criticism: 'When she touches, as she chooses to touch, on the lives and problems of working people, her personal observation and conclusion surrender, virtually without a fight, to the general structure of feeling about these matters which was the common property of her generation'.[4] In a sense this is true. In trying to relate the social analysis of, say, *Middlemarch* to the thinkers who influenced George Eliot one is conscious that the novel is a different, and superior, kind of intellectual endeavour. But with *Felix Holt* one does not have the sense of a comprehension beyond the range of a Comte or a Spencer. Dr Williams's criticism, however, clearly involves the belief that George Eliot should have come to a different conclusion about Radicalism. 'It has passed too long for a kind of maturity and depth in experience to argue that politics and political attachments are only possible to superficial minds'.[5] While applauding the motive behind that remark I should point out that it could equally be applied to *Anna Karenina,* and that Dr Williams would need to alter his terms radically in order to say why the following cannot be dismissed in terms of 'structure of feeling'.

'Constantine considered his brother to be a man of great intellect, noble in the highest sense of the word, and gifted with the power of working for the general welfare. But the older he grew and the more intimately he came to know his brother, the oftener the thought occurred to him that the power of working for the general welfare—a power of which he felt himself entirely destitute—was not a virtue but rather a lack of something: not a lack of kindly honesty and noble desires and tastes, but a lack of the power of living, of what is called heart—the aspiration which makes a man choose one out of all the innumerable paths of life that present themselves, and desire that alone. The better he knew his brother, the more he noticed that Koznyshev and many other social workers were not led to this love for the common good by their hearts, but because they had reasoned out in their minds that it was a good thing to do that kind of work, and took to it accordingly.'[6]

The difference between this and what is offered in *Felix Holt* can be defined by a phrase that Dr Williams uses elsewhere: it is an 'articulated experience'.[7] In the complex drama of Levin's relation to the peasants, his inability to think of them and generalise about them as a class, his transitory desire to live as a peasant himself and the destruction of that desire by the sight of Kitty, we have something for which there is no equivalent in *Felix Holt*. It is not simply a matter of Felix's social experience being different from George Eliot's. The crucial fact is that Felix is not a working-man at all, and that his experience is irrelevant to the medium[8] in which he is placed.

In this connection Samuel Bamford's *Passages in the Life of a Radical* is very useful. Bamford was a Radical weaver in Middleton, Lancashire, during the period of serious industrial unrest in the second decade of the nineteenth century. He was deeply involved in political activity, and was present at the demonstration in St Peter's Field, Manchester, which became what was to be known as the Peterloo Massacre. Subsequently he became a journalist and the author of several books, of which the *Passages,* published in 1844, is the best-known. George Eliot read the book before beginning *Felix Holt,* and the uses she made of it are fairly evident.[9] What seems remarkable is that she did not make more use of it—or rather, that it did not more deeply penetrate her imagination. One use she obviously had for Bamford can be seen in his judgements on popular violence and on the Chartist movement in particular:

'It was not until we became infested by spies, incendiaries, and their dupes—distracting, misleading, and betraying—that physical force was mentioned amongst us. After that our moral power waned; and what we gained by the accession of demagogues, we lost by their criminal violence, and the estrangement of real friends.'[10]

'One evening spent in the aquirement of useful knowledge,—in rational conversation,—in the promotion of kindly feelings,—in the restraints of sobriety,—in the comforting of families,—in the blessings of children, and in the improvement of their hearts and understandings,—in the devisements of cheerful economy and industry,—in the feeling of mercy towards all God's creatures, and of love of all goodness, for his sake; one evening so spent, were to thyself and thy country, worth more than thou hast seen, heard, or done, at Radical or Chartist meetings, since sun-light or torch-light first illuminated them.'[11]

This evidence that a working-man with much experience of Radical agitation subscribed to the view of individual self-improvement ('the self-knowledge, and self-control of a reformed people')[12] before administrative change must have given George Eliot confidence in putting her views in the mouth of a 'Radical' and a 'working-man'. But this use confirms the view that her imaginative response to Bamford was remarkably small. For such expressions of opinion are the least interesting part of the book. They seem to come from the comfortable London journalist rather than the rebellious Middleton weaver. The reconstruction of the events leading up to and following the Peterloo Massacre, and the vivid and humorous characterisation of such individuals as 'Orator' Hunt and 'Doctor' Healy, as well as of Bamford himself, suggest a world of Radical activity quite different from that of unscrupulous agents like Johnson manipulating illiterate oafs like Dredge. It is the variety, humour and vigour of the world Bamford re-creates, and the many-faceted individual that he shows himself to be, that mark the poverty of George Eliot's response to her subject. Lawrence's phrase 'man alive', by which he defined the greatness of great novels, is more applicable to Bamford's narrative than to George Eliot's. Even his weaknesses have this quality:

'And thou, too, poor, and beautiful, and innocent, Lavinia Robinson; what heart but responds to thy affliction! It was midnight, and there came a deep moan, that told of a grief not to be comforted; of a wounded spirit which could not be borne. Soft, but hasty footsteps approached; and again, tones were heard almost too plaintive for human woe. Then, there was a pause, and a plunge, and a choking, bubbling scream; and all was silent around that Bridge of Tears!'[13]

Though I do not of course ask for maudlin sentimentality, this is a note entirely missing in *Felix Holt*. If one thinks of Dickens one can see the place such feelings might have in an imaginative response to popular distress. Dickens's sentimentality—when it is still sentimentality and has not been transformed into something else—is annoying because he is a great writer and one feels entitled to something better. But the capacity for such a simple, over-loaded response as this is present as a pressure behind some of Dickens's greatest writing.

Equally important, when we think of *Felix Holt,* is the straightforward historical detail of the *Passages*. Bamford is a leader, but he is entirely *of* the people. He sees them not as a mass but as individuals, much as Tolstoy's Levin sees the peasants. The difference from *Felix Holt* can be seen in the following passage:

> 'Felix was sanguine; he saw some pleasant faces among the miners when they were washed on Sundays; they might be taught to spend their wages better. . . .
>
> "I'll lay hold of them by their fatherhood," said Felix; "I'll take one of their little fellows and set him in the midst. Till they can show there's something they love better than swilling themselves with ale, extension of the suffrage can never mean anything for them but extension of boozing. . . . "
>
> He had fixed his choice on a certain Mike Brindle. . . . Brindle was one of the head miners; he had a bright good-natured face, and had given especial attention to certain performances with a magnet which Felix carried in his pocket.' (Chapter 11)

No working-man, however educated, would be at that distance from the miners. He would, for example, be able to detect a pleasant face even when it was not washed. But he would not stand in anything like the relation to them implied by 'pleasant faces'. He would be interested in their individual characters; 'boozing' would not have for him the narrow symbolic quality it has for Felix (we often see Bamford getting drunk). He would, as Bamford does, speak to them in dialect; Bamford is quite capable of speaking 'standard English', but he habitually uses dialect to his friends, as well as for satirical effect to those in authority. There is no affectation or condescension in this—it is natural for him, as an educated working-man, to have two distinct forms of speech.

Furthermore, though Felix voluntarily embraces the working-man's life, and is proud of his willingness to suffer poverty, the details of that life are not present in the novel at all. We see nothing of his relations with his employer. We are told that he 'made himself a journeyman to Mr Prowd the watchmaker' (Chapter 4), but Mr Prowd makes no appearance in the novel. Not only is watchmaking an untypical pursuit for a working-man, but George Eliot avoids showing Felix in a relationship which he might resent as much as the miners resent Spratt.

The most significant general conclusion then, to which a reading of the *Passages* leads us, is that Felix is not simply an unsuccessful attempt to create an intelligent working-man of the early 1830s, (or even of the middle '60s), the failure being attributable to her lack of first-hand experience, or to her share in the 'general structure of feeling'. Her reading of Bamford could not have left her innocent of some of the aspects of that failure; and we must rather conclude that she made no attempt at the necessary imaginative effort. She was not interested in Felix as a working-man. The 'Address to Working Men by Felix Holt' that George Eliot wrote at the request of John Blackwood for his Magazine, has its significance here. As Jerome Thale puts it, 'That George Eliot could transpose Felix from fiction to reality may be an indication of the way he is conceived in the novel'.[14] Perhaps the only other character in George Eliot's fiction whom one can imagine being used in a similar way is Daniel Deronda. Deronda, too, is a failure, but the similarity reveals a special weakness in Felix. Deronda is conceived as a man with no roots in society, or rather, as one who has been alienated from his roots. His abstractness is partly disguised by his being a special case—there is no sharp historical focus to expose it. The special weakness of Felix is that he is, as it were, *posing* as an English working-man; as a member, unlike Deronda, of a definable class of whom we may have relevant historically-based expectations.

It is ironical that George Eliot's much-quoted insistence on the importance of the 'medium in which a character moves' was made with reference to *Romola* in which, as W.

J. Harvey says, the protagonist is 'basically aloof from the life created around her'.[15] The same may be said of Fedalma in *The Spanish Gypsy,* in which there is a similarly earnest and laboured attempt to show a broad range of social life, which seems suspiciously like 'local colour'. In both these cases one may say that George Eliot's problem is partly that the societies themselves are theoretically conceived. She may well have felt an apparently justified confidence that the theories which her own social experience supported, would not fail to be vivified and sanctioned by any society she might choose to portray. There is, after all, no such thing as an exception to a law. It remains true, however, that Romola and Fedalma are detachable from their respective societies in a way that Arthur Donnithorne and Maggie Tulliver are not. It seems, from the evidence, that George Eliot needed the felt pressure of known social experience in order to realise the relation of the individual to his society.

Felix, as I have said, is another character who does not relate to his medium, who remains 'aloof' from it. He is not, however, an identical case. The temptation here is to draw a parallel between the English working classes of 1832, and Renaissance Florence and Spain: George Eliot lacked direct experience of both, and both remain theoretic. But it is dangerous to draw a parallel between a 'class' and a 'society'. Those elements in the society of *Felix Holt* represented by Transome and Jermyn are very well portrayed, and one is certainly not tempted to call George Eliot's understanding of them 'theoretic'. Many of the pressures on Felix derive from this part of the novel: from the corruption which issues from the conflicts of Transome, Jermyn and Johnson. Certainly one does feel the absence of convincing working-class life in the novel, but here the comparison with *Romola* reveals a contrast. However uneasy one may be in reading the 'background' of *Romola,* there is certainly a lot of it (too much, very often) and George Eliot has tried hard. She characteristically portrays her minor figures as existing in their own right, living from their own centres of experience and aspiration. In *Romola* the result of this is that they seem irrelevant, but in her successful fiction this method is essential to the social analysis: because other people are independently pursuing their interests, the protagonist is not free to pursue his. This happens in *Felix Holt* with Harold, Jermyn and Johnson. What is remarkable about the working-men in the novel is not only that there is so little of them but that they are not strictly social agents at all, but rather a kind of social putty. They make only two substantial appearances in the novel, in Chapters 11 and 33. In the first case they are shown succumbing to Johnson's guile, and in the second they appear as a mob. The mob itself might have seemed an excellent opportunity for showing in detail and in microcosm the influence of disparate individual motives on general social movement, but George Eliot takes no advantage of it. She seems simply not to have been interested in the workers as individuals, and the result is a flagrant disregard for her own principles of social analysis. Because they are not conceived as social agents but as passive material to be worked on by appeals either to their lower or higher natures —in the form of 'booze' or education—the analysis is radically unbalanced.

We have, then, two negative propositions: George Eliot was not, in the figure of Felix, trying seriously to create a working-class leader, and she was not interested in the working classes in general as social agents. What, then, was her purpose in writing this part of the novel? The answer, I think, lies in the very theoretical conception of Felix. That he is theoretically conceived is not of course a new suggestion, but the emphasis has tended to fall on the fact that he is a 'mouthpiece'. That he certainly is, but as an *explanation* of the failure it is unsatisfactory. From all that we know of George Eliot's preoccupations and methods, we must surely say that the 'mouthpiece' effect is a symptom, not the source, of the failure. To say that it is the source would be to suppose an aesthetic crudity and naivety that we know her to have been far removed from. The effect is indeed crude and naive, but we must look for a more sophisticated cause.

George Eliot's view of society was consistent and intellectual. Her intellectuality was a strong feature of her creative power, but this does not mean, of course, that her intellect was identical with her creativity. The social ideas formulated in 'An Address to Working Men', in the review of Riehl, and in the note on 'Historic Guidance' are not, as they stand, superior to those of Mill, Comte and Spencer. They are, if anything, rather inferior. This is just a way of saying that she was essentially a novelist. When her creative powers fail, one sometimes sees the antecedent ideas in their undigested crudity; and it is this, no doubt, which gave rise to the false, though long current, view of the relation between the intellectual and the genius. The particular formulation I have in mind here is one from her essay on Riehl, already quoted in Chapter One:

> 'The external conditions which society has inherited from the past are but the manifestation of inherited internal conditions in the human beings who compose it; the internal conditions and the external are related to each other as the organism and its medium, and development can take place only by the gradual consentaneous development of both.'

This idea, in various forms, can be traced throughout George Eliot's work, but its relevance varies according to the different ways in which it is manifested. Consider the following analysis of the pressure of social circumstances on Mrs Transome.

> 'She always thought that the dangerous French writers were wicked and that her reading of them was a sin; but many sinful things were highly agreeable to her, and many things which she did not doubt to be good and true were dull and meaningless. She found ridicule of Biblical characters very amusing, and she was interested in stories of illicit passion: but she believed all the while that truth and safety lay in due attendance on prayers and sermons, in the admirable doctrines and ritual of the Church of England, equally remote from Puritanism and Popery; in fact, in such a view of this world and the next as would preserve the existing arrangements of English society quite unshaken, keeping down the obtrusiveness of the vulgar and the discontent of the poor. The history of the Jews, she knew, ought to be preferred to any profane history; the Pagans, of course, were vicious, and their religions quite nonsensical, considered as religions but classical learning came from the Pagans; the Greeks were famous for sculpture; the Italians for painting; the middle ages were dark and Papistical; but now Christianity went hand in hand with civilisation, and the providential government of the world, though a little confused and entangled in foreign countries, in our own favoured land was clearly seen to be

carried forward on Tory and Church of England principles, sustained by the succession of the House of Brunswick, and by sound English divines. For Miss Lingon had had a superior governess, who held that a woman should be able to write a good letter, and to express herself with propriety on general subjects. And it is astonishing how effective this education appeared in a handsome girl, who sat supremely well on horseback, sang and played a little, painted small figures in water-colours, had a naughty sparkle in her eyes when she made a daring quotation, and an air of serious dignity when she recited something from her store of correct opinions. But however such a stock of ideas may be made to tell in elegant society, and during a few seasons in town, no amount of bloom and beauty can make them a perennial source of interest in things not personal; and the notion that what is true and, in general, good for mankind, is stupid and drug-like, is not a safe theoretic basis in circumstances of temptation and difficulty.' (Chapter 1)

Mrs Transome's tragedy is that the established, inherited codes of principle and conduct do not claim her reverence, and yet she has not the originality, courage or independence to establish a firm basis of her own. The result is that she lives in a moral vacuum. In George Eliot, every individual life is a point of growth from the accumulation of past experience, adding to and extending that experience: ideally, the development of individual and society is, as she puts it, 'consentaneous'. The key to what is wrong with Mrs Transome's relation to accepted values is that her 'stock of ideas' is not 'a perennial source of interest in things not personal'. Her rejection of inherited ideas is in the service of a petty egoism; she does not achieve a coherent, impersonal stance apart from them.

The following is a major contribution to our understanding of Mrs Transome:

'If she had only been more haggard and less majestic, those who had glimpses of her outward life might have said she was a tyrannical, griping harridan, with a tongue like a razor. No one said exaclty that; but they never said anything like the full truth about her, or divined what was hidden under that outward life—a woman's keen sensibility and dread, which lay screened behind all her petty habits and narrow notions, as some quivering thing with eyes and a throbbing heart may lie crouching behind withered rubbish.' (Chapter 1)

The tragedy is shaped by social conditions, but without the 'woman's keen sensibility and dread', so powerfully imaged as a frightened animal, there would be no tragedy. The conflict between Mrs Transome and her son is not merely, or even mainly, a conflict of social change, but one of enduring conditions:

> 'Day after day, year after year, had yielded blanks; new cares had come, bringing other desires for results quite beyond her grasp, which must also be watched for in the lottery; and all the while the round-limbed pet had been growing into a strong youth, who liked many things better than his mother's caresses, and who had a much keener consciousness of his independent existence than of his relation to her.' (ibid.)

It is in such passages as this, above all, that we see a realisation of George Eliot's theory of tragedy: the 'adjustment of our individual needs to the dire necessities of our lot', and the 'irreparable collision between the individual and the general'.[16] In comparison the emphasis on heredity in *The Spanish Gypsy*, to which the theorising specifically refers, is unsubtle and doctrinal. Unlike Zarca's demands on Fedalma, the impersonal forces working in Mrs Transome are shown to be real and genuinely inescapable—there is no need for recourse to theories of hereditary duty.

If the tragedy is centred on Mrs Transome's lot as a woman and a mother, conditioned by her failure to construct a standing-ground of principle, it is acted out in terms of the individual's failure to escape from habits of feeling and action. In Harold's case this appears most significantly in his prejudice about women.

> ' "Women, very properly, don't change their views, but keep to the notions in which they have been brought up. It doesn't signify what they think—they are not called upon to judge or to act. You must really leave me to take my own course in these matters, which properly belong to men." ' (Chapter 2)

'These matters', here, refers to his intention to stand as a Radical candidate; but the issue has much wider connotations than the pain that this intention causes to his mother. 'Keeping to the notions in which they have been brought up' is, we have already seen, not a simple matter, and

Harold's attitude implicitly denies the possibility of drama in a woman's life—even the kind of drama that has accounted for his own existence. When he similarly insists, against his mother's advice, on filing a bill against Jermyn, he commits the crucial act in a tragedy that seems made of the very stuff of county life: in which the powers of unexamined assumptions—about the relation of culture to principle, of men to women, of the past to the present—combine for maximum effect on the fates of the individuals through whom they work.

The part played by Jermyn in this tragedy is, of course, conditioned by a different set of assumptions:

> 'A man of sixty, with an unsuspicious wife and daughters capable of shrieking and fainting at a sudden revelation, and of looking at him reproachfully in their daily misery under a shabby lot to which he had reduced them—with a mind and with habits dried hard by the years—with no glimpse of an endurable standing-ground except where he could domineer and be prosperous according to the ambitions of pushing middle-class gentility—such a man is likely to find the prospect of worldly ruin ghastly enough to drive him to the most uninviting means of escape.' (Chapter 42)

This analysis is no more crudely 'social' than that of the pressures which formed Mrs Transome's moral nature. Jermyn's feelings as a father and husband are not so potently and sympathetically present as Mrs Transome's motherhood: that is George Eliot's tact—Jermyn's power over his former mistress is dependent on his most private self not being conceived as a 'quivering thing with eyes and a throbbing heart'. And his fatherhood being so closely woven with his social ambition is a part of his 'moral vulgarity'. It is Mrs Transome's vulnerability to the domination of both Jermyn and her son that places her beyond that peculiarly devastating judgement. Nevertheless, his actions would be incomprehensible if he were not sensitive to the reproachful looks of his wife and daughters; he is morally vulgar but not morally dead. The persuasiveness of George Eliot's social analysis is dependent on her grasp of the individual human reality on which social pressures operate, without which the 'social' would have no meaning. The analysis of the pressures on Jermyn reveals and explains a seeming paradox. That the inherited feelings and assumptions of the county aristocracy should impede individual development and freedom of choice—free, that is, not absolutely but as expressing maximum individuality—is not hard to grasp; those feelings and assumptions are essentially static and conservative, and include a strong sense (expressed in Mrs Transome's horror at Harold's Radicalism) of class loyalty.

But Jermyn belongs to the rising class. He is the forerunner of Victorian individualism. His class is 'pushing'. (He was responsible for the attempt to turn Treby into a Spa, for which Sir Maximus Debarry 'never forgave the too persuasive attorney'. The Spa failed but Sir Maximus, having lost money on it, was forced to lease a building and land for what was intended as a benevolent college and eventually became a tape factory. Thus Jermyn, though not himself an industrialist, is shown to be one of the forces in the process by which Treby 'gradually passed from being simply a respectable market-town . . . and took on the more complex life brought by mines and manufactures' (Chapter 3). It is highly characteristic of George Eliot that she should show the process, and Jermyn's influence, to be so involved and indirect.) George Eliot exposes the false contrast of 'static' aristocracy and 'dynamic' middle-class; she also exposes, by implication, the falsity of the concept of 'individualism' that we associate with the Victorians. It is not merely a matter of the shrewd association of 'pushing' and 'gentility', though that phrase has extraordinary force and penetration. She shows that the dynamic process itself produces 'a mind and habits dried hard by the years'. These habits and feelings which impede the relative freedom that George Eliot considered essential are not, like those of the Transomes, purely 'inherited'. The desire for gentility is inherited—'and be prosperous according to the ambitions of pushing middle-class gentility' suggests the absence of an individually worked-out ambition —but the crucial habits are, as it were, a kind of sediment, 'dried hard', of the dynamism of his career.

Johnson, the agent, is a smaller conception than Jermyn; he is, frankly, a device for linking the Transome-Jermyn world and that of Felix Holt. But he is not the less convincing for being a device, nor for the close correspondence of his values and those of his employer:

> 'Being a man who aimed at respectability, a family man, who had a good church-pew, subscribed for engravings of banquet pictures where there were portraits of political celebrities, and wished his children to be more unquestionably genteel than their father, he presented all the more numerous handles of wordly motive by which a judicious superior might keep a hold on him. But this useful regard to respectability had its inconvenience in relation to such a superior: it was the mark of some vanity and some pride, which, if they were not touched just in the right handling-place, were liable to become raw and sensitive.'
>
> (Chapter 29)

Johnson's vulgarity is closer to the surface than Jermyn's; he is almost a parody of Jermyn. In him too, there is the emphasis (though muted) on fatherhood, and its close connection with social ambition. Jermyn's failure to handle Johnson—his insensitivity to his employee's vanity and pride —reflects Harold's failure to handle Jermyn. In both cases the individual's habits of thought and feeling are a vehicle for the egoism which causes enmity and opposition of interests:

> 'Jermyn had often been unconsciously disagreeable to Johnson, over and above the constant offence of being an ostentatious patron. He would never let Johnson dine with his wife and daughters; he would not himself dine at Johnson's house when he was in town. He often did what was equivalent to pooh-poohing his conversation by not even appearing to listen, and by suddenly cutting it short with a query on a new subject.'
>
> (ibid.)

These offences exactly parallel Harold's treatment of Jermyn:

> ' "A fourth candidate of good position, who should coalesce with Mr Debarry—a—"
> Here Mr Jermyn hesitated for the third time, and Harold broke in.
> "That will not be my line of action, so we need not discuss it." '
>
> (Chapter 2)

> 'Harold, who, underneath all the tendencies which had made him a Liberal, had intense personal pride, thought, "Confound the fellow—with his Mrs Jermyn! Does he think we are on a footing for me to know anything about his wife?" ' (Chapter 2)

'Intense personal pride' is in a way a misleading phrase; for it does not mean that Harold's pride is an expression of strong individuality. Rather, his irritation with Jermyn derives from his unquestioned class-assumptions. Thus in both the Harold-Jermyn and the Jermyn-Johnson relationships George Eliot shows that these assumptions are the allies of egoism and that egoism is not a form of free, healthy individuality.

In this analysis of the Transome drama I have introduced some ideas from outside the novel, but my purpose has been to show that the relevance of those ideas is very limited. One might extend the 'experiments in life' analogy by saying that in scientific practice the experiment does not merely confirm the hypothesis but realises it, and in realising extends and modifies it. The reality will almost invariably extend beyond the scientist's foreshadowing of it in his hypothesis. The hypothesis will not, therefore, suffice as an account of the experimental findings.

In *Felix Holt* there would be no need to refer to the hypothesis if it were not that a large part of the novel seems to need explanation from outside. There is clearly a lack of unity in the novel; or, there is a lack of unity in our reading which seems to reflect something in the novel. And yet one can imagine George Eliot exclaiming, as she did about *Daniel Deronda*, 'I meant everything in the book to be related to everything else there.'[17] Clearly, an attempt to understand what George Eliot was trying to do with Felix must be based on the question, in what way did she mean the different parts to be related?

It is here that the sense in which Felix is a theoretic character can be more precisely defined. It is not, as I have said, simply a matter of his being a 'mouthpiece', but rather of the way in which he is conceived in relation to the Transomes and Jermyn. One might begin with his class-loyalty:

' "I mean to stick to the class I belong to—people who don't follow the fashions. . . . That's how the working men are left to foolish devices and keep worsening themselves: the best heads among them forsake their born comrades, and go in for a house with a high door-step and a brass knocker." '   (Chapter 5)

'If the past is not to bind us, where can duty lie? We should have no law but the inclination of the moment.'[13] That dictum, which is so close to the heart of the very different drama of *The Mill on the Floss,* is present here as well, under a different kind of definition. And just as there are complexities and contradictions in its working-out in the earlier novel, there are similar difficulties here. Personal loyalty in Maggie becomes class loyalty in Felix. The new form has the rational advantage of the argument that if the best of a class desert it, the class as a whole will degenerate; but the staple of the position is the belief in living in accordance with the forces that have formed you:

> ' "O yes, your ringed and scented men of the people!—I won't be one of them. Let a man once throttle himself with a satin stock, and he'll get new wants and new motives. Metamorphosis will have begun at his neck-joint, and it will go on till it has changed his likings first and then his reasoning, which will follow his likings as the feet of a hungry dog follow his nose." '
>
> (ibid.)

The rugged metaphorical language is a part of George Eliot's attempt to give Felix a distinctive voice; and it is just because of the attempted ventriloquism, the forced forthrightness, that the author's preconceptions show through with especial clarity. Change your way of life and you cut yourself loose from the sources of principle. The word 'metamorphosis' is peculiarly loaded, and the play on 'likings' is a remarkably blatant piece of sophistry. If you change your likings your reasoning will become subordinate to them, and you will live by your animal appetites, like a hungry dog: the vitiating element being, not the strength of the likings, or the weakness of the moral nature, but simply the fact of change. Original likings are, by implication, pure and subordinate to reason.

But the main difficulty is the way in which this relates to the rest of the novel. 'Ringed and scented' reminds us of Jermyn and Johnson; and if Johnson is a 'man of the people' who has opted for gentility and thereby surrendered the life of principle, the much more important and poignant case of Jermyn is different. The 'pushing' ambition which hardens his moral nature is a part of his own class-heritage.

Similarly, the parts played in the tragedy by Mrs Transome and Harold are determined by the inadequacy of the gentry's stock of assumptions in the face of a complex moral situation.

Perhaps a more interesting and adequate account of Felix's grounds for action is given in the following conversation with Esther:

> ' "I can't help caring very much what happens to me. And you seem to care so little about yourself."
> "You are thoroughly mistaken," said Felix. "It is just because I'm a very ambitious fellow, with very hungry passions, wanting a great deal to satisfy me, that I have chosen to give up what people call worldly good. At least that has been one determining reason. It all depends on what a man gets into his consciousness—what life thrusts into his mind, so that it becomes present to him as remorse is present to the guilty, or a mechanical problem to an inventive genius." '   (Chapter 27)

Felix is clearly at home in sophisticated argument about determinism: the play of 'chosen' against 'determining reason' comes directly from George Eliot's balancing of determinism and free will. Felix's class-loyalty is represented as a choice: that is, as something very different from Mrs Transome's blind Church and Tory partisanship. George Eliot seems to be presenting him as a man on whom hereditary claims and determining circumstances are *rationally* coercive: who has placed himself in such a relation to them that he can make a choice, even though in reality he has no alternative. It is the fact of rational choice that determines the quality of his loyalty, and defines Felix as a man who has achieved the essential freedom of a willing and rational acceptance of the past.

Felix is theoretically conceived in terms of a certain ideal relation to hereditary and environmental pressures; he is not conceived as a working-man. His class-loyalty, therefore, which is so essential to the conception, is entirely illusory; he does not behave to the miners as a fellow-worker, but as a mentor from outside the circle of working-class life. 'What life thrusts into his mind' can only be, for Felix, what it is like to be a working-man, and because that precise pressure is not a part of his conception, the character is vitiated; he becomes not only theoretical but irrelevant to the situation

in which he is placed. The conception requires some definition of the pressures and assumptions of working-class life,
to lay beside and contrast with those of the middle-class and
the gentry. If the 'ringed and scented men of the people' are
contemptible because they are men of the people, how does
this contempt relate to such a man as Jermyn, who is living
according to the assumptions of his own class? Because Felix's
character is theoretical, an important issue is blurred: is it
the relation in which he stands to his class, or the intrinsic
qualities of the class itself which accounts for Felix's
superiority? External evidence and the presentation of the
miners (though this is so artistically infelicitous that it almost
has the status of external evidence) suggest the former, but
the novel is too confused to either confirm or extend the
hypothesis.

8
Middlemarch

Middlemarch is George Eliot's most coherent, most inclusive and (if we except the much shorter *Silas Marner*) most nearly flawless novel. If it contains nothing greater than the Transome story in *Felix Holt*, and perhaps nothing *as* great as Gwendolen's story in *Daniel Deronda*, it has in its scope and consistency elements of greatness that make it unique, not only among her own works, but in the whole of English fiction. As a picture of English society *Felix Holt* is seriously inadequate, and *Daniel Deronda* is virtually limited to a single class. The added dimensions of *Middlemarch* are its subtle exploration of class differences, class relations and class interests, from the gentry through the finely distinguished gradations of the middle-class to (in a single scene) the agricultural labourers; and its depth of historical reference thoroughly persuades the reader that the characters belong to a particular time and place—an essential part of their reality. George Eliot read in Auguste Comte that the individual man is a fiction; only the species is real, since the individual is dependent on the species. What makes George Eliot not only a great artist but also a greater thinker than Comte is her perception of the equal truth that the species is dependent for its reality on the individuals who compose it. The creator of Lydgate, Dorothea and Bulstrode (who significantly refused to write a Comtist Utopia) is clearly convinced of the reality and precious importance of the individual human being. But George Eliot is equally aware of the half-truth that Comte taught her. An individual can only be himself, can only be real, in the particular social and historical circumstances that he inhabits.

This thorough attention to 'the medium in which a

character moves' can produce—or did produce in the novel's early readers—two conflicting impressions. One is an overwhelming admiration for the 'reality' of the fictional world. The other is a depressing sense of a deterministic process quenching effort and aspiration. This impression is less common among modern readers, perhaps because the kind of social and historical determinism that the novel undoubtedly does embody has gained much wider acceptance in the past hundred years. George Eliot's is not the mechanistic determinism which argues that freedom and responsibility are mischievous illusions that get in the way of an artificially-induced happiness. Lydgate fails, and Dorothea (a very different case) falls short of her early ideals, largely because of complex social and historical circumstances. There are determining factors in both these cases, but the destinies of both Lydgate and Dorothea are partly shaped by acts of conscious moral responsibility which are not visibly determined.

The other impression—the overwhelming sense of reality —is perhaps what most readers would refer to when asked to account for their admiration of the novel. *Middlemarch* does contain numerous examples of verbal and structural patterning—that is, of patterns not present in reality, whose function is to direct the reader's attention and suggest judgements. There is the famous web imagery, which draws attention to the complex interdependence of the lives; there is the fish imagery associated with Casaubon; there are the numerous parallels, usually revealing important differences, in the lives of the various characters. There is also, especially in the account of the relations between Dorothea and Casaubon, a highly developed poetic rendering of the inner life—what F. R. Leavis has called 'psychological notation'[1]— the effect of which is to give the most private, most tenuous and unrecognised experience the status of a perceived reality:

> 'Mr Casaubon had never had a strong bodily frame, and his soul was sensitive without being enthusiastic: it was too languid to thrill out of self-consciousness into passionate delight; it went on fluttering in the swampy ground where it was hatched, thinking of its wings and never flying.'   (Chapter 29)

This is only one of the many examples that could be taken

from the treatment of Mr Casaubon alone. It is the means by which George Eliot communicates and inspires a very rare kind of sympathy. It is quite different from the sympathy canvassed for Romola, Felix Holt, Daniel Deronda and occasionally Dorothea, which often consists of flattering the character. The passage quoted is typical in its suggestion of Casaubon's inward squalor. George Eliot does sometimes say that she is sorry for Casaubon and wishes the reader to share her pity, but it is not these direct appeals which inspire the real sympathy: it is the recognition that this miserable centre of egotism is the self that Casaubon has to live with, and that the suffering that his egotism causes to others is less than that which it causes to himself. It is not a sympathy that withholds judgement—the testament in which his poisoned nature finally expresses itself is hateful—but the judgement called for is more akin to that which is prompted by self-knowledge than that which we normally apply to other people. We know Casaubon in a way in which, in real life, we only know ourselves, and the exposure that George Eliot subjects him to would be terrible if that were not in itself a cause for radical sympathy.

The creation of Casaubon is characteristic of George Eliot, but it is not in this that the peculiar greatness of *Middlemarch* lies. (One sees a superb example of this same art in Mrs Transome, and also in Gwendolen Harleth.) It is an important part of the sense of reality referred to, and it is one of the surest signs that George Eliot recognised the reality of the individual. But most readers when testifying to that sense of reality would probably refer first to the feeling that the world of the novel extends beyond its pages, that the fictional reality is embedded in a further reality of which George Eliot has an equally sure grasp. One means by which this feeling is created is the extensive and almost invariably casual historical reference. Professor Jerome Beaty has given an excellent account of this technique in his essay 'History by Indirection: the Era of Reform in *Middlemarch*'.[2] The first Parliamentary Reform Bill and the development of the railways are prominent at particular moments in the novel. More characteristic are the passing references to the death of the politician William Huskisson on the railway, the suicide of Sir Samuel Romilly, the *volte-face* of Sir Robert

Peel and the Duke of Wellington on the question of Catholic Emancipation, the death of George IV, the threat of cholera, the publication of Louis's book on fever and of Robert Brown's 'Microscopic Observations on the Pollen of Plants'. The phrase 'a Tory Ministry passing Liberal measures' (Chapter 37) is even a paraphrase of a remark made by Huskisson in Parliament: 'a Tory administration governing on Whig principles'.[3] In its attention to individual lives at a specified date and its emphasis on process *Middlemarch* is essentially a historical novel (not just a better novel but a better *historical* novel than *Romola*). But as Professor Beaty points out we are not, as in the classic *genre* initiated by Scott, or as in *War and Peace,* thrust into the centre of the events we have learnt about in history lessons. We experience 'history' as it was experienced by the obscure inhabitants of a provincial town. George Eliot conceived of history as a slow progress operating through the minute adjustments of individual lives, and even such a great event as the impending Reform Bill is seen mainly as the comedy of Mr Brooke's candidature and the almost accidental introduction to politics of the future Liberal M.P. Will Ladislaw.

Another important way in which the depth and extension of the novel's world is suggested is the precise social identification of the characters. At the beginning of this chapter I used the phrase *'picture* of English society'—a very inadequate description of *Middlemarch*. The author herself calls it a *'Study* of Provincial life', and the study entails analysis. The characters are representative; their representativeness suggests a structure and an extension beyond what is actually presented. Furthermore, the structure is fluid and the suggested extension is one of time both backward and forward as well as of place. This technique can best be shown by an example: the domestic conversation of the Vincy family:

' "Well, my dear, you will not find any Middlemarch young man who has not something against him."

"But"—here Rosamond's face broke into a smile which suddenly revealed two dimples. She herself thought unfavourably of these dimples and smiled little in general society. "But I shall not marry any Middlemarch young man."

"So it seems, my love, for you have as good as refused the pick of them; and if there's better to be had, I'm sure there's no girl better deserves it."

"Excuse me, mamma—I wish you would not say, 'the pick of them.'"

"Why, what else are they?"

"I mean, mamma, it is rather a vulgar expression."

"Very likely, my dear; I never was a good speaker. What should I say?"

"The best of them."

"Why, that seems just as plain and common. If I had had time to think, I should have said, 'the most superior young men.' But with your education you must know."

"What must Rosy know, mother?" said Mr Fred, who had slid in unobserved through the half-open door while the ladies were bending over their work, and now going up to the fire stood with his back towards it, warming the soles of his slippers.

"Whether it's right to say 'superior young men,'" said Mrs Vincy, ringing the bell.

"Oh, there are so many superior teas and sugars now. Superior is getting to be shopkeepers' slang."

"Are you beginning to dislike slang, then?" said Rosamond, with mild gravity.

"Only the wrong sort. All choice of words is slang. It marks a class."

"There is correct English: that is not slang."

"I beg your pardon: correct English is the slang of prigs who write history and essays. And the strongest slang of all is the slang of poets". . . .

"What would you think of me if I came down two hours after every one else and ordered grilled bone?"

"I should think you were an uncommonly fast young lady." said Fred, eating his toast with the utmost composure.

"I cannot see why brothers are to make themselves disagreeable, any more than sisters."

"I don't make myself disagreeable; it is you who find me so. Disagreeable is a word that describes your feelings and not my actions."

"I think it describes the smell of grilled bone."

"Not at all. It describes a sensation in your little nose associated with certain finicking notions which are the classics of Mrs Lemon's school. Look at my mother: you don't see her objecting to everything except what she does herself. She is my notion of a pleasant woman."'   (Chapter 11)

Mrs Vincy is an innkeeper's daughter who has 'risen' by marrying a member of a leading Middlemarch manufacturing family. She has retained some of the cheerful vulgarity and vigorous idiomatic English of her origins. As in all 'rising' families the children are given an education that is considered superior to the parents', but a distinction is necessarily made between the son and the daughter. Rosamond is sent to Mrs Lemon's school where she learns only the social skills necessary to make her a desirable wife after the accepted pattern—accepted not only among the Vincys' peers in Middlemarch but also, we see, by Lydgate the baronet's nephew. Fred is sent to Cambridge where, for all the shortcomings of English universities at that date, he does genuinely widen his social and intellectual horizons. All this complex social differentiation and movement is revealed in this scene, when Rosamond objects to her mother's idiomatic speech, Mrs Vincy defers to the genteel standards and restricted vocabulary that the family has acknowledged by sending Rosamond to that school, and Fred with the easy manners and comparatively unblinkered outlook of a university man prefers the honest vulgarity of his mother to Rosamond's genteel notions.

When we look beyond the confines of the scene, we see that the analysis is still more complex. Although objectively Rosamond's education is as bad as can be it is spectacularly successful in helping her to procure a marriage into the gentry—to whose houses the manufacturers of Middlemarch are invited, but not their wives and daughters. Fred's life, on the other hand, takes a direction to which his education is quite irrelevant: he becomes the assistant of Caleb Garth and marries his daughter Mary. Mention of the Garths introduces another social and moral dimension— for George Eliot's social analysis is never independent of values. In Mrs Vincy's view Fred's marriage into the Garth family is a disaster. She despises Mrs Garth for having been a schoolteacher, the Garths generally for living 'in a poor way' and flatters her own status by supposing that the Garths are angling for Fred as a husband for Mary. In fact the Garths are the only middle-class characters (if we except the very different case of Bulstrode) whose values are entirely independent of the idea of rank, and by their very different standards Fred is as undesirable an addition to the family as Mary is to Mrs Vincy, Although Fred has gained something from his university education, its main function has been to prepare him for a gentleman's life in the Church. By abandoning that direction and allying himself with the Garths, he also abandons the values that determine social movement in his world: by Vincy standards his work for Caleb and marriage to Mary are of course a severe disappointment. The world he enters is one in which the dignity of creative labour is the supreme value, and one which George Eliot thoroughly endorses. The Garths' rectitude, acknowledgement of necessity and contempt for parasites are founded on the experience and valuation of practical work as a source of self-respect and improvement in the world:

> ' "You must be sure of two things: you must love your work, and not be always looking over the edge of it, wanting your play to begin. And the other is, you must not be ashamed of your work, and think it would be more honourable to you to be doing something else." '   (Chapter 56)

> ' " . . . it's a fine thing to come to a man when he's seen into the nature of business: to have the chance of getting a bit of the country into good fettle, as they say, and putting men into the right way with their farming, and getting a bit of good contriving and solid building done—that those who are living and those who come after will be the better for." '
>   (Chapter 40)

These attitudes provide a critical perspective not only on the Vincys' world, where employment is subordinate to status, but also on the world of Dorothea: 'the stifling oppression of that gentlewoman's world, where everything was done for her and none asked her aid' (Chapter 28). We are doubtless intended to regard Caleb as an exceptional individual, but he is fortunate (like Adam Bede) in being a member of a class, or more accurately participant in a way of life, which sustains such attitudes and the moral strength which they provide. The only person in the novel who has an activity corresponding to Caleb's is Lydgate but, as will emerge, in his case there is a conflict between the values inherent in his work and those he derives from his class.

The sustenance that Caleb Garth's values derive from his social circumstances makes him unusual among George Eliot's exceptional individuals. I have argued in Chapter 1 and in Chapter 3 that she customarily presents the relation between such a character and his social environment as one of conflict, and that there is also a conflict within herself between the ideas of continuity and of progress: the exceptional individual develops new forms of life and thought but in doing so he must not cut himself off from his own past. In *Middlemarch* she continues and extends her investigation of this conflict, particularly in the stories of Dorothea and Lydgate. One measure of the book's greatness is the extent to which she freed herself from the weaknesses that vitiated this investigation in *The Mill on the Floss* and the related attempt (more complex and of a different nature from the case of Caleb Garth) to express an ideal relation between the individual and his social inheritance in *Felix Holt*. The attempt in *Felix Holt* fails because working-class life is not truly presented, so that no conclusions can be validly formed. In *The Mill on the Floss* the potentially fruitful conflict between Maggie's superiority and the ties which bind her to her inferiors is denied resolution (or even a fully honest expression) by the didactic insistence on the sanctity of the past.

But something has been learned from *Felix Holt*. I have suggested that the portrayal of the Transomes and of Jermyn raises the unanswered question, whether Felix's supposed strength derives from his relation to the assumptions of his class, or from the nature of those assumptions. More important, for George Eliot's development, we have the recognition that inherited values do not necessarily command the respect she accorded to the Dodson code; in Jermyn and Harold, the influence of past associations makes not for moral strength, but for 'moral vulgarity'. This insight passes into *Middlemarch,* and is essential to the strength of its social analysis. Lydgate's 'spots of commonness', we are told,

'lay in the complexion of his prejudices, which, in spite of noble intention and sympathy, were half of them such as are found in ordinary men of the world: that distinction of mind which belonged to his intellectual ardour, did not penetrate his feeling and judgement about furniture, or women, or the desirability of its being known (without his telling) that he was better born than other country surgeons. He did not mean to think of furniture at present; but whenever he did so it was to be feared that neither biology nor schemes of reform would lift him above the vulgarity of feeling that there would be an incompatibility in his furniture not being of the best.'   (Chapter 15)

Lydgate's prejudice about women is almost the first thing we learn about him:

'She [Dorothea] did not look at things from the proper feminine angle. The society of such women was about as relaxing as going from your work to teach the second form, instead of reclining in a paradise with sweet laughs for bird-notes, and blue eyes for a heaven.'   (Chapter 11)

His prejudices are, in fact, those of Harold Transome. The similarity goes further: as Harold's Radicalism remains external to him, leaving his hereditary feelings untouched, so Lydgate's scientific habits of thought are sealed off from his personal life:

' . . . he was no radical in relation to anything but medical reform and the prosecution of discovery. In the rest of practical life he walked by hereditary habit.'   (Chapter 36)

(I have not, as this quotation shows, imposed the word 'hereditary' from outside the novel.) But there is a crucial difference between Lydgate and Harold. The externality of Harold's Radicalism is its own condemnation: it is superficial and essentially frivolous. Lydgate's scientific and medical career, however, is completely serious, and its seriousness is essential to his tragedy. The construction of the tragedy, moreover, is more tightly-knit than in *Felix Holt*. In the earlier novel, the arrogance of the landed gentry conflicts with the 'ambitions of pushing middle-class gentility', but the conflict is largely brought about by external circumstance: the plot suffers from its excess of machinery. In *Middlemarch*, middle-class gentility is represented by Rosamond, and the conflict is more intimate and more complicated than in *Felix Holt*. There is, in the first place, the irony that it is Lydgate's aristocratic prejudice about women that makes him Rosamond's victim, and his prejudice about furniture that further enmeshes him. Moreover, the conflict on Lydgate's side is not a matter merely of hereditary notions, but of an intensely original and impersonal ambition.

But the superiority of *Middlemarch* to its predecessors is not a matter of George Eliot's having come to different or more accurate conclusions about the individual and society. Rather it is that her interest in sociological theory with its accompanying moral and emotional intensity does not make itself felt here at the expense of the novel's coherence and verisimilitude. Contrary to what was once the orthodox view, it is the earlier novels and not *Middlemarch* in which theory is obtrusively present. In order to pursue this question, we will turn for the moment from Lydgate's career, and consider the treatment of Dorothea.

To judge by the alteration she made in the conclusion of the novel, George Eliot was confused about the extent to which Dorothea's mistakes could be blamed on her social circumstances. In the 'Finale' to the first edition, the following passage appears:

> 'Certainly those determining acts of her life were not ideally beautiful. They were the mixed result of young and noble impulse struggling under prosaic conditions. Among the many remarks passed on her mistakes, it was never said in the neighbourhood of Middlemarch that such mistakes could not have happened if the society into which she was born had not smiled on propositions of marriage from a sickly man to a girl less than half his own age—on modes of education which make a woman's knowledge another name for motley ignorance—on rules of conduct which are in flat contradiction with its own loudly-asserted beliefs. While this is the social air in which mortals begin to breathe, there will be collisions such as those in Dorothea's life, where great feelings will take the aspect of error, and great faith the aspect of illusion.'

Subsequently, she altered the passage to the following:

> 'Certainly those determining acts of her life were not ideally beautiful. They were the mixed result of young and noble impulse struggling amidst the conditions of an imperfect social state, in which great feelings will often take the aspect of error, and great faith the aspect of illusion.'

One cannot regret the change. Whatever the answer to the vexed question of how far George Eliot damagingly identified with Dorothea, she certainly did so when she wrote the first of the passages. That reference to 'prosaic conditions', for example, does not come from the author who was so clear-sighted about the 'working-day' world. What is most interesting, however, is the suggestion that Dorothea's marriage to Casaubon could be blamed on the complaisance of her social world. It is as if George Eliot forgot her brilliant rendering of the horror with which Sir James, Celia and Mrs Cadwallader viewed the marriage.[4]

Too much emphasis, however, should not be placed on a passage which George Eliot expunged from the novel. Rather, it will be useful to consider Dorothea's musings after it has first occurred to her that Mr Casaubon may be intending to marry her:

> 'There would be nothing trivial about our lives. Everyday things with us would mean the greatest things. It would be like marrying Pascal. I should learn to see the truth by the same light as great men have seen it by. And then I should know what to do, when I got older: I should see how it was possible to lead a grand life here—now—in England. I don't feel sure about doing good in any way now: everything seems like going on a mission to a people whose language I don't know;—unless it were building good cottages—there can be no doubt about that. Oh, I hope I should be able to get the people well housed in Lowick! I will draw plenty of plans while I have time.'
>
> (Chapter 3)

One peculiarity of Dorothea's mind is that it is continually moving between the immediately practical and the vaguely theoretical. So, in this prevision of life with Casaubon she imagines both 'the greatest things' and the building of cottages. There is no reason to suppose that we are to take the same attitude to both these ambitions. The vague 'grand life' is clearly presented ironically: 'It would be like marrying Pascal'. The building of cottages later (Chapter 56) receives the approval of Caleb Garth, the representative of uncompromisingly unideal virtue. What Dorothea does not understand is that the 'grand life' which she would enter by marrying Pascal, or Milton, or Hooker, or Mr Casaubon, does not encompass the building of cottages:

'Mr. Casaubon apparently did not care about building cottages, and diverted the talk to the extremely narrow accommodation which was to be had in the dwellings of the ancient Egyptians, as if to check a too high standard.' (Chapter 3)

The one ambition which Dorothea, in her prevision, was sure of having satisfied, is a matter of complete indifference to Mr Casaubon. The irony is doubled by the fact that, immediately after Dorothea's prevision, and immediately before Casaubon's expression of indifference, Sir James Chettam rides up and—in addition to making a fool of himself by offering her a Maltese puppy—shows an active interest in the building of cottages. The sane, healthy and practical side of her ambition would be fulfilled by Sir James—the suitor who falls within the expectations of her society—and is frustrated by Mr Casaubon.

The point is not, of course, that Dorothea should have married Sir James. Dorothea is the victim of two linked illusions. One is about the mind and character of Mr Casaubon; the other, more fundamental, is about the nature of her own intellectual and spiritual needs. The implied criticism of her society is not that it 'smiled' on the marriage with Casaubon, nor that it was too worldly for the satisfaction of Dorothea's theoretic ardour. It is that the society did not provide an environment in which such a nature as Dorothea's could develop healthily:

'The intensity of her religious disposition, the coercion it exercised over her life, was but one aspect of a nature altogether ardent, theoretic, and intellectually consequent: and with such a nature struggling in the bonds of a narrow teaching, hemmed in by a social life which seemed nothing but a labyrinth of petty courses, a walled-in maze of small paths that led no whither, the outcome was sure to strike others as at once exaggeration and inconsistency.' (Chapter 3)

The image for Dorothea's social life brilliantly foreshadows the later descriptions of Casaubon's mind. The life marked out for Dorothea has no ends—it 'led no whither'—and she marries a man whose mind consists of 'anterooms and winding passages which seemed to lead nowhither' (Chapter 20). Dorothea's social world has given her no clear conception of the ends to which her ardour should be directed. She does not simply make an error of judgement when she takes Casaubon for Pascal; she has no means of distinguishing between the two. Her confusion is expressed in terms of her desire for knowledge:

' . . . how could she be confident that one-roomed cottages were not for the glory of God, when men who knew the classics appeared to conciliate indifference to the cottages with zeal for the glory? Perhaps even Hebrew might be necessary—at least the alphabet and a few roots—in order to arrive at the core of things, and judge soundly on the social duties of the Christian.'

(Chapter 7)

Dorothea's vagueness about ends is at the root of the comedy here: the incongruity of Hebrew roots and 'social duties'. Behind the comedy lies the fact that Dorothea's social world has provided her with no coherent view of social duties, to enable her to perceive the incongruity. A passage from George Eliot's essay on 'Woman in France' is relevant here:

'Those famous *habitués* of the Hôtel de Rambouillet did not, apparently, first lay themselves out to entertain the ladies with grimacing "small-talk", and then take each other by the sword-knot to discuss matters of real interest in a corner; they rather sought to present their best ideas in the guise most acceptable to intelligent and accomplished women. . . . in such a circle, women would not become *bas bleus* or dreamy moralizers, ignorant of the world and of human nature, but intelligent observers of character and events.'[5]

Dorothea is consistently presented in the early parts of the novel as 'ignorant of the world and of human nature', and with this passage in mind, it is not hard to relate her ignorance to the prejudices of her society.

' "Well, but now, Casaubon, such deep studies, classics, mathematics, that kind of thing, are too taxing for a woman—too taxing, you know."
"Dorothea is learning to read the characters simply," said Mr Casaubon, evading the question. "She had the very considerate thought of saving my eyes."
"Ah, well, without understanding, you know—that may not be too bad. But there is a lightness in the feminine mind—a touch and go—music, the fine arts, that kind of thing—they should

study those up to a certain point, women should; but in a light
way, you know." '
(Chapter 7)

Beneath the obvious point about Mr Brooke and the world
he represents, there is a deeper irony. For Mr Brooke it is
quite clear that reading ancient tongues without understanding 'may not be too bad'; and this conversation follows
almost immediately after the passage in which Dorothea
wonders whether the Hebrew alphabet might not clarify her
conception of social duty. This double irony is apparent
throughout the early chapters. The doubleness is necessary
in order to avoid the feeling that the society is being
measured and found wanting by the standard of Dorothea's
own aspirations. For example, the point of the following
passage seems straightforward enough:

> 'A young lady of some birth and fortune, who knelt suddenly
> down on a brick floor by the side of a sick labourer and prayed
> fervidly as if she thought herself living in the time of the
> Apostles—who had strange whims of fasting like a Papist, and of
> sitting up at night to read old theological books! Such a wife
> might awaken you some fine morning with a new scheme for
> the application of her income which would interfere with
> political economy and the keeping of saddle-horses: a man
> would naturally think twice before he risked himself in such
> fellowship. Women were expected to have weak opinions; but
> the great safeguard of society and of domestic life was, that
> opinions were not acted on.' (Chapter 1)

The prospective husbands among the local gentry are afraid
for their worldly complacency with such a wife as Dorothea.
But on the other hand, there is surely a suggestion that such
a wife would be really inconvenient and impractical—
because, for one thing, she does not understand political
economy and is not expected to understand it: in the words
of Mr Brooke, 'Young ladies don't understand political
economy, you know'. To be expected to possess irreproach-
able Christian sentiments, while being barred from understanding the mechanics of the practical world, would be
supportable only to a woman who accepted that 'opinions
were not acted on'. More serious-minded and ardent women
are likely to develop dangerous notions that bear little relation to reality.

This could serve as a gloss on the phrase 'dreamy moralizers' in the 'Woman in France' essay. Dorothea in fact shares this attribute with Maggie Tulliver. Both girls live in unreal moral worlds: Dorothea 'looking forward' to giving up riding is reminiscent of Maggie's delusive hope of joy in renunciation. They differ markedly, however, in their development, and that difference is an important element in the superiority of *Middlemarch*. Dorothea, we are told, had 'the advantage over most girls that she had contemplated her marriage chiefly as the beginning of new duties'. This, in fact, is her salvation; for although the duties of her marriage turn out to be very different from what she expected, she is at least partly prepared for them. Whereas the problem with Maggie's renunciation of Stephen was that the reader was not allowed to consider the probability that that marriage might be one of 'new duties' rather than of 'easy delicious leaning'. Dorothea's career, in fact, illuminates the falsity of Maggie's moral dilemma.

Dorothea's unreal notions repeatedly cause pain to Casaubon—as, for example, when she presses him about publishing his work, and about helping Ladislaw. Her moral nature makes contact with reality when she sees that the marriage must rest on her strength, and not on his. This happens conclusively in the fine scene in which Casaubon, having learnt from Lydgate the truth about his condition, repels her pity, and she is thereby thrown into a fit of antagonism:

'If he had drawn her towards him, she would never have surveyed him—never have said, "Is he worth living for?" but would have felt him simply a part of her own life. Now she said bitterly, "It is his fault, not mine." In the jar of her whole being, Pity was overthrown. Was it her fault that she had believed in him— had believed in his worthiness?—And what, exactly, was he?— She was able enough to estimate him—she who waited on his glances with trembling, and shut her best soul in prison, paying it only hidden visits, that she might be petty enough to please him. In such a crisis as this, some women begin to hate.'

(Chapter 42)

The resolution comes the same night when Casaubon at last comes down to her:

'When her husband stood opposite to her, she saw that his face was more haggard. He started slightly on seeing her, and she looked up at him beseechingly, without speaking.

"Dorothea!" he said, with a gentle surprise in his tone. "Were you waiting for me?"

"Yes, I did not like to disturb you."

"Come, my dear, come. You are young, and need not to extend your life by watching."

When the kind quiet melancholy of that speech fell on Dorothea's ears, she felt something like the thankfulness that might well up in us if we had narrowly escaped hurting a lamed creature. She put her hands into her husband's, and they went along the broad corridor together.' (Chapter 42)

This is a magnificent moment, and its simple persuasiveness is an example of the real superiority of *Middlemarch* to its predecessors—it is not merely a matter of a false doctrine having given way to a true one. There is no didactic pressure here at all, but behind this and the whole of Dorothea's relation to Casaubon is the implicit recognition that the moral nature grows through daily experience, and that the influence of past associations is modified by that experience. The marriage remains a failure: when Dorothea begins to pity Casaubon she is partly recognising the failure, and taking upon herself the responsibility that it should cause her husband as little pain as possible. If the failure was inherent in the ignorance with which both parties entered the marriage, we are made to see that ultimately it is through Casaubon's fault, and not Dorothea's, that the failure is not less complete.

It would be disingenuous to pretend that in this novel George Eliot has completely emancipated herself from the doctrine of the sanctity of the past. Her career does not show a progressive movement away from didacticism, and indeed in *Daniel Deronda* we see the doctrine again assuming the crude racial form that it took in *The Spanish Gypsy*. However, if we look at Dorothea's career in the widest perspective it seems to represent a complete emancipation. She is the only one of George Eliot's heroines who effects a complete break with her past associations, and is shown to be justified in doing so. Dorothea does this in intention at least, when she goes to live in London with Ladislaw: it is hard not to feel that the reconciliation with her family in the Finale is merely a compromise. Whatever qualifications might be hinted at about the success of her career, it is certainly not suggested that she has cut herself morally adrift. This situation has been arrived at, however, by a dubious route, and in one crucial incident an accident is introduced which radically alters the course of events.

This incident is Casaubon's desire to make Dorothea promise to 'avoid doing what I should deprecate, and apply yourself to do what I should desire' (Chapter 48), and the fact that he dies before she can make the promise. Dorothea takes his request to refer to the completion and publication of his work. 'She had no presentiment that the power which her husband wished to establish over her future action had relation to anything else than his work' (ibid). The other possibility, of course, is that she should promise not to marry Will Ladislaw, but for the present argument it is necessary only to consider the possibility that occurs to Dorothea herself, since it is only in relation to that that she acts, and since it would effectively preclude marriage to Will in any case. She has three possible courses of action. One is to make the promise and fulfil it. The second is to refuse to promise. The third is to lie. Only the first two seem to occur to Dorothea, and yet in the terms in which she puts the question to herself, there is no obvious reason why she should not lie:

'Was it right, even to soothe his grief—would it be possible, even if she promised—to work as in a treadmill fruitlessly?

And yet, could she deny him? Could she say, "I refuse to content this pining hunger"? It would be refusing to do for him dead, what she was almost sure to do for him living.

. . . And now, if she were to say, "No! if you die, I will put no finger to your work"—it seemed as if she would be crushing that bruised heart.' (Chapter 48)

It is clearly not a question of whether the 'Key to All Mythologies' ought to be finished—that question has already been decided in the negative, even by Dorothea—but of whether Casaubon ought to be occasioned the greatest possible pain by disappointing him while still alive. It is his belief that the work should be finished that matters.

161

It would not be right to 'work as in a treadmill fruitlessly', but there is no obvious way in which it can also seem right to tell him so. The only answer is to lie. This may be a starkly utilitarian suggestion, and there are excellent reasons for believing that one should never make a false promise. It is possible that George Eliot believed this,[6] and even more lying is ignored in the book it seems to be a question of likely that Dorothea would have believed it. The point is that the issue is not what it seems. Because the possibility of whether one should abandon all self-responsibility for the rest of one's life, working at a task which one knows to be futile, in order to save a loved one from pain and bitter disappointment. In real life, the question would surely be, whether it is right to make a delusive promise in order to avoid making the terrible choice that faces Dorothea, when the other person will never know that the promise will not be fulfilled. The difference is between the right to individual happiness in relation to another person's happiness, and the importance of moral integrity and abstract concepts of good.

Dorothea decides to make the promise, and her decision is glossed as follows:

> 'Neither law nor the world's opinion compelled her to this—only her husband's nature and her own compassion, only the ideal and not the real yoke of marriage.' (ibid.)

There is a profound disingenuousness in the use of the words 'real and 'ideal' here; a disingenuousness which reflects the difference between the apparent and the real nature of the dilemma. In the book's terms, the 'ideal yoke' of marriage demands that Dorothea should sacrifice herself; but in that case what is the real yoke? In 'real' marriage is one partner at liberty to cause the other such pain as Casaubon would feel if Dorothea refused him? And is the real therefore inferior to the ideal? What George Eliot later says about Rosamond's belief that Will would have been a more suitable husband for herself than Lydgate is relevant here:

> 'No notion could have been falser than this, for Rosamond's discontent in her marriage was due to the conditions of marriage itself, to its demand for self-suppression and tolerance, and not to the nature of her husband.' (Chapter 75)

That is, the *reality* of marriage calls for self-suppression. It is hard to see how, in this context, the distinction between real and ideal could have any meaning. The difference might seem to be between truly moral marriage and what 'the world's opion' demands, but the suppressed possibility shows that it is really between marriage as a spiritual bond transcending the life together on earth, demanding absolute truth, and marriage in which one may make a false promise, to save one's partner from pain. In the latter case, the words ideal and real can be readily understood. By suppressing the possibility that Dorothea might lie, and by her disingenuous use of the words 'real' and 'ideal', George Eliot is passing off one distinction in the guise of the other, and making the reader who disagrees with Dorothea's decision seem morally shabbier than he is.

Casaubon's death, of course, releases Dorothea, but it is not hard to see that if he had lived another day, her position would have been very similar to Maggie Tulliver's. She would have promised to finish the 'Key to All Mythologies', and possibly also promised not to marry Will Ladislaw. Adherence to that promise would inevitably involve the feeling by which Maggie acts: 'If the past is not to bind us, where can duty lie?' Her only reason against breaking it would be, that to do so would cause a breach in her own moral nature, or in an ideal to which she had attached herself:

> 'Bound by a pledge given from the depths of her pity, she would have been capable of undertaking a toil which her judgement whispered was vain for all uses except that consecration of faithfulness which is a supreme use.' (Chapter 50)

This comes from the moral world of Maggie Tulliver, and in 'that consecration of faithfulness which is a supreme use', there is the same moral insistence that marks the end of *The Mill on the Floss*. The phrase presents a marked contrast to 'Rosamond's discontent in her marriage was due to the conditions of marriage itself . . . ' where, with a matter-of-fact tone, and the absence of quasi-religious vocabulary ('supreme', 'consecration'), George Eliot is clearly confident that she is expressing a self-evident moral truth.

But Dorothea's faithfulness, unlike Maggie's, is not put to the test, and as a consequence the emancipation represented by marriage with Will is too cheaply bought. In parenthesis, I will comment here on the feeling of many readers that this emancipation is also damaged by George Eliot's failure to make them share her valuation of Ladislaw, and that the scenes between Will and Dorothea are stilted and sanctimonious:

> 'They were looking at each other like two fond children who were talking confidentially of birds.
> "What is *your* religion?" said Dorothea. "I mean—not what you know about religion, but the belief that helps you most?"
> "To love what is good and beautiful when I see it," said Will. "But I am a rebel: I don't feel bound, as you do, to submit to what I don't like."
> "But if you like what is good, that comes to the same thing," said Dorothea, smiling.'   (Chapter 39)

This comes only two chapters after the following speech by Mr Brooke:

> ' "He seems to me a kind of Shelley, you know. . . . I don't mean as to anything objectionable—laxities or atheism, or anything of that kind, you know—Ladislaw's sentiments in every way I am sure are good. . . . But he has the same sort of enthusiasm for liberty, freedom, emancipation—a fine thing under guidance— under guidance, you know." '   (Chapter 37)

The irony here seems assured, yet in the exchange with Dorothea George Eliot appears to be offering Ladislaw as precisely a kind of Shelley without 'anything objectionable'. The atmosphere of sanctimony which surrounds their talk puts out of court the question of whether Ladislaw, like the real Shelley, might find marriage among the things he didn't like, and might refuse to submit to it. He is the only character in her novels who is allowed to express such a moral attitude and yet behave virtuously.

The aspirations of Will Ladislaw, most uncharacteristic of George Eliot, were shared by her contemporary Matthew Arnold. When Edward Dowden's biography revealed the consequences to Shelley's private life of his refusal to submit, Arnold complained, 'Our ideal Shelley was the true Shelley after all; what has been gained by making us at moments doubt it?'[7] Another testament to Arnold's need to believe in an ideal Shelley is 'The Scholar-Gypsy': 'Roaming the countryside, a truant boy'. The hero of Arnold's poem is conceived as an extreme contrast to the preoccupations and moral tone of the Victorian intellectual; he represents above all an envied freedom. But this freedom is made safe by the word 'boy'. A truant *man* would raise disturbing and incongruous thoughts. Ladislaw might be called George Eliot's Scholar-Gypsy: both are idealisations of the Romantic Poet as represented by Shelley, and although George Eliot is ironic about Ladislaw's Romantic enthusiasm and conviction of genius, the irony does not touch the central issue of his freedom from restraint. Like Arnold, she stresses her hero's boyishness—'They were looking at each other like two fond children.' The character is sentimental because he lacks the adult energies that would make his freedom problematic, and which make the real Shelley a less comfortable but more interesting figure than the ideal one.

The equivocation about Casaubon's dying wish shows us that George Eliot has still not resolved the problem of the individual's relation to his past, but the implications in *Middlemarch* are not nearly so extensive as in *The Mill on the Floss*. In the earlier novel, she was concerned with 'young natures in many generations, that in the onward tendency of human things have risen above the mental level of the generation before them, to which they have been nevertheless tied by the strongest fibres of their hearts' (Book 4, Chapter 1), and I have suggested that her concentration on working out the implications of the last phrase left her no way of expressing Maggie's elevation, that would not seem to involve a thwarting of the sources of her moral nature. In *Middlemarch* George Eliot has not lost her grasp of the ties which bind the individual to his heritage, but here she stresses their influence on the form which Dorothea's moral nature takes: the tradition into which she is born has certain expectations of women, and these expectations make her a 'dreamy moralizer'. The Brooke-Chettam-Cadwallader traditions are no more imperfect than the Dodson traditions, but they are treated with far less respect, because George Eliot sees that Dorothea can survive morally, and be independent of them.

Mr Paris gives an admirable expository analysis which I shall quote here:

> 'The sympathetic tendencies may be encouraged by tradition, but sympathy is antecedent to tradition and potentially superior to it. The individual who has a strongly sympathetic nature combined with profound personal experience and the ability to imagine the inward states of others has a moral life independent of tradition; he has a truer sense of good and evil and a more highly developed conscience than tradition could supply.'[8]

This is relevant to both novels, but it must be said of Maggie that if her sympathetic tendencies are *antecedent* to tradition they are not strictly *independent* of it. Both Maggie and Dorothea encounter 'profound personal experience', but it is only in Dorothea that this experience is accompanied by a growing independence and ability to cope with life.

The issue is partly that of determinism. Dorothea seems a freer being than Maggie; yet it is with reference to Dorothea's career that George Eliot says, 'there is no creature whose inward being is so strong that it is not greatly determined by what lies outside it' (Finale). This sentence has undoubtedly contributed to the view that *Middlemarch* is a grimly deterministic novel, and the associated view that Dorothea's career is a gloomy example of failed ideals:

> ' . . . that we are to trace the history of a "foundress of nothing, whose loving heart-beats and sobs after an unattained goodness tremble off and are dispersed among hindrances", seems to me the fiat not so much of realism as of that deficiency in the faculties of insight which only the stimulus of faith can supply. The true idealism of life undoubtedly often leads to failure and grief and outward ruin immeasurable; but only infidelity to it, selfish recoil from it, leads to that quenching and exhaustion of spirit in which the finest characters of George Eliot's works are so often allowed to flicker out their lives.'[9]

The application of this last sentence to Dorothea seems to me the result of a serious misreading of the novel; but it will be noticed that Hutton takes his quotation from the Prelude, and the note on which the novel ends, though it picks up the theme of the Prelude, is in quite a different key:

'But the effect of her being on those around her was incalculably diffusive: for the growing good of the world is partly dependent on unhistoric acts; and that things are not so ill with you and me as they might have been, is half owing to the number who lived faithfully a hidden life, and rest in unvisited tombs.'

(Finale)

In *Middlemarch: Critical Approaches to the Novel* Professor Beaty points out that in the manuscript 'partly dependent' reads 'chiefly dependent', and the last word of the novel is 'nobly' instead of 'tombs'.[10] But even in the more muted final version George Eliot does not seem to be describing a 'quenching and exhaustion of spirit'. The Prelude, in fact, seems to me misleading. It is worth asking how much value George Eliot really attached to 'the reform of a religious order' in comparison to the 'unhistoric acts' on which 'the growing good of the world' depends. Such an act, clearly, is Dorothea's second visit to Rosamond, after she has discovered Rosamond and Will together. Dorothea's 'resolve' recalls George Eliot's protest, in a letter to Mrs Ponsonby, against crude 'necessitarianism';

'I shall not be satisfied with your philosophy till you have conciliated necessitarianism—I hate the ugly word—with the practice of willing strongly, willing to will strongly, and so on. . . .'[11]

The 'irony of events' appears to have conspired cruelly to separate Dorothea from Will, but events are overcome by Dorothea's act of 'solidarity': 'She was a part of that involuntary palpitating life, and could neither look out on it from her luxurious shelter as a mere spectator, nor hide her eyes in selfish complaining' (Chapter 80). (If we imagine the use Hardy might have made of the situation, we can see something of the quality of George Eliot's belief in responsibility.)

'It always remains true that if we had been greater, circumstances would have been less strong against us' (Chapter 58). Dorothea's visit to Rosamond might be taken as a positive exposition of this comment, but the comment is actually applied to Lydgate, where it has of course a negative force. Mr Paris places this extract beside the statement in the Finale that 'there is no creature whose inward being is so strong that it is not greatly determined by what lies outside it', and concludes that whereas Dorothea's mistakes result 'chiefly from defects in her social medium', Lydgate's failure is 'more the result of his own deficiencies than of circumstances'.[12] I think that this is a simplification, implying a wrong kind of comparison between the characters. The outward circumstances that influence Dorothea's career are those social traditions which make her early aspirations so impractical and dangerous. There is a parallel in Lydgate, in those aspects of his character which he has in common with Harold Transome: those inherited assumptions which evade his habits of intelligent inquiry. But Lydgate's aspirations, unlike Dorothea's, have been formed independently of social traditions. Dorothea's major mistake—her marriage with Casaubon—is a commentary on the aspirations that she sought to satisfy thereby; Lydgate's mistakes—notably his marriage with Rosamond and his inept handling of his patients and his profession—form barriers to the fulfilment of aspirations that remain noble and practical in conception.

Their mistakes, therefore, are not parallel and do not have a parallel relation to defects in the social medium. Lydgate's failure is a failure to carry out a beneficial public activity: the double activity of enlightened medical practice and scientific research. The novel shows us vividly those conditions of society which militate against his medical practice, and they are so formidable as to make any balancing of personal and social responsibility a precarious exercise—and one which I do not propose to undertake.

But Lydgate faces another difficulty: one which is buried very deep in the novel's historical perspective, and which the late Professor W. J. Harvey has very usefully pointed out. Professor Harvey makes the important comparison between Lydgate and Casaubon, with the help of some historical information about their intellectual backgrounds. There seems to be a clear schematic link between the characters: both are engaged in arduous research; both fail; Casaubon's work is overshadowed by that of his German contemporaries, while Lydgate is afraid of being overtaken by 'some plodding fellow of a German'. However,

'while the irony of Casaubon is that he is in ignorance of the real work already done by German scholars in the near-past, the irony of Lydgate is that he is just too soon for the real work to be done, again by German scholars, in the near future. . . . Casaubon's mistake is his own fault, Lydgate's mistake is an accident of history. In his day his microscope would not have been good enough for the work to be done; . . . the crucial break-through by the German biologists, Schwann and Scheider, was to come a few years later in 1838-9. By that time Lydgate had dwindled to a fashionable practice and a treatise on Gout. Poor Lydgate—his research, like his medical practice, is just a little too premature.'[13]

All this is hinted by George Eliot's remark that Lydgate put the question arising from Bichat's work 'not quite in the way required by the awaiting answer'. Thus we have a concrete historical example of the way in which the exceptional individual is limited by the stage of human development in which he is living. Lydgate had no way of finding the right answer in 1829; and the reason why he was not in a position to profit by the improved conditions a few years later links, with a significant irony, this historical example with those other more evident examples which operate in his medical practice and private life.

Lydgate's concern for medical reform is as deeply rooted in historical detail as his scientific research. In Chapter 16 he makes himself unpopular by associating himself—in the presence of Mr Chichely the coroner with Wakley's[14] campaign to place the coronership in the hands of medically-qualified men. This leads Dr Sprague to say,

'"I disapprove of Wakley . . . no man more: he is an ill-intentioned fellow, who would sacrifice the respectability of the profession, which everyone knows depends on the London Colleges, for the sake of getting some notoriety for himself. . . . But Wakley is right sometimes," the Doctor added, judicially. "I could mention one or two points in which Wakley is in the right."'

Wakley's biographer, who takes this passage as his epigraph, comments:

'George Eliot was accurate, as only she could be, in thus describing Dr Sprague as muddled and uncertain in his estimate. She has in doing so exactly recorded the way in which many worthy members of the profession regarded Wakley while his general work of reform was in its fierce inception.'[15]

Thus the introduction of Wakley's name does not merely give one a thrill of recognising that actual historical events were occurring at the same time as the fiction, but gives the habits of mind of the Middlemarch doctors an accurate and representative historical significance.

But the key chapter is Chapter 45, which traces the course of Lydgate's career and reputation in Middlemarch. The major theme of this chapter is the way in which popular ignorance and professional prejudice interact, so that almost everything he does contributes to his eventual fall. The reaction to his refusal to supply drugs is an obvious case in which the two come together in simple combination. There are more complex cases, however, in which Lydgate's genuine successes create hostility. One such case is that of Nancy Nash, who has a painful lump which Dr Minchin diagnoses as a tumour, but which Lydgate successfully treats as cramp. Popular opinion, however, persists in regarding it as an 'amazing case of tumour, not clearly distinguishable from cancer, and considered the more awful for being of the wandering sort'.

Thus Lydgate, to his own vexation, is the subject of 'the sort of prestige which an incompetent and unscrupulous man would desire', and at the same time Dr Minchin learns from Lydgate's house-surgeon that his own diagnosis had been wrong, and 'privately pronounced that it was indecent in a general practitioner to contradict a physician's diagnosis in that open manner, and afterwards agreed with Wrench that Lydgate was disagreeably inattentive to etiquette.' (Wrench, too, bases his judgement of Lydgate's etiquette on having been proved wrong by the newcomer in the case of Fred Vincy.)

The whole situation is concisely conveyed in a single comic incident in this chapter, which is worth quoting in full:

'Mr Toller remarked one day, smilingly, to Mrs Taft, that "Bulstrode had found a man to suit him in Lydgate; a charlatan in religion is sure to like other sorts of charlatans."

"Yes, indeed, I can imagine," said Mrs Taft, keeping the number of thirty stitches in her mind all the while; "there are so many of that sort. I remember Mr Cheshire, with his irons, trying to make people straight when the Almighty had made them crooked."

"No, no," said Mr Toller, "Cheshire was all right—all fair and above board. But there's St John Long—that's the kind of fellow we call a charlatan, advertising cures in ways nobody knows anything about: a fellow who wants to make a noise by pretending to go deeper than other people. The other day he was pretending to tap a man's brain and get quicksilver out of it."

"Good gracious! what dreadful trifling with people's constitutions!" said Mrs Taft.'

Professor Beaty's phrase, 'History by Indirection', can be as well applied to the medical history in the novel as to the political. There is a deeply buried irony in the mention of St John Long. In Chapter 16, Lydgate suffered through being associated with Thomas Wakley and the *Lancet,* and now he is compared with the charlatan whom Wakley himself was active in exposing, and whose escape from justice Wakley blamed on the medical incompetence of coroners.[16] The comparison, originating in Mr Toller's prejudice, is passed on to Mrs Taft, whose own idea of charlatanism is defined by the tattered remnants of the age-old theological opposition to medicine (earlier we have been told that some people held that Lydgate's 'power of resuscitating persons as good as dead was an equivocal recommendation, and might interfere with providential favours'). The fact that Mrs Taft keeps 'the number of thirty stitches carefully in her mind all the while' during this conversation is a fine example of how the pettiest details combine with more easily identifiable social defects to militate against Lydgate. Her lack of attention to what Toller is saying evidently leaves her in some confusion about the distinction between Lydgate and St John Long:

'"Good gracious! what dreadful trifling with people's constitutions!" said Mrs Taft.

After this, it came to be held in various quarters that Lydgate played even with respectable constitutions for his own purposes, and how much more likely that in his flighty experimenting he should make sixes and sevens of hospital patients.'

The chapter ends with a scene between Lydgate and Rosamond, in which Rosamond for the first time clearly takes her place among the hindrances to his work. One of Lydgate's indiscretions in Middlemarch has been his request to open the body of a dead patient, and he tells Rosamond of his hero Vesalius, who had to learn anatomy by digging up dead bodies ' "Oh!" said Rosamond, with a look of disgust on her pretty face, "I am very glad you are not Vesalius. I should have thought he might find some less horrible way than that." ' One can hardly blame Rosamond for this reaction: indeed one may wonder what even Dorothea would have thought of a husband digging up dead bodies. But Rosamond's distaste takes a more general form: 'I do *not* think it is a nice profession, dear'. We are reminded that marriage with Rosamond subjects Lydgate to social pressures quite outside the medical sphere:

> 'No one quicker than Rosamond to see causes and effects which lay within the track of her own tastes and interests: she had seen clearly Lydgate's pre-eminence in Middlemarch society, and could go on imaginatively tracing still more agreeable social effects when his talent should have advanced him; but for her, his professional and scientific ambition had no other relation to these desirable effects than if they had been the fortunate discovery of an ill-smelling oil.'   (Chapter 58)

Rosamond is drawn to Lydgate by an attraction quite separate from his distinction as a doctor and man of science; and Lydgate's own prejudices allow him to encourage that attraction without inquiring into its source. One peculiarity of Rosamond's mind is that she is quite incapable of seeing causes and effects *outside* 'the track of her own tastes and interests'. 'The essence of stupidity is egoism', George Eliot says of her in a passage deleted in proof;[17] but she might equally have said 'the essence of egoism is stupidity'. Rosamond cannot feel the pressure, not only of other people's needs, but of external objects. Her own emotional life is carried on almost independently of reality, and she cannot conceive of an emotional state which is not entirely self-bounded and self-motivated. Thus, she describes Lydgate as 'disagreeable' or 'out of humour' when he is pressed by material anxiety, and does not relate the two facts. It is difficult to separate out the influences of nature and nurture. Rosamond is clearly an egoist 'by nature'; but her education at Mrs Lemon's school and the social expectations it represents—being an imitation of the education and social expectations of the class to which Dorothea Brooke belongs—do not include training the mind to apprehend reality. The only truly 'educational' experiences that Rosamond encounters are Will's outburst after Dorothea's first visit, and Dorothea's behaviour during her second visit:

'Rosamond, while these poisoned weapons were being hurled at her, was almost losing the sense of her identity, and seemed to be waking into some new terrible existence. . . . What another nature felt in opposition to her own was being burnt and bitten into her consciousness.' (Chapter 78)

'It was a newer crisis in Rosamond's experience than even Dorothea could imagine: she was under the first great shock that had shattered her dream-world in which she had been easily confident of herself and critical of others; and this strange unexpected manifestation of feeling in a woman whom she had approached with a shrinking aversion and dread, as one who must necessarily have a jealous hatred towards her, made her soul totter all the more with a sense that she had been walking in an unknown world which had just broken in upon her.' (Chapter 81)

Dorothea's gentlewoman's education makes her a 'dreamy moralizer', and she learns by experience to attach her ardour to real and not imagined objects. Rosamond's imitation-gentlewoman's education makes her a dreaming egoist, and she learns by experience—if only briefly—that the world does not centre upon herself.

We have seen that these social influences, of which Rosamond is the most powerful example, are ironically linked to the fact that, historically, Lydgate was working too early to be able to come to the correct conclusions in his research. It is his dependence on, and defeat by, the immediate social conditions that leaves him unable to profit when, in broader historical terms, the right moment comes. Thus his story might at first seem to be a simple deterministic case-history. This would be a simplification, however, and some weight should be placed on the reason which Lydgate gives Dorothea for not continuing his work at the hospital:

' "It is impossible for me now to do anything—to take any step without considering my wife's happiness. The thing that I might like to do if I were alone, is become impossible to me. I can't see her miserable. She married me without knowing what she was going into, and it might have been better for her if she had not married me."

"I know, I know—you could not give her pain, if you were not obliged to do it," said Dorothea, with keen memory of her own life.'

(Chapter 76)

If Lydgate's love for Rosamond began in self-indulgent folly, it ends in a self-denying devotion that is here explicitly compared with Dorothea's devotion to Casaubon. However strong the socially-determining influences on his failure, ultimately it is because he chooses to take the consequences of his marriage to Rosamond, rather than sacrifice her happiness, that he renounces his ambition. This is most movingly expressed at the end of Chapter 81: 'Lydgate had accepted his narrowed lot with sad resignation. He had chosen this fragile creature, and had taken the burthen of her life upon his arms. He must walk as he could, carrying that burthen pitifully.' Lydgate's story remains a tragedy, and there is no suggestion that his failure is mitigated by the 'incalculably diffusive' effect of 'unhistoric acts'. It is, however, a token of the novel's quality that, despite everything, Lydgate's last decisive act is one of conscious moral responsibility, and not of forced acquiescence to the determining powers. It is also a reminder to the critic looking for 'social' interpretations that he does so at the peril of his own humanity.

George Eliot's central religious belief, a belief which she derived from or found confirmed in Feuerbach, was that 'the idea of God, so far as it has been a high spiritual influence, is the ideal of a goodness entirely human.'[18] This 'goodness entirely human' is Feuerbach's 'True, or Anthropological' essence of Christianity, and this belief informs George Eliot's sympathetic portrayal of Methodists and Evangelicals in *Adam Bede* and *Janet's Repentance*. This identification of the source of what is good in Christianity is, however, accompanied in Feuerbach's analysis by another emphasis:

'Faith in Providence is faith in one's own worth, the faith of man in himself; hence the beneficent consequences of this faith, but hence also false humility, religious arrogance, which, it is true, does not rely on itself, but only because it commits the care of itself to the blessed God. God concerns himself about me; he has in view my happiness, my salvation; he wills that I shall be blest; but that is my will also : thus, my interest is God's interest, my own will is God's will, my own aim is God's aim,— God's love for me nothing else than my self-love deified.'[19]

George Eliot chose to make Mr Bulstrode, her study of a corrupt Christian conscience, an Evangelical not only because she had been Evangelical herself but because Evangelicalism was, in its own view and according to the terms of Feuerbach's analysis, an extremely pure form of Christianity. The Evangelicals described the mass of Churchmen as 'nominal Christians' who, if not entirely vicious, lived by essentially pagan standards of behaviour which would have been readily understood by a virtuous Greek or Roman. In the words of William Wilberforce, the leader of the movement for forty years from its inception in the 1780s,

'the grand distinction, which subsists between the true Christian and all other Religionists ... is concerning the nature of this holiness, *and the way in which it is to be obtained.*'

The 'nominal' Christians 'conceive it is to be *obtained by their own natural unassisted efforts*', but the true Christian *'knows that this holiness is not to* PRECEDE *his reconciliation to God, and be its* CAUSE*; but to* FOLLOW *it, and be its* EFFECT. *That in short it is by* FAITH IN CHRIST *only that he is to be justified in the sight of God.'*[20] The category of nominal Christians included the vast majority of clergymen. Such clergymen are strongly represented in George Eliot's works: by Mr Gilfil in *Scenes of Clerical Life*, Mr Irwine in *Adam Bede*, Mr Lingon in *Felix Holt*, Mr Farebrother and Mr Cadwallader in *Middlemarch* and Mr Gascoigne in *Daniel Deronda*. These clergymen, most of them admirable, preach not about justification by faith and imputed righteousness, like the Evangelical Amos Barton and Mr Tyke, but 'short moral sermons'. In other words they work on the principle that 'holiness is to precede reconciliation to God, and be its cause.' In *Adam Bede* George Eliot says that she can imagine some of her readers exclaiming that Mr Irwine is no better than a pagan (Chapter 17), and she justifies the charge by telling us that he 'found a savouriness in a quotation from Sophocles or Theocritus that was quite absent from any text in Isaiah or Amos' (Chapter 5). The only book we see him reading is Aeschylus, and the moral advice he gives to Arthur is entirely Greek in spirit. In *Middlemarch* when Dorothea has to choose the new incumbent for Lowick on Casaubon's death she reads a volume of Mr Tyke's sermons and decides that 'such sermons would be of no use at Lowick—I mean, about imputed righteousness and the prophesies in the Apocalypse.' She accepts Lydgate's argument in favour of Farebrother, that 'His position is not quite like that of the Apostles: he is only a parson among parishioners whose lives he has to try and make better' (Chapter 50). In the Evangelical view, such attitudes were simply not Christian.

Bulstrode is Tyke's sponsor and his career is George Eliot's examination—in the spirit of the passage quoted earlier from Feuerbach—of the assumption that reconciliation with God precedes conversion. An historical example of the consequences of this belief can be seen in the leader of the powerful Evangelical group at Cambridge, Charles Simeon:

'In the most conspicuous way, Charles Simeon's every act was the product of an elevated, unintermittent and entirely acceptable righteousness that he was intensely and unintermittently aware of . . . . in what may have been his most eminent service (out of many) to the Reformation, the collection of Evangelical gold to buy places in the church, he regarded without a moment's questioning as wholly admirable a practice that if it had been the High Church party's he would at once have seen as unscrupulous and unchristian.'[21]

' "To this hour do I reap the benefits of these habits [of early economy]," he wrote; "for though my income is now very large, I never indulge in any extravagance. I have, it is true, my establishment on rather a high scale in comparison of others; but I never throw away my money in foolish indulgences, nor spend more of my income upon myself than I believe God himself approves." '[22]

This is not to suggest that Simeon was a Bulstrode, who not only made himself rich but did so crookedly. The quotation in the second of these passages does, however, indicate that an assumption of a familiar relationship with God could allow a man of undoubted good faith to justify his personal comfort by reference to God's will:

> 'It was a principle with Mr Bulstrode to gain as much power as possible, that he might use it for the glory of God. He went through a great deal of spiritual conflict and inward argument in order to adjust his motives, and make clear to himself what God's glory required. But, as we have seen, his motives were not always rightly appreciated.' (Chapter 16)

This is the same habit of thought as Charles Simeon's justification of the purchase of livings for Evangelicals, when he would condemn it in others. It is his *motives* that Bulstrode tries to adjust, not necessarily his actions. When he is faced with the temptation of causing Raffles's death he tells himself 'intention was everything in the question of right and wrong' (Chapter 70). This is the opposite of George Eliot's belief; she was concerned to show that the consequences of deeds are independent of intentions.

The sharp division made by Evangelicals between true Christians and others—the mark of the true Christian being, before all else, his claim to have experienced conversion—naturally encouraged the application of separate standards of behaviour. The man who is God's chosen vessel judges his own actions according to their usefulness to God's cause:

> 'Bulstrode's standard had been his serviceableness to God's cause: "I am sinful and nought—a vessel to be consecrated by use—but use me!"—had been the mould into which he had constrained his immense need of being something important and predominating.' (Chapter 61)

It had been the conviction that his possession of Mrs Dunkirk's fortune would be pleasing and serviceable to God, that consciously motivated his concealment of her daughter's existence—the cause of his eventual crisis and humiliation:

> 'Could it be for God's service that this fortune should in any considerable proportion go to a young woman and her husband

who were given up to the lightest pursuits, and might scatter it abroad in triviality—people who seemed to lie outside the path of remarkable providences?'   (ibid.)

Similar reasoning prompts the killing of Raffles:

'Raffles dead was the image that brought release, and indirectly he prayed for that way of release, beseeching that, if it were possible, the rest of his days here below might be freed from the threat of an ignominy which would break him utterly as an instrument of God's service.'   (Chapter 70)

The utter plausibility of this reasoning illustrates the potential for corruption of a belief which makes moral action secondary to, and not a direct expression of, the will of God. This displacement of morality is central to George Eliot's rejection of Christianity:

'There is no general doctrine which is not capable of eating out our morality if unchecked by the deep-seated habit of direct fellow-feeling with individual men.'   (Chapter 61)

In the same paragraph she insists that such reasoning as Bulstrode's is not 'peculiar to evangelical belief' and in *Janet's Repentance* she portrayed an Evangelical clergyman untainted by such corruption. Nevertheless, with Bulstrode's career she demonstrates conclusively that Evangelicalism is no protection against a powerful egotism.

I may have suggested that Bulstrode's story is merely a dissection of a faith that George Eliot had rejected, and of a man who used that faith for his own selfish interests. It is of course far other than that. What makes Bulstrode's case poignant is that despite his egotism, love of power and moral equivocation he has the quality that makes him, even in his corrupted state, a finer human type than the Hawleys and the Hackbutts who condemn him: the desire to be better than he is and belief in 'something else than his own greed . . . a conscience or standard to which he more or less adapts himself' (Chapter 61). The scene of his unmasking has a very different effect on the reader from the exposure of Pecksniff or Uriah Heep. Although the love of domination that aroused the hatred of his neighbours really was hateful, a large part of their resentment is at being exposed to a more strenuous mode of existence. Bulstrode has been a Pharisee, but the pleasure of his accusers is exactly like the pleasure of the Pharisees when they thought they had trapped Jesus by confronting him with the adultress.

George Eliot takes as her epigraph to Chapter 85 Bunyan's account of Mr Malice, Mr Love-lust and the rest condemning Faithful to death, and comments,

'When immortal Bunyan makes his picture of the persecuting passions bringing in their verdict of guilty, who pities Faithful? That is a rare and blessed lot which some greatest men have not attained, to know ourselves guiltless before a condemning crowd—to be sure that what we are denounced for is solely the good in us. The pitiable lot is that of the man who could not call himself a martyr even though he were to persuade himself that the men who stoned him were but ugly passions incarnate —who knows that he is stoned, not for professing the Right, but for not being the man he professed to be.'

A part of our judgement of Bulstrode must be the acknowledgement that he would have recognised the truth of this, whereas some of his accusers would have condemned Faithful with equal satisfaction.

An important element in Bulstrode's faith—of Christian belief generally, but more prominently of Evangelical belief —is the concept of Providence: that God is perpetually intervening on behalf of His servants. Mention of Providence in *Middlemarch* is not confined to Bulstrode. Two other characters who are shown to have an implicit belief in a Providential arrangement of events are—at first sight surprisingly—Fred and Rosamond Vincy. At the opening of Chapter 27 George Eliot uses the metaphor of a surface covered with scratches which, when a candle is brought near, give the illusion of a concentric pattern:

'These things are a parable. The scratches are events, and the candle is the egoism of any person now absent—of Miss Vincy, for example. Rosamond had a Providence of her own who had kindly made her more charming than other girls, and who seemed to have arranged Fred's illness and Mr. Wrench's mistake in order to bring her and Lydgate within effective proximity.'

Satirical references to Providence in *Middlemarch* are so numerous that one could almost call it—despite George Eliot's dislike of attacks on religion—her one positively anti-Christian novel. Fred Vincy's whole career until his regeneration by the Garths, can be seen as a parody of this Christian belief. Fred's vice is his assumption that events will arrange themselves for his convenience, without any effort of his own. When he gets into debt with Bambridge and then renews the bill with Caleb Garth's signature he is confident that he will be able to repay within the specified time:

> 'You will hardly demand that his confidence should have a basis in external facts; such confidence, we know, is something less coarse and materialistic: it is a comfortable disposition leading us to expect that the wisdom of providence or the folly of our friends, the mysteries of luck or the still greater mystery of our high individual value in the universe, will bring about agreeable issues, such as are consistent with our good taste in costume, and our general preference for the best style of thing.'
>
> (Chapter 23)

When Featherstone gives Fred some banknotes 'they actually presented the absurdity of being less than his hopefulness had decided that they must be. What can the fitness of things mean, if not their fitness to a man's expectations? Failing this, absurdity and atheism gape behind him' (Chapter 14). Elsewhere in Fred's story, and with reference to a different belief, George Eliot makes the most explicitly anti-Christian statement in all her novels. Having told us that Fred's first pain at having caused the loss of Caleb's money was 'the sense that he must seem dishonourable' and not the actual consequences for the Garths, she comments: 'Indeed we are most of us brought up in the notion that the highest motive for not doing a wrong is something irrespective of the beings who would suffer the wrong' (Chapter 24).

Fred's attitudes would of course be as unacceptable to a true Christian as they are to George Eliot. The Christian Providence is not an arrangement for personal comfort but an expression of God's will. Its best fruit is resignation to personal sorrow and joy in good not our own. However, Fred's belief in his 'high individual value in the universe' differs from the Christian's only in its narrowness, egotism and worldly reference. Morally this is a very wide difference, but in George Eliot's view both beliefs are equally delusive. 'Why should one expect the truth to be consoling?'[23] she is reported as saying by Edith Simcox. Fred's assumptions are not intended as a personal satire on pure-hearted Christians, such as her Aunt Samuel Evans, whom she revered. A parallel is intended, however, between Fred and Rosamond's untheological Providence and the corrupt Christian belief of Bulstrode whose God is equally, though less simply, identified with his own ego. But there is also a wider reference. George Eliot sees the Christian belief as an example of the human tendency to interpret reality in a consoling or flattering manner, the Christian 'candle' being not petty egotism but the corporate aspirations of the human race. The delusiveness of Providence is highlighted by its appearance in a novel so closely organised on the strictest principles of causation.

The most pertinent contrast to Fred's assumptions are those of Caleb Garth:

'Though he had never regarded himself as other than an orthodox Christian, and would argue on prevenient grace if the subject were proposed to him, I think his virtual divinities were good practical schemes, accurate work, and the faithful completion of undertakings: his prince of darkness was a slack workman. But there was no spirit of denial in Caleb, and the world seemed so wondrous to him that he was ready to accept any number of systems, like any number of firmaments, if they did not obviously interfere with the best land drainage, solid building, correct measuring, and judicious boring (for coal). In fact, he had a reverential soul with a strong practical intelligence.' (Chapter 24)

The last sentence expresses George Eliot's ideal. The 'reverential soul' is the awareness of 'the mystery that lies under the processes'[24] without which men cannot maintain a spontaneous and sympathetic relation to the world and to others, and are in danger of the callous calculating cynicism that afflicts Tito Melema in *Romola* or the poisonous *ennui* of Grandcourt in *Daniel Deronda*. George Eliot hated rationalistic arrogance more than any religious dogma: 'of all intolerance, the intolerance calling itself philosophical is the most odious to me.'[25] But Caleb's interpretation of all that is not genuinely beyond his comprehension is based on principles derived from the observation of cause and effect in creative practical work. He is thus, together with his wife and daughter who share his attitudes, the only character who consistently interprets reality on principles that are harmonious with those by which the novel's world is created.

One of Lydgate's favourite sayings is that 'a man's mind must be continually expanding and shrinking between the whole human horizon and the horizon of an object-glass' (Chapter 63). This is an excellent description of the method by which the novel is created. The world of the novel, the object of investigation, expands and shrinks in just this way, from the most intimate, barely conscious experience of Dorothea or Casaubon, of Lydgate or Bulstrode, to their relations with others, their immediate social worlds, and the larger social worlds and historical developments of whose influence on their lives they are unaware. This sense of reality derives from George Eliot's resolution of the questions of individual and species, determinism and free will—a resolution that is made much more convincingly than in her explicit statements in letters and journals. Perhaps the most important, though submerged, reason why we see her world as real is that in it the individual and the species are—in contrast to Comte's one-sided formula—interdependent, and while the operation of powerful determining forces is clearly presented, the characters make real choices and are responsible for their own lives.

9
Daniel Deronda

Daniel Deronda contains the extremes, in George Eliot's novels, of unqualified theoretical assertion and genuine experimental art. Critical opinion, as in the case of *Felix Holt,* has been virtually unanimous about the respective merits of the two parts, a unanimity which in this case dates back to its very first readers. My purpose here is not to alter the general preference for Gwendolen's story over the Jewish section, but the novel is such a striking illustration of the differing relations between George Eliot's beliefs and her art and is, at its best, such a magnificent achievement, possibly surpassing even *Middlemarch,* that it is a pleasurable necessity to pay some extended attention to it.

It is worth noticing George Eliot's response to the criticisms of the novel's first readers since it has a bearing on this argument. It reveals what is perhaps her least pleasing characteristic—a vein of self-righteous disdain for her readers, which had first shown itself in some of the authorial commentaries in *Scenes of Clerical Life*.[1] In a letter to Mme Bodichon she refers contemptuously to 'the laudation of readers who cut the book into scraps and talk of nothing in it but Gwendolen. I meant everything in the book to be related to everything else there'.[2] And to Harriet Beecher Stowe she wrote:

'As to the Jewish element in "Deronda", I expected from first to last in writing it, that it would create much stronger resistance and even repulsion than it has actually met with. But precisely because I felt that the usual attitude of Christians towards Jews is—I hardly know whether to say more impious or more stupid when viewed in the light of their professed principles, I therefore felt urged to treat Jews with such sympathy and understanding as my nature and knowledge could attain to.'[3]

There are two points of interest here. One is the virtual acknowledgement of special pleading, which is present both in her attitude to the Jews generally and more particularly in the character of Deronda, who never frees himself from the author's protective insistence that we should admire him. The second is that here and in all her and Lewes's other complaints about the reading public's lack of sympathy, this is attributed not to a failure to respond to George Eliot's art, but to a prior lack of sympathy with the subject. No doubt the reading public was anti-Semitic to a considerable extent, but it is very likely that the authority of George Eliot at the height of her influence would have supported an artistic treatment of her subject in overcoming such prejudice. What she actually did, on the contrary, was of a nature to encourage the expression of anti-Semitic feeling, as exasperation at the insistence, inflexibility and humourlessness of her writing.

Her attribution of the unfavourable response to the subject-matter rather than to her art may partly have been defensive, but it also indicates the kind of interest she had in this part of the novel. It is not the public's blindness to the artistic creations of Deronda, Mordecai and Mirah that distresses her, but their blindness to her intention and to her convictions. Yet (and this is no real paradox) it is a deficiency in George Eliot's own sympathy with her characters which creates this resistance. By sympathy I mean not the conscious partiality that we can see in the treatment of Deronda, but what I have called the essence of the novelist's art, the sympathetic immersion in the actual and the individual which *creates* character, independent, self-responsible, suffering and sturdily real.

A few extracts will show the various ways in which George Eliot actually repels, in the case of Deronda, the kind of sympathy that the reader is compelled to feel for Gwendolen, and how this is a symptom of the novelist's own lack of real sympathy with the characters towards whom she is partial. The qualities that create this repulsion are an abstractness of analysis which suggests that the author's imagination does not spontaneously conceive of the character in particular situations (numerous critics have commented on her difficulty in giving Deronda even a convincing physical posture, relying on the trick of holding his coat-collar); explicit partiality expressing itself in laudatory language; and a habit of presenting the character's mental processes in the form of an argument which clearly comes direct from the author.

The following passage, from Chapter 32, is particularly revealing, being preceded by the statement that 'any one wishing to understand the effect of after-events on Deronda should know a little more of what he was at five-and-twenty than was evident in ordinary intercourse'. This occurs almost halfway through the novel, and although Gwendolen has been the centre of attention for most of the time, Deronda has had more words devoted to him than, for example, Grandcourt, whom we know well from the four superb pages (Chapter 12) in which we see him at home with Lush and his dogs. The necessity of a formal analysis of the hero at this late hour suggests some lack of confidence in what has already been done:

'His early-awakened sensibility and reflectiveness had developed into a many-sided sympathy, which threatened to hinder any persistent course of action: as soon as he took up any antagonism, though only in thought, he seemed to himself like the Sabine warriors in the memorable story—with nothing to meet his spear but flesh of his flesh, and objects that he loved. His imagination had so wrought itself to the habit of seeing things as they probably appeared to others, that a strong partisanship, unless it were against an immediate oppression, had become an insincerity for him. His plenteous, flexible sympathy had ended by falling into one current with that reflective analysis which tends to neutralise sympathy. Few men were able to keep themselves clearer of vices than he; yet he hated vices mildly, being used to think of them less in the abstract than as a part of mixed human natures having an individual history, which it was the bent of his mind to trace with understanding and pity.'

This is not the prose of a novelist. It is more like that of a reflective but unimaginative biographer—though George Eliot does not have the biographer's advantage of real incidents to hand to flesh out the abstractions. One of the meanings of the insistence that a novelist must be a verbal artist is that he should not rely as heavily as this on items of general moral and emotional currency, leaving the reader to provide his own life-giving particularities. *Sensibility, reflectiveness, sympathy, imagination, insincerity, understanding, pity:* a novelist should not of course totally eschew these important words but he should awaken them from the slumber which is their most common and comfortable form of existence in our minds. Their effect here is to glide past the reader's attention, leaving only a vague sense that the hero's weakness is being described, but that it is a weakness attainable only by a great nature. Thus abstractness and protective partiality co-operate, as they do in the following example of mental processes presented in the form of argument:

'At least, Deronda argued, Mordecai's visionary excitability was hardly a reason for concluding beforehand that he was not worth listening to except for pity's sake. Suppose he had introduced himself as one of the strictest reasoners: do they form a body of men hitherto free from false conclusions and illusory speculations? The driest argument has its hallucinations, too hastily concluding that its net will now at last be large enough to hold the universe. Men may dream in demonstrations, and cut out an illusory world in the shape of axioms, definitions, and propositions, with a final exclusion of fact signed Q.E.D. No formulas for thinking will save us mortals from mistake in our imperfect apprehension of the matter to be thought about. And since the unemotional intellect may carry us into a mathematical dreamland where nothing is but what is not, perhaps an emotional intellect may have absorbed into its passionate vision of possibilities some truth of what will be—the more comprehensive massive life feeding theory with new material, as the sensibility of the artist seizes combinations which science explains and justifies.'   (Chapter 41)

Now this is an excellent piece of writing, an expression of George Eliot's fine mind vigorously applying itself to a question which is of supreme importance to her. But that is exactly the trouble. The reader is puzzled to know just whose argument he is following and in what context it belongs: that of George Eliot's intellectual life, or Deronda's. And this intensifies the suspicion that Deronda does not have a free existence, independent of his creator's protection; that he does not have, in the truest sense, her sympathy. Deronda's mind would of course operate in the form of argument as Gwendolen's, with whom I shall be comparing him, would not. But here we are not conscious of his mind as a medium for the argument. The argument exists outside him, as something attributed to him.

It should be mentioned here that there are examples in great novels of characters who have a special relation to their author and who are not open to the criticism I am making of Deronda. Julien Sorel in *Le Rouge et le Noir*, Levin in *Anna Karenina*, Birkin in *Women in Love* and Nerzhin in *The First Circle* are examples. But in all these cases, although the novels are not in the ordinary sense autobiographical, and the characters are not intended as representations of the authors, there is a pressure of autobiographical experience and an effort by the author to be honest about himself. Although the characters express thoughts which we can imagine being expressed identically by the authors in their own persons, the authors have exposed themselves sufficiently in the characters for there to be no problem about whose mind we are meeting. At the same time there is no sense of the character being under the author's protection, because the author has no protection to give, being himself at risk; and although most readers admire all these characters, the admiration is not canvassed in a manner at all like this: 'With exquisite instinct, Deronda, before he opened his lips, placed his palm gently on Mordecai's straining hand— an act just then equal to many speeches' (Chapter 40).

Gwendolen's character is much more readily and confidently established than Deronda's, and there could not be greater contrast than that between the formal account of Deronda in Chapter 32 and the following.

> ' "Why did you marry again, mamma? It would have been nicer if you had not."
> Mrs. Davilow coloured deeply, a slight convulsive movement passed over her face, and straightway shutting up the memorials she said, with a violence quite unusual in her—
> "You have no feeling, child!"
> Gwendolen, who was fond of her mamma, felt hurt and ashamed, and had never since dared to ask a question about her father.
> This was not the only instance in which she had brought on

herself the pain of some filial compunction. It was always arranged, when possible, that she should have a small bed in her mamma's room; for Mrs Davilow's motherly tenderness clung chiefly to her eldest girl, who had been born in her happier time. One night under an attack of pain she found that the specific regularly placed by her bedside had been forgotten, and begged Gwendolen to get out of bed and reach it for her. That healthy young lady, snug and warm as a rosy infant in her little couch, objected to step out into the cold, and lying perfectly still, grumbled a refusal. Mrs. Davilow went without the medicine and never reproached her daughter; but the next day Gwendolen was keenly conscious of what must be in her mamma's mind, and tried to make amends by caresses which cost her no effort. Having always been the pet and pride of the household, waited on by mother, sisters, governess, and maids, as if she had been a princess in exile, she naturally found it difficult to think her own pleasure less important than others made it, and when it was positively thwarted felt an astonished resentment apt, in her cruder days, to vent itself in one of those passionate acts which look like a contradiction of habitual tendencies. Though never even as a child thoughtlessly cruel, nay, delighting to rescue drowning insects and watch their recovery, there was a disagreeable silent remembrance of her having strangled her sister's canary-bird in a final fit of exasperation at its shrill singing which had again and again jarringly interrupted her own. She had taken pains to buy a white mouse for her sister in retribution, and though inwardly excusing herself on the ground of a peculiar sensitiveness which was a mark of her general superiority, the thought of that infelonious murder had always made her wince.'   (Chapter 3)

It is not illegitimate to compare this with the passage describing Deronda's character since, despite the completely different methods, the two passages perform the same function: presenting to the reader the 'habit' or 'bias' (to use terms which George Eliot frequently uses in talking about Deronda) of the character's mind. The specificity exemplified in this passage is not of course always superior to abstractness but the important thing to note is how easily, when writing of Gwendolen, George Eliot's mind runs to specific incidents. It is as if she cannot help imagining Gwendolen in action. The very thought of her, like the thought of a real person, is inescapably bound up with what she did. There has been a tendency in modern criticism to be contemptuous of the idea that the test of a fictional character is whether we can imagine his life outside the novel. Such imaginings are certainly not part of the novel and should be kept in their place but they can be an indication of how thoroughly the *novelist* has imagined the character, and they are likely to be proportionate to the wealth of lively detail within the novel. One feels that a character such as Gwendolen has *possessed* the novelist, and thus gained her independence; and this gives the impression (of course illusory and often dangerous) that she could actually walk out of the novel. It is only when the character achieves this independence that the 'experiment in life' can be said to occur.

It should also be noted that this passage and the Deronda description have opposite relations to the moral currency. The word which is always in the background and often actually used of Gwendolen is 'egoism'. This passage provides a series of sharp impressions which keep the word alive in our minds as well as demonstrating exactly how it applies to Gwendolen. No equivalent service is provided for those words by which we are supposed to understand Deronda.[4] In what concerns Gwendolen the novelist is doing a poet's work on language, while with Deronda she is not.

George Eliot has said that she meant everything in *Daniel Deronda* to be related to everything else there, and while she did not suceed in creating an integrated work of art, the dogmas enacted in the Jewish part have a strong bearing on the story of Gwendolen. My criticism of the individual characters, that despite the partiality there is no real sympathy, applies equally to Zionism itself. The criticism here is similar to that of *Felix Holt:* that the 'particular programme' of social action is not taken seriously enough. This is best conveyed by reference to the response I find myself making to Mordecai's words when Deronda announces that he is a Jew:

'Mordecai's answer was uttered in Hebrew, and in no more than a loud whisper. It was in the liturgical words which express the religious bond: "Our God, and the God of our fathers."'

(Chapter 63)

189

My response is 'What on earth can this mean to Deronda?' I then find myself reflecting that the word God has no place in Deronda's vocabulary; that although he describes himself as a Christian before his discovery of his lineage, we are given no indication of what his religious sentiments and loyalties are. When, later in the same chapter, he refuses to be a passive medium for Mordecai's ideas, he says, 'Don't ask me to deny my spiritual parentage, when I am finding the clue of my life in the recognition of my natural parentage'. What sense can the reader make of this? How can he represent to himself the synthesis, or conflict, of Deronda's gentile upbringing and his Jewish affiliation? The reader seems to be invited here to consider this problem, but he is not given the means even to make a start. Neither Christianity nor Judaism is presented in the novel as a distinctive system of thought and faith. Christianity, or gentile civilisation, represents *merely* environmental influence. Judaism represents *merely* hereditary instinct and duty. This seems to be undeniable on the evidence of the novel, and is supported by the close resemblance of the moral scheme to that of *The Spanish Gypsy*. This strange lapse, in a writer who took religion so seriously, is difficult to account for; but it may well have something to do with the Feuerbachian interpretation of religion which, as argued in Chapter One, strongly influenced George Eliot:

> 'The fellowship between man and man which has been the principle of development, social and moral, is not dependent on conceptions of what is not man: and . . . the idea of God, so far as it has been a high spiritual influence, is the ideal of a goodness entirely human (i.e., an exaltation of the human).'[5]

This is the conception which enabled George Eliot, despite her loss of faith, not only to recognise the value of religion, but to love and revere its noblest manifestations. What she appears to have lost sight of in *Daniel Deronda* is that there is a difference between the essence of religion, and the reality of its presence in men of genuine religious faith. She was, in fact, most successful in this respect in her earliest work, perhaps because in dealing with Evangelical Christianity the truth was immediately present to her. The faith of Edgar

Tryan in *Janet's Repentance* and of Dinah Morris in *Adam Bede* is clearly reducible to the Feuerbachian essence, but it is also clearly dependent for its operation on 'conceptions of what is not man'. Even Savonarola is nothing if not a Catholic. But in *Daniel Deronda* Mordecai himself, although he uses religious language, does not impress one as a man with a body of religious beliefs to which a man needs to be converted. What Deronda is converted to is the idea of race. The discovery of his birth is the answer not to any religious yearning but to the need expressed here:

> 'But how and whence was the needed event to come?—the influence that would justify partiality, and make him what he longed to be yet was unable to make himself—an organic part of social life, instead of roaming in it like a yearning disembodied spirit, stirred with a vague social passion, but without fixed local habitation to render fellowship real?'   (Chapter 32)

In this way the weakness of this part of the novel is similar to that of *Felix Holt*. In both cases George Eliot is working from an analytic reduction of inherited influences and loyalties, and in both cases she fails to provide adequate 'experimental' conditions because of an inadequate interest in (or sympathy with) the particularities of the cases under observation.

George Eliot may have been misled by her personal sympathy for the Jews into believing that it could be creatively linked with the expression of her beliefs in submission to the past, sympathy with the wider life of man, and 'noble partiality' or loving attachment to particular objects. What criticism reveals is that the Jewish element in the story is present only as a channel for these beliefs. It is, as it were, a receptacle rather than a medium.

Deronda himself represents a submission to the past as extreme as any in George Eliot's novels following the career of Maggie Tulliver. He is an embodiment of the Comtean principle of continuity. In the first paragraph of the first chapter in which he is the centre of attention (16) we are told that 'the lad had a passion for history, eager to know how time had been filled up since the Flood' and, three chapters later, that 'one of his favourite protests was against the severance of past and present history'. Deronda's strongest affirmation of his belief is made in his second interview with his mother:

'"The effects prepared by generations are likely to triumph over a contrivance which would bend them all to the satisfaction of self. Your will was strong, but my grandfather's trust which you accepted and did not fulfil—what you call his yoke—is the expression of something stronger, with deeper, farther-spreading roots, knit into the foundations of sacredness for all men. You renounced me—you still banish me—as a son"—there was an involuntary movement of indignation in Deronda's voice—"But that stronger Something has determined that I shall be all the more the grandson whom also you willed to annihilate."'

(Chapter 53)

This 'stronger Something' could at first glance be interpreted to be a suggestion of the supernatural. In fact the best name for it is Necessity, and here George Eliot's mind has not travelled very far from her advice to John Chapman on appointing an editor for the *Westminster Review* in 1852.[6]

But the Necessity referred to by Deronda is clearly not a blind, amoral Fate. In one of its manifestations at least it bears a striking resemblance to the convenient determinism of *Romola*. When Deronda finds Mirah he is literally drifting, and the discovery of Mirah is the beginning of the process which prepares him to welcome the truth about his birth. But another, more specifically human aspect of the 'stronger Something' is referred to by Deronda in his meeting with Mordecai after his return to England:

'"It is through your inspiration that I have discerned what may be my life's task. It is you who have given shape to what, I believe, was an inherited yearning—the effect of brooding, passionate thoughts in many ancestors—thoughts that seem to have been intensely present in my grandfather. Suppose the stolen offspring of some mountain tribe brought up in a city of the plain, or one with an inherited genius for painting, and born blind—the ancestral life would lie within them as a dim longing for unknown objects and sensations, and the spell-bound habit of their inherited frames would be like a cunningly-wrought musical instrument, never played on, but quivering throughout in uneasy mysterious moanings of its intricate structure that, under the right touch, gives music. Something like that, I think, has been my experience."'

(Chapter 63)

In other words, one of the forces that Deronda's mother has attempted to defy for the satisfaction of her selfish purposes is evolution, understood in terms of the inheritance of acquired characteristics.[7] For, although the instances cited for comparison do not involve acquired characteristics (though George Eliot may have thought they did), Deronda's 'inherited yearning' does. The 'brooding, passionate thoughts' of his ancestors are, in an inchoate form, biologically transmitted. George Eliot probably had this kind of inheritance at least partly in mind when she referred in a letter to John Morley to 'the moral evolution':

'As a fact of mere zoological evolution, woman seems to me to have the worse share in existence. But for that very reason I would the more contend that in the moral evolution we have "an art which does mend nature." It is the function of love in the largest sense, to mitigate the harshness of all fatalities.'[8]

Part of the moral evolution is the development of moral traditions in societies, which is the basis of George Eliot's conservatism. This is far more important in her novels than biological inheritance, and is fairly obviously more susceptible of demonstration by the methods of her art, as well as being more unquestionably true. But in both Deronda and Fedalma, the biological inheritance of moral characteristics (though only in Deronda's case unambiguously *acquired* characteristics) is shown to operate in opposition to social influence, and to be more coercive.

However, this should not be over-emphasised. It is not the basis of George Eliot's belief in dependence on the past, merely a supporting argument. Its interest for the reader is that it helps to illustrate the theoretical nature of this part of the novel: for, if we happen not to believe in the inheritance of acquired characteristics, there is nothing in Deronda's history to persuade us that we may be wrong.

A more central and permanent affirmation of continuity comes from Mordecai, in the discussion at the working men's club:

' "I too claim to be a rational Jew. But what is it to be rational— what is it to feel the light of the divine reason growing stronger within and without? It is to see more and more of the hidden

bonds that bind and consecrate changes as a dependent growth—
yea, consecrate it with kinship: the past becomes my parent,
and the future stretches towards me the appealing arms of
children. Is it rational to drain away the sap of special kindred
that makes the families of man rich in interchanged wealth,
and various as the forests are various with the glory of the cedar
and the palm?" '   (Chapter 42)

This serves to remind us that Mordecai's speeches are not
merely wordy unrealities; it also emphasises the nature of
his appeal to Deronda, and the fact that George Eliot's
interest is less in the particular issue of Zionism than in the
general questions for which Zionism serves as an occasion.
In addition it is one of the passages which have a genuine
moral bearing on Gwendolen's story. However, the character
of Mordecai presents new problems. The criticisms I have
levelled so far concern the inadequacy of the art as an experimental medium for George Eliot's preconceptions. The
treatment of Mordecai, however, presents contradictions that
suggest either a surprising modification in George Eliot's
beliefs, or a more radically distorting partiality than any so
far discussed. Consider the following account of Mordecai's
feelings when he sees Deronda approaching down the river.

'Mordecai lifted his cap and waved it—feeling in that moment
that his inward prophecy was fulfilled. Obstacles, incongruities,
all melted into the sense of completion with which his soul was
flooded by this outward satisfaction of his longing. His exultation was not widely different from that of the experimenter,
bending over the first stirrings of change that correspond to what
in the fervour of concentrated prevision his thought has fore-
shadowed. The prefigured friend had come from the golden
background, and had signalled to him: this actually was: the
rest was to be.'   (Chapter 40)

This can be compared with George Eliot's comment on the
Arrowpoints' astonishment that their daughter should fall in
love with Klesmer: 'The truth is something different from
the habitual lazy combinations begotten by our wishes'
(Chapter 22). The independence of reality in relation to our
wishes, and the danger of the common habit of building
forecasts on the basis of what we desire, are of course among
the most important truths illustrated by Gwendolen's career.

The question is why George Eliot supposes Mordecai to be an exception to this law. His prophecies are not of course 'lazy combinations', and his desires are not narrowly personal but generous and altruistic. Nevertheless, it remains true that in his case George Eliot reverses her habitual portrayal of the relation between internal and external, and fashions a reality entirely in accordance with Mordecai's prevision. Her apology for this is made at the beginning of Chapter 38:

> ' "Second sight" is a flag over disputed grounds. But it is matter of common knowledge that there are persons whose yearnings, conceptions—nay, travelled conclusions—continually take the form of images which have a foreshadowing power: the deed they would do starts up before them in complete shape, making a coercive type; the event they hunger for or dread rises into vision with a seed-like growth, feeding itself fast on unnumbered impressions . . . . sometimes it may be that their natures have manifold openings, like the hundred-gated Thebes, where there may naturally be a greater and more miscellaneous inrush than through a narrow beadle-watched portal.'

This is, again, not an acknowledgement of the supernatural, but a suggestion of an intense refinement of the natural. However, such a sensitive receptiveness to impressions is contradicted by much of what we see of Mordecai: the fact, for example, that 'he had no interest in the fact of Deronda's appearance at the Cohens' beyond its relation to his own ideal purpose' (Chapter 40), and his statement that 'In new places the outer world presses on me and narrows the inward vision' (Chapter 42). On numerous occasions in George Eliot's work an appreciative responsiveness to the outside world effects or represents the escape from self—Dorothea's experience on the morning after discovering Will with Rosamond being perhaps the paradigm. Similarly, an appreciation of other people's being and needs irrespective of their relation to oneself is a cardinal element of the moral life. It is true that Mordecai is dying and that his obsession is an impersonal one, but this does not make it any less unlikely that he would correspond to the type of clairvoyant as George Eliot describes it.

To propose that the author should have written an altogether different work from the one actually produced is perhaps the greatest impertinence of criticism, and one against which George Eliot herself protested. But one way of explaining why Mordecai fails to engage the reader's sympathy is to say that the author exempts him from tragedy. The tragic possibilities of the trust he places in Deronda are several times referred to but he, Deronda and Mirah move in a world in which the tragic conditions of life are suspended. For them there is no conflict between the individual and the general; their world is other than our world not because they are greater than we but because their author has connived at the removal of all 'obstacles and incongruities' from their path. Thus partiality excludes sympathy. George Eliot's most nearly tragic characters, such as Mrs Transome and Gwendolen Harleth, represent a fairly common order of experience. The ability to perceive tragedy *there* is a large part of her greatness. But the tragedy of the great nature, who is thwarted despite having escaped from self, was beyond her. She attempted it in Savonarola and in Zarca, but neither of these can be seriously compared with the major figures in her great works. Her nearest approach is with Lydgate, whose ambition is pure and impersonal, but even here Lydgate's 'commonness' is a major element in his tragedy. In *Deronda,* George Eliot sacrificed tragedy to didacticism. Not only Mordecai's vision, but her own, is exempted from obstacles and incongruities—which are the lifeblood of her experimental art. When we turn to Gwendolen, it is with relief at meeting a creature who inhabits our own world of tragic conflict; when those early readers talked 'only of Gwendolen' they were moved by the spirit of the great George Eliot.

Both the opening and the conclusion of *Daniel Deronda* are the most original in all George Eliot's novels. The book opens, without any introductory material, with Deronda's speculations about Gwendolen. It closes, at least as far as Gwendolen is concerned, at a moment of pain, without any projection into the future.

The opening is remarkable, not so much because it presents the action at an advanced stage before the account of the preceding development, as for its statement, dramati-

cally and symbolically, of all the novel's major concerns, and
of the forces which are to shape the action. By symbols I
mean—as with all George Eliot's effective symbols—realities
which suggest or condense many other realities.

The most obvious symbol is Gwendolen's gambling. This
incident is referred to many times later in the novel, and
becomes a kind of shorthand between Gwendolen and
Deronda when, in their snatched conversations at fashionable
gatherings, Gwendolen reveals the difficulties of her life, and
Deronda attempts to encourage her painfully growing moral
awareness. Her marriage to Grandcourt, and its results, are
described as 'this last great gambling loss' which Gwendolen
bears, in public, 'with an air of perfect self-possession'
(Chapter 36) as, in the opening chapter, she bears her losses
at Leubronn. This is not merely a literary device. Gambling
is a paradigm of the superstitions spun from the undisciplined and ignorant ego. The gambler conceives of a
degenerate Providence which will modify the laws of probability in his favour:

> 'She had begun to believe in her luck, others had begun to
> believe in it: she had visions of being followed by a *cortège* who
> would worship her as a goddess of luck and watch her play as a
> directing augury.'   (Chapter 1)

For George Eliot gambling also represents all forms of
desire for gain or pleasure which are inseparable from desire
for other people's loss or pain. It is thus that gambling
becomes associated in Gwendolen's mind with the wrong she
has done to Lydia Glasher.

When, in Chapter 2, Gwendolen receives the letter from
her mother announcing the family's ruin, her first impulse
is not compassion for her mother—'There was no inward
exclamation of "Poor mamma!"'—but of 'bitter vexation
that she had lost her gains at roulette'. Thus her inability to
accept the inevitable hinders the spirit of fellowship in
misfortune which can begin to overcome it. This prefigures
her refusal, when she returns home, to admit the necessity
of going to live at Sawyer's Cottage, or to co-operate with
her family's efforts to meet the crisis. It is a part of the
severe imbalance in Gwendolen's conception of things: her

197

imprisonment in self making her closed both to personal claims and to impersonal necessity.

A crucial element in Gwendolen's raw moral condition, and in her future development, is unobtrusively indicated in the sale of her turquoise necklace. The stones

'had belonged to a chain once her father's; but she had never known her father; and the necklace was in all respects the ornament she could most conveniently part with. Who supposes that it is an impossible contradiction to be superstitious and rationalising at the same time? Roulette encourages a romantic superstition as to the chances of the game, and the most prosaic rationalism as to human sentiments which stand in the way of raising needful money.'
                                                        (Chapter 2)

The reader of *Romola* will recognise this as a kind of *motif* for the egotist's rejection of the claims of the past. When Tito sells Baldassarre's ring, it is an important stage in his gradual determination not to seek out and rescue his captive foster-father, and George Eliot emphasises his scepticism about the 'superstitious' value of inanimate objects.[9] In Gwendolen's case the *motif* is more subtly handled, and the action more plausible—'she had never known her father', whereas Tito owed everything to Baldassarre's devotion. Here it is not the blatant action of a callous egotist, but an indication of Gwendolen's moral disinheritance, her dangerous freedom from sanctities. George Eliot's commentary might seem too explicit, but it is perhaps too early in the novel to expect the reader to respond unaided.

Deronda anonymously retrieves and returns the necklace which becomes, like the roulette, a personal (not just a literary) metaphor for his relation to Gwendolen (which is itself both launched and epitomised in the two opening chapters). After her marriage, she clumsily displays it—giving herself away to her husband—as a sign to Deronda that she accepts his rebuke.

The necklace figures in another scene which again marvellously suggests the way in which George Eliot uses symbols as an intrinsic part of the characters' emotional life. Gwendolen and her mother are discussing the sale of jewellery to raise a little money after the loss of their fortune.

' "Why, how came you to put that pocket-handkerchief in here?"

It was the handkerchief [Deronda's] with the corner torn off which Gwendolen had thrust in with the turquoise necklace.

"It happened to be with the necklace—I was in a hurry," said Gwendolen, taking the handkerchief away and putting it in her pocket. Don't sell the necklace, mamma," she added, a new feeling having come over her about that rescue of it which had formerly been so offensive.

"No, dear, no; it was made out of your dear father's chain. And I should prefer not selling the other things. None of them are of any great value." '   (Chapter 24)

George Eliot says of this 'new feeling' that it 'came from that streak of superstition in her which attached itself both to her confidence and her terror. . . . Why she should suddenly determine not to part with the necklace was not much clearer to her than why she should sometimes have been frightened to find herself in the fields alone'. We are made aware of Gwendolen's 'streak of superstition' early in the novel, when the picture of the figure fleeing from the dead face is suddenly revealed by the opening of a shutter in Chapter 3 and again, more strikingly, in Chapter 6 when she is acting the part of Hermione in a charade: 'She looked like a statue into which a soul of Fear had entered: her pallid lips were parted; her eyes, usually narrowed under their long lashes, were dilated and fixed'. This susceptibility is a manifestation of what can best be described by Shelley's phrase, 'the mystery within'. This is something quite different from the mysteries of Mordecai's second sight and Deronda's inherited thoughts. It is what makes the symbolism of the necklace in relation to Gwendolen something different from the symbolism of the ring in relation to Tito. It is what makes us acknowledge other people as more than automata, and since the novelist's most difficult task is to make the reader acknowledge *his* people as more than automata, it constitutes the difference between a work of art and a narrative scheme. What makes Gwendolen a vivid presence to the reader is the continuity between the inward and the outward, between herself and her actions, so that what she does is herself:

'One day, indeed, he [Grandcourt] had kissed not her cheek but her neck a little below her ear; and Gwendolen, taken by surprise, had started up with a marked agitation which made him rise too and say, "I beg your pardon—did I annoy you?" "Oh, it was nothing," said Gwendolen, rather afraid of herself, "only I cannot bear—to be kissed under my ear." She sat down again with a little playful laugh, but all the while she felt her heart beating with a vague fear: she was no longer at liberty to flout him as she had flouted poor Rex.' (Chapter 29)

That *is* Gwendolen. She is completely there in everything that she does, and this or any number of other incidents could be used as a substantial basis for an exploration of her character.

To return to the dialogue concerning the necklace—one of the first signs of Gwendolen's moral development is that what had formerly been a neutral object to be exchanged for money becomes a thing of value which has or represents (for Gwendolen there is no distinction) a claim on her. And at the same time that this awakening takes place in Gwendolen, her mother is seen responding to the claim that Gwendolen had originally been blind to. So the subject is quietly developed, without strain or distortion, and in a thoroughly imagined human medium.

Gwendolen is George Eliot's last and greatest study in egotism. This statement, however, needs qualification. Rosamond Vincy was a great achievement: the character whom, by her own account, George Eliot had most difficulty in rendering—whom she felt to be most alien. And although George Eliot succeeded in eliminating most of the animus which found expression in the manuscript, Rosamond does inspire a kind of horror, as of a creature not quite fully human—a horror of vacancy, of nullity. However, as George Eliot says, 'We are all of us born in moral stupidity, taking the world as an udder to feed our supreme selves.'[10] The triumph of Rosamond was not enough. It remained for George Eliot to portray egotism as a human condition—fully, vigorously and sympathetically human; not an absence but a misdirection of vitality and passion.

At first Gwendolen might appear to be no more than Rosamond seen 'from the inside'—

'But her thoughts never dwelt on marriage as the fulfilment of her ambition; the dramas in which she imagined herself a heroine were not wrought up to that close. To be very much sued or hopelessly sighed for as a bride was indeed an indispensable and agreeable guarantee of womanly power; but to become a wife and wear all the domestic fetters of that condition, was on the whole a vexatious necessity.'   (Chapter 4)

Rosamond, of course, *does* want to marry, but Gwendolen's fantasies resemble Rosamond's *after* her marriage (about Will Ladislaw, for example)—a difference which indicates Gwendolen's superiority. Another resemblance, and one of the cardinal manifestations of egotism, is the reference of everything to the will.

'Other people *allowed* themselves to be made slaves of, and to have their lives blown hither and thither like empty ships in which no will was present; it was not to be so with her. . . . '
ibid. (My italics.)

' "It is Sawyer's Cottage we are to go to."
At first, Gwendolen remained silent, paling with anger—justifiable anger, in her opinion. Then she said with haughtiness—
"That is impossible. Something else than that ought to have been thought of. My uncle ought not to allow that. I will not submit to it." '   (Chapter 21)

This closely resembles Rosamond's reaction to Lydgate's attempts to economise. Both girls are fatally shut off from reality and blind to necessity. The difference between them is perhaps first made evident in the striking revelation of 'the mystery within' to which I have already referred. In the charade scene Gwendolen's behaviour is startling, but it is vividly and fully human in a way that Rosamond never attains to:

'Herr Klesmer, who had been good-natured enough to seat himself at the piano, struck a thunderous chord—but in the same instant, and before Hermione had put forth her foot, the movable panel, which was on a line with the piano, flew open on the right opposite the stage and disclosed the picture of the dead face and the fleeing figure, brought out in pale definiteness by the position of the wax-lights. Every one was startled, but all eyes in the act of turning towards the opened panel were recalled by a piercing cry from Gwendolen, who stood without change of attitude, but with a change of expression that was terrifying in its terror. She stood like a statue into which a soul of Fear had entered. . . .

What she unwillingly recognised, and would have been glad for others to be unaware of, was that liability of hers to fits of spiritual dread, though this fountain of awe within her had not found its way into connection with the religion taught her or with any human relations. She was ashamed and frightened, as at what might happen again, in remembering her tremor on suddenly finding herself alone, when, for example, she was walking without companionship and there came some rapid change in the light. Solitude in any wide scene impressed her with an undefined feeling of immeasurable existence aloof from her, in the midst of which she was helplessly incapable of asserting herself. The little astronomy taught her at school used sometimes to set her imagination at work in a way that made her tremble : but always when someone joined her she recovered her indifference to the vastness in which she seemed an exile; she found again her usual world in which her will was of some avail. . . . '

(Chapter 6)

Again, the whole of Gwendolen is there : her egotism, her habitual narrowness of outlook, her exceptional imaginative susceptibility. The revelation of the picture would not have so unhinged a Rosamond Vincy; but neither would it have so affected a person who habitually faced and acknowledged the challenges to self—death and conscience—that the painting portrays. Gwendolen's susceptibility to changes in the light and to the vastness of the universe reveals the same condition : the imagination, enemy to the ego, is alive but imprisoned within the ego. Within the human, social world she is safe because there her claims for her self are acknowledged and encouraged, as we see again and again, not only by her indulgent mother but even by her sensible and worldly-wise uncle. Her moral education is the discovery that this safety is an illusion created by the éclat of her personality and the peculiarities of her social position; and that in fact the indocile forces and threats that she perceives in the painting and in the stars exist in the human world also. One of George Eliot's sharpest comments on Gwendolen is that perhaps her 'potent charm' is not a necessary condition of success in getting her own way and that she knows of other people enjoying similar power who have in common only 'a strong determination to have what was pleasant, with a total fearlessness in making themselves disagreeable or dangerous when they did not get it' (Chapter 4). This is an early warning of Grandcourt, who is Gwendolen's precise nemesis. It also wards off a too ready sympathy with Gwendolen. Nevertheless, there are many other determinants of her character besides her innate disposition and one of them, her social position, is worth paying particular attention to. As early as 1844 George Eliot had a contemptuous opinion of the 'young lady':

> 'I do not think it was kind to Strauss . . . to tell him that a *young lady* was translating his book. I am sure he must have some twinges of alarm to think he was dependent on that most contemptible specimen of the human being for his English reputation.'[11]

In her later novels she seems to have passed beyond this easy contempt, and begun to contemplate the young lady as a remarkably poignant subject for her special preoccupations: the relation of the individual to reality, the escape from the enclosed self, the discovery of the laws on which life depends, the power of ignorance to foster egotism. The first young lady of any importance in the novels is Esther Lyon in *Felix Holt*, but the potential is most thoroughly exploited in the three beautifully imagined and various young women: Dorothea, Rosamond and Gwendolen. Barbara Hardy has observed in *The Novels of George Eliot*[12] that George Eliot always gives a full account, or *curriculum vitae*, of her female characters' education. She was not a femininst, and believed that a woman's natural sphere of influence is domestic and private; but she also believed that to become a complete and tolerable human being, a woman must be thoroughly educated, not in decorative accomplishments but in an understanding of reality. The young lady is probably the most essentially ignorant class in her society, the inadequacies of her education not being compensated for by any appreciable direct knowledge of the world. There is reference in the previous chapter to the effects of this ignorance on the lives of Dorothea and Rosamond. Gwendolen's case is the most poignant and pathetic of the three. Her delusions about the effectiveness of her own will are fostered by her ignorance of the world except in its moments of leisure, when men take pleasure in deferring to young ladies. This is consummately suggested in the episode of her rudeness to Mr Lush:

'Certainly, Gwendolen's refusal of the burnous from Mr Lush was open to the interpretation that she wished to receive it from Mr Grandcourt. But she, poor child, had had no design in this action, and was simply following her antipathy and inclination, confiding in them as she did in the more reflective judgements into which they entered as sap into leafage. Gwendolen had no sense that these men were dark enigmas to her, or that she needed any help in drawing conclusions about them—Mr. Grandcourt at least. The chief question was, how far his character and ways might answer her wishes; and unless she were satisfied about that, she had said to herself that she would not accept his offer.'   (Chapter 11)

Gwendolen's situation is even more succinctly expressed in the pathetic question that she puts to her mother, when she has become engaged to Grandcourt, knowing about Mrs Glasher, and has heard the rumour that Deronda is Sir Hugo Mallinger's illegitimate son: 'Mamma, have men generally children before they are married?'

This kind of ignorance was probably almost universal among young women of Gwendolen's class. So too, one imagines, was the kind illustrated in Gwendolen's failure to understand why the money lost in Grapnell and Co.'s irresponsible speculations cannot be retrieved by 'law'. 'Young ladies don't understand political economy, you know'. But Gwendolen is an extreme case. The following little incident occurs after the financial collapse, when she is replying to Grandcourt's note.

'Before addressing the note she said, "Pray ring the bell, mamma, if there is anyone to answer it." She really did not know who did the work of the house.'   (Chapter 26)

This is extreme, but Gwendolen's general ignorance of reality is very much of the period.

But what needs emphasising is Gwendolen's peculiarity,

her uniqueness among George Eliot's egotists. The incident of the charade persuades poor Rex 'more than ever that she must be instinct with all feeling, and not only readier to respond to a worshipful love, but able to love better than other girls' (Chapter 6). This recalls the irony of Lydgate's susceptibility to Rosamond, and we have seen that Gwendolen's egotism, her very inability to love, is an important factor in that incident. Rex's misconstruction is ironic, but it is not the dreadful, chilling irony of the scene in which Lydgate is trapped into proposing to Rosamond: 'In half an hour he left the house an engaged man, whose soul was not his own, but the woman's to whom he had bound himself' (Chapter 31). Gwendolen's is the egotism of a full, passionate nature, and therefore she is vulnerable. There is evidence of this, though perhaps only with hindsight, even in this early conversation:

> ' "I wish you had given me your perfectly straight nose; it would have done for any sort of character—a nose of all work. Mine is only a happy nose; it would not do so well for tragedy."
>
> "Oh, my dear, any nose will do to be miserable with in this world," said Mrs Davilow, with a deep, weary sigh, throwing her black bonnet on the table, and resting her elbow near it.
>
> "Now, mamma," said Gwendolen, in a strongly remonstrant tone, turning away from the glass with an air of vexation, "don't begin to be dull here. It spoils all my pleasure, and everything may be so happy now. What have you to be gloomy about now? . . .
>
> "Well, but what is the use of my being charming, if it is to end in my being dull and not minding anything? Is that what marriage always comes to?"
>
> "No, child, certainly not. Marriage is the only happy state for a woman, as I trust you will prove."
>
> "I will not put up with it if it is not a happy state. I am determined to be happy." '   (Chapter 3)

How poignant, and how beautifully executed, is the contrast between the young girl's pert confidence and the mother's experienced disillusion, running to gloomy epigram. The poignancy is largely in the presence of the mother's warning example—and yet Mrs Davilow, despite her dreadful experience, encourages, by her conventional wisdom, Gwendolen's brash reference of everything to the will. When her mother tells her that 'marriage is the only happy state for a woman', we see that Gwendolen's assurance is not all stupid blindness. And how, with the opposite warning of 'Jocosa' the lugubrious governess, can one say that Mrs Davilow's words are not true? The world's messages are confusing and Gwendolen is so brash, so unused, so vulnerable. The sense of vulnerability gains in definition and intensity when she rejects Rex's advances:

'The perception that poor Rex wanted to be tender made her curl up and harden like a sea-anemone at the touch of a finger. . . .
"Pray don't make love to me! I hate it." She looked at him fiercely.
Rex turned pale and was silent, but could not take his eyes off her, and the impetus was not yet exhausted that made hers dart death at him. Gwendolen herself could not have foreseen that she should feel in this way. It was all a sudden, new experience to her. The day before she had been quite aware that her cousin was in love with her—she did not mind how much, so that he said nothing about it; and if any one had asked her why she objected to love-making speeches, she would have said laughingly, "Oh, I am tired of them all in the books." But now the life of passion had begun negatively in her. She felt passionately averse to this volunteered love. . . . '

Mrs Davilow enters and finds her daughter crying—

'Gwendolen gave way, and letting her head rest against her mother, cried out sobbingly, "Oh mamma, what can become of my life? there is nothing worth living for!"
"Why, dear?" said Mrs Davilow. Usually she herself had been rebuked by her daughter for involuntary signs of despair.
"I shall never love anybody. I can't love people. I hate them."
"The time will come, dear, the time will come."
Gwendolen was more and more convulsed with sobbing; but putting her arms around her mother's neck with an almost painful clinging, she said brokenly, "I can't bear any one to be very near me but you." '
(Chapter 7)

The novels of Charles Dickens are full of characters who behind a more or less comically grotesque appearance carry a horrifying inability to love or to need love. George Eliot, too, has her Featherstones, Riggs and Grandcourts. Gwendolen, clearly, is not one of these. She is not indifferent to Rex:

in one of the most superb and suggestive phrases in the novel we are told that 'the life of passion had begun negatively in her'. More, she is frightened and made miserable by her revulsion from normal, healthy, youthful love. Gwendolen cannot be happy because she has not the control over herself which the egotist needs. There are parts of herself which are disconcertingly independent of her will. In other words, in contrast to Rosamond and Grandcourt, who are too dead to know joy, Gwendolen is too alive to be happy. This fact about Gwendolen is subsequently shown, with extraordinary insight, to be an essential element in the development of the moral life within her. She does not know whether she will accept Grandcourt:

> 'Even in Gwendolen's mind that result was one of two likelihoods that presented themselves alternately, one of two decisions towards which she was being precipitated, as if they were two sides of a boundary-line, and she did not know on which she should fall. This subjection to a possible self, a self not to be absolutely predicted about, caused her some astonishment and terror: her favourite key of life—doing as she liked—seemed to fail her, and she could not foresee what at a given moment she might like to do.' (Chapter 13)

In the issues suggested here, and in their working-out in the drama (above all in the scene of Grandcourt's proposal) we are witnesses to a profundity and subtlety of investigation unequalled anywhere in George Eliot's work: the most important part of this pre-eminence being that the 'self not to be absolutely predicted about' is more consistently a motive and presence in Gwendolen's character than in any other. If as a person she is the antithesis of Mrs Garth, as a creation she is the antithesis of Tito Melema.

In commenting on the phrase 'the life of passion had begun negatively in her' it is necessary to observe, at the risk of appearing a typically obtrusive modern critic, that an essential part of the conception of Gwendolen concerns her sexuality. Numerous critics have commented on George Eliot's subtle suggestion that Dorothea and Casaubon's marriage is unconsummated, or otherwise sexually a failure. While I acknowledge this, it is not in fact very interesting Such a marriage would so obviously be a sexual failure that little art is needed to suggest it; and sex is otherwise unimportant to Dorothea (least of all in her relation to Ladislaw) or in the novel generally. The marriage whose sexual implications are much more interesting is that of Gwendolen and Grandcourt. *Daniel Deronda* seems to me to be the novel in which George Eliot had something to say about the relation of sexual feeling to the whole of life, and in which she might have profited from the possibility of greater explicitness (not *much* greater, I had better add). Gwendolen is her first sexually alive heroine after Maggie Tulliver, who is one of the few heroines in Victorian fiction in whom passionate sexual feeling is shown operating independently of, if not in opposition to, the moral and social consciousness. One cannot talk about the sexuality of Romola, Esther Lyon, Dorothea or Mary Garth; but in the scene with Rex, when Grandcourt kisses her neck, and in the railway carriage after the wedding—

'Gwendolen had been at her liveliest during the journey, chatting incessantly, ignoring any change in their mutual position since yesterday; and Grandcourt had been rather ecstatically quiescent, while she turned his gentle seizure of her hand into a grasp of his hand by both hers, with an increased vivacity as of a kitten that will not sit quiet to be petted.' (Chapter 31)

—Gwendolen's sexuality is *electrically,* though 'negatively' alive. Professor Haight suggests that George Eliot may have been attempting to portray a feminine psychology similar to that of such 'morbidly passionate' women as Edith Simcox, who was obsessively attached to the novelist:

'Gwendolen Harleth, whose intricate character George Eliot was creating when she first knew Edith, has a similar physical aversion to men. Though Grandcourt is frightful enough to justify it in his case, her rejection of Rex's love suggests a latent homosexual streak. Gwendolen confesses to having been jealous of her stepfather, and sleeps in her mother's bed till the day of her marriage.'[13]

This seems to me a perverse interpretation. Gwendolen does not confess to being 'jealous' of her stepfather; she says (Chapter 56), 'I did not like my father-in-law to come home'; for which, to judge by what we hear of him, there might be many good reasons. The statement that she sleeps in her mother's bed until the day of her marriage is based on the fact that once, after her engagement, she goes to her mother's bed in the early morning because she can't sleep. It is true, we have seen, that her mother is the only person whom Gwendolen can love. But this is a symptom of her failure to grow up, not of homosexuality. The mother is the child's protection against the world, intensively so when there is no father. In the case of a 'spoiled child' (N.B. the title of the first Book) this protection is unduly prolonged and with it the child's belief in the effectiveness of her own will. All other people are a threat to Gwendolen; she can love her mother because she, by her invariable submissiveness, has created the little world in which Gwendolen is omnipotent. And Gwendolen is no more capable of loving other women than of loving men. Certainly Gwendolen is sexually abnormal, but this has nothing to do with homosexuality. It is the abnormality of egoism, an aversion to other people in proportion to their passionate attachment to her, to the claims they implicitly make upon her. Thus she accepts Grandcourt where she vehemently rejected Rex, and is delighted when, after her acceptance, he refrains from the most natural actions of a lover. 'She thought his manners as a lover more agreeable than any she had seen described. She had no alarm lest he meant to kiss her . . . ' (Chapter 27).

The interest of Gwendolen's sexuality then, is not an isolated freak. In her study of a passionate egotist George Eliot includes the impulses that in a sympathetic individual most determine attachment. Gwendolen's passionate self, unable to form relationships, is lawless and destructive. She is the kind of woman whom another novelist might have shown engaged in destructive love-affairs. The interest lapses after the marriage, partly perhaps because Gwendolen comes increasingly under the influence of Deronda, perhaps because it would have been more difficult to handle within her limits of reticence. However, in the earlier part of the novel it contributes greatly to Gwendolen's pre-eminence as a vivid presence, and to that completeness of internal motivation which is the opposite of theoretical assertion.

The centre of Gwendolen's story, the incident which can most suitably be described as the channel into which all her previous experience flows and from which her subsequent life emerges most drastically changed, is of course the accep-

G.E.—O

tance of Grandcourt in Chapter 27. This is also an incident which strongly raises the question of determinism. Dr Leavis's commentary on this states the issue of free will and determinism as well as it can be stated. (The relevant passage from the novel is too long to be conveniently quoted here.)

'It will be noted how beautifully the status of Gwendolen's spontaneously acted self is defined by her relieved and easy assumption of it once the phase of tense negativity has issued in "Yes". And it was clearly not this self that pronounced the "Yes"; nor does it come from a profound integrated self. George Eliot's way of putting it is significant: " 'Yes' came as gravely from Gwendolen's lips as if she had been answering to her name in a court of justice." This is a response that issues out of something like an abeyance of will; it is determined for her. No acquiescence could look less like an expression of free choice. Yet we don't feel that Gwendolen is therefore not to be judged as a moral agent. The "Yes" is a true expression of her moral economy; that the play of tensions should have as its upshot this response has been established by habits of valuation and by essential choices lived.'[14]

This is surely very much George Eliot's sense of the matter. Leavis supports his comment about Gwendolen's 'spontaneously acted self' by citing the passage already quoted, concerning the 'self not to be absolutely predicted about'. Throughout this long scene Gwendolen's refractory, will-free self is as consistently present as it is in the shorter extracts which I have used to illustrate it. It is this that prevents any suspicion of the diagrammatic in Gwendolen's 'moral economy'. The 'essential choices lived' include such obvious things as her failure to refuse Grandcourt when his note first arrived and her flight to Leubronn at a time when to stay and refuse him would have been much easier than it is now (the family fortunes being still intact); but also the radical and constant habit of consulting only her own pleasure and will in everything that she does. If this seems, despite the vividness of Gwendolen's presence and the appearance of inward motivation, another example, like Tito, of the novelist hunting down the character, let me add to Leavis's assessment a note on an incident that might easily pass unnoticed. The following occurs immediately before the arrival of Grandcourt's note:

'She rose from the low ottoman where she had been sitting purposeless, and walked up and down the drawing-room, resting her elbow on one palm while she leaned down her cheek on the other, and a slow tear fell. She thought, "I have always, ever since I was little, felt that mamma was not a happy woman; and now I daresay I shall be more unhappy than she has been." Her mind dwelt for a few moments on the picture of herself losing her youth and ceasing to enjoy—not minding whether she did this or that: but such picturing inevitably brought back the image of her mother. "Poor mamma! it will be still worse for her now. I can get a little money for her—that is all I shall care about now." And then with an entirely new movement of her imagination, she saw her mother getting quite old and white, and herself no longer young but faded, and their two faces meeting still with memory and love, and she knowing what was in her mother's mind—"Poor Gwen too is sad and faded now"—and then for the first time she sobbed, not in anger but with a sort of tender misery.'   (Chapter 26)

There is a lot of self-pity mixed with it, but this is nevertheless and unambiguously Gwendolen's first movement of real sympathy towards another person. Only shortly before in time, though much earlier in the novel, when Mrs Davilow's letter arrives at Leubronn, we have been told that 'There was no inward exclamation of "Poor Mamma!"' The action of this feeling in the proposal scene is almost impossibly complex. Grandcourt is perfectly aware that Gwendolen knows about Mrs Glasher, and so his campaign is the more carefully designed. One of his most telling strokes is this—

'"You will tell me now, I hope, that Mrs Davilow's loss of fortune will not trouble you further. You will trust me to prevent it from weighing upon her. You will give me the claim to provide against that."
   The little pauses and refined drawlings with which this speech was uttered, gave time for Gwendolen to go through the dream of a life. As the words penetrated her, they had the effect of a draught of wine, which suddenly makes all things easier, desirable things not so wrong, and people in general less disagreeable. She had a momentary phantasmal love for this man who chose his words so well, and who was a mere incarnation of delicate homage.'   (Chapter 27)

The concern for her mother makes 'all things easier', not, as we might expect, more difficult. George Eliot's perception of the way in which this sympathetic element enters into Gwendolen's moral choice is astonishing in its subtlety and rightness (that 'momentary phantasmal love' is superb). It becomes absorbed into her wish that all things should be easy; it is not an alien element among her egotistical promptings but an oil to ease their movement. After her marriage she cannot bear to have this one disinterested motive taken away, and in its service of her other motives we see that in fact it is not disinterested at all: at the crucial moment, it operates as a moral anaesthetic. But her sympathetic motion towards her mother remains what it is, her first escape from self, and its timing and effect persuade us that it is not good enough to say that we determine our evil actions by an anterior sequence or habit of selfishness, and vice versa. Gwendolen's first experience of sympathy makes her acceptance of Grandcourt easier and more inevitable, makes her less free.

Surely, if we are looking for the potential of tragedy, we shall find it in such elements as this.

I have described Grandcourt as Gwendolen's precise Nemesis. In her passionate egotist's revulsion from healthy natural life, with its warm, spontaneous claims, she is an easy prey to the cold egotist whose claims are subtly inhuman and who knows how to disguise them. She marries the man with the minimum of vitality because she supposes that this will give her the maximum freedom. It's not that she deserves what she gets: if we think of Nemesis as something deserved we are doing what George Eliot does in 'The Spanish Gypsy' and the other part of Deronda—sacrificing tragedy to didacticism. Perhaps it is because we inherit such an intensely moral and retributive outlook that we need the Greek word, and have no English equivalent for it. This is a good point at which to recall that George Eliot's interest in Greek tragedy is a symptom of an outlook less hidebound by traditional moral values than is commonly supposed. The case is very well put by R. T. Jones, in talking about Mary Garth's guilt at having prejudiced Fred's fortunes by refusing to comply with Featherstone's last wishes, even though she could not have acted otherwise. Caleb sympathises with her but Mrs Garth insists that she has no reason to feel guilty. Jones comments:

> 'If one incurs guilt through one's own fault, one can repent and seek forgiveness; but it is more difficult to deal with guilt innocently incurred. The Greek tragedians knew about such guilt; but later moralists have been inclined to ignore it, stressing the quality of the intention, rather than the actual consequences of the action.'[15]

This is one way in which the attention to Necessity (which is undoubtedly what attracted her to the Greek tragedians) leads her to moral conclusions radically different from the Christian. The idea of Nemesis, which has no place in Christian morality, is another.

Grandcourt is the furthest refinement of pure will, in whom the freedom from claims and dependence is seen to be virtual imbecility—though not of a kind to make him less dangerous. Not all the determining elements in Gwendolen's moral career occur in her own person. Grandcourt was expected to propose to her *before* Mrs Glasher made her revelation, but 'to desist then, when all expectation was to the contrary, became another gratification of mere will, sublimely independent of definite motive' (Chapter 14). George Eliot is still troubled by the vacuity that she perceived in Rosamond Vincy, and while giving us in Gwendolen a very different kind of egotistical young lady, she does not shirk that horror, but rather pursues it to its extreme:

> 'Grandcourt's passions were of the intermittent, flickering kind: never flaming out strongly. But a great deal of life goes on without strong passion: myriads of cravats are carefully tied, dinners attended, even speeches made proposing the health of august personages, without the zest arising from a strong desire. And a man may make a good appearance in high social positions —may be supposed to know the classics, to have his reserves on science, a strong though repressed opinion on politics, and all the sentiments of the English gentleman, at a small expense of vital energy. Also, he may be obstinate or persistent at the same low rate, and may even show sudden impulses which have a false air of daemonic strength because they seem inexplicable, though perhaps their secret lies merely in the want of regulated channels for the soul to move in—good and sufficient ducts of

habit without which our nature easily turns to mere ooze and mud, and at any pressure yields nothing but a spurt or a puddle.'

(Chapter 15)

At first it seems a mystery that a man so completely null can be so powerful and so dangerous. Partly of course his power rests in his inherited wealth and rank. But it is his very nullity that makes him invulnerable and, because lawless, dangerous. Like Gwendolen he cannot love, but unlike her he is not pained by this because he has no passionate self which needs to love. He is lawless *because* he has no connection with other people, or with external standards and ideals, or with disinterested activity. He does have one standard, that of the gentleman, and we can see in the passage quoted that, as with Gwendolen, the study of egotism includes the study of the social conditions that foster it. On numerous occasions throughout the novel, George Eliot seems to be posing the question, What does the idea of the gentleman amount to? What is its substance? Dickens conducts a similar and more thoroughgoing investigation in *Little Dorrit*, in the persons of Gowan, Blandois and the Barnacles. Dickens's conviction is that everything of value in the idea of the gentleman is attainable by men of any class, without leaving their class. Ham Peggotty and Joe Gargery are gentlemen; Betty Higden and Lizzie Hexam are ladies. Anything beyond this is merely the basis of pernicious claims on behalf of such people as Henry Gowan, who is Dickens's Grandcourt. George Eliot is less radical. In men of ordinary intelligence and goodwill, such as Sir James Chettam, Sir Hugo Mallinger and Mr Gascoigne, the idea of the gentleman is a source of disinterestedness, a fortifying and livable if not entirely coherent code. But her criticisms are as penetrating as Dickens's:

> ' "I don't think he (Deronda) would come. He is too clever and learned to care about *us*," said Gwendolen, thinking it useful for her husband to be told (privately) that it was possible for him to be looked down upon.
> "I never saw that make much difference in a man. Either he is a gentleman, or he is not," said Grandcourt.' (Chapter 35)

In Grandcourt, then, the idea of the gentleman fortifies something quite other than disinterestedness. And not only in him. In the superb comic scene in Chapter 22, when the 'expectant peer' Mr Bult, whom we have no reason to suppose a Grandcourt, confidently slights Herr Klesmer, he is acting upon the same easy caste-based assumption of superiority. In the same chapter, when Catherine Arrowpoint announces her engagement to Klesmer her mother, who had been proud to extend her patronage to him, calls him a 'mountebank'. We see the same spirit again in the reaction to Klesmer's outlandish appearance at the archery meeting (Chapter 10): 'What extreme guys those artistic fellows usually are!'

Klesmer is a figure of major importance. It is he who makes the first explicit and unanswerable challenge to Gwendolen's assumptions of superiority, when she consults him about going on the stage. In fact he is of more real importance than George Eliot intended. His influence on Gwendolen is intended to be preliminary and ancillary to Deronda's; but he is a so much more completely imagined character and vivid presence than Deronda, the convincing type of the real cosmopolitan artist, that the great chapter (23) in which he shatters Gwendolen's illusions is more necessary than it might otherwise have been. Gwendolen's confrontation with reality, with disinterested and impersonal standards and activities, begins there and is developed in the much more stilted conversations with Deronda. The part played by Deronda damages Gwendolen's story less than it would otherwise have done, partly because the development begins with Klesmer: it is convincingly launched.

The investigation of the ethos of the gentry, in which Klesmer plays a major rôle, includes of course the study of the 'young lady' which I have already discussed. One of the major barriers between the young lady and reality is the easy assumption of superiority which we have seen in Grandcourt, Bult and the Arrowpoints. This passage follows the interview with Klesmer:

'At home, at school, among acquaintances, she had been used to have her conscious superiority admitted; and she had moved in a society where everything, from low arithmetic to high art, is of the amateur kind politely supposed to fall short of perfection only because gentlemen and ladies are not obliged to do more than they like—otherwise they would probably give forth abler writings and show themselves more commanding artists than any the world is at present obliged to put up with.'

The life of the artist and the furtherance of a racial destiny are very different activities, but in relation to Gwendolen they have the same meaning: the disinterested pursuit of objects for the objects' sake, not for the satisfaction of the ego. The difference in the novel is that Klesmer's function is dramatic and created, while Deronda's is schematic and referential. Gwendolen becomes somewhat statuesque in her scenes with Deronda, as Dorothea does with Ladislaw; but Gwendolen suffers less than Dorothea, perhaps because Deronda is a worse failure than Ladislaw and so impinges less on the heroine, certainly because Gwendolen's intensely real life must go on independently of Deronda—he is not an answer or a destination, merely a guide. And there is nothing sentimental in the scenes between them. George Eliot's partiality for Deronda is more abstract, less warm than her partiality for Ladislaw who, if we might say it without impertinence, more closely resembles an idealisation of G. H. Lewes, as well as of Shelley.

Deronda's career tells on our understanding of Gwendolen's in an abstract, referential manner. The sanctity of the past, 'noble partiality', submission to necessity, devotion to impersonal pursuits are stated and purportedly vindicated in the smooth medium of Deronda's world. There are numerous points in Gwendolen's story at which we can see these ideas controlling and illuminating George Eliot's sense of reality. An understanding of the theoretic basis of the Jewish part highlights such things as the symbolism of the necklace and the lament which opens Chapter 3: 'Pity that Offendene was not the home of Miss Harleth's childhood, or endeared to her by family memories! A human life, I think, should be well rooted in some spot of a native land. . . . ' George Eliot 'meant everything in the book to be related to everything else there'. Deronda's story gives us a set of ideas and a language which we cannot help to some extent applying to the rest. But we should not be too free in making the application. The implied invitation is inevitably a didactic one and therefore, if didacticism is indeed hostile

to tragedy, impoverishing. It would be wrong to reverse Henry James's phrase, and say that at her best George Eliot proceeds from the concrete to the abstract; the truth is rather that the concrete is more important than the abstract, the human life which is the medium of the experiment matters more than the theoretic basis. This can be clarified by comparing the situations of Deronda and Gwendolen at the end of the novel. Deronda's career is purely exemplary, and we can account for his departure to the East and his future activities only in terms of the moral ideas that they exemplify: they do not have the effect of overwhelming and chastening realities. This is true of the ends of most Victorian novels, including *Middlemarch*: the married lives of Dorothea and Ladislaw, Fred and Mary, are merely graceful flourishes. But Gwendolen's life is pure reality to the end. The real culmination of her story is this, her account of Grandcourt's drowning:

> ' "I saw him sink, and my heart gave a leap as if it were going out of me. I think I did not move. I kept my hands tight. It was long enough for me to be glad, and yet to think it was no use—he would come up again. And he *was* come—farther off— the boat had moved. It was all like lightning. 'The rope!' he called out in a voice—not his own—I hear it now—and I stooped for the rope—I felt I must—I felt sure he could swim, and he would come back whether or not, and I dreaded him. That was in my mind—he would come back. But he was gone down again, and I had the rope in my hand—no, there he was again—his face above the water—and he cried again—and I held my hand, and my heart said, 'Die!'—and he sank; and I felt 'It is done—I am wicked, I am lost!'—and I had the rope in my hand—I don't know what I thought—I was leaping away from myself—I would have saved him then. I was leaping away from my crime, and there it was—close to me as I fell—there was the dead face—dead, dead. It can never be altered. That was what happened. That was what I did. You know it all. It can never be altered." '
>
> (Chapter 56)

This, like her acceptance of Grandcourt, is a complete expression of Gwendolen's 'moral economy'. It is the true outcome of what she has been, and of what her relations with her husband have been. Deronda is comforted by the account—Gwendolen is less 'guilty' than her use of the word had led him to fear. That he should be comforted is dramatically right, but I doubt that we ought completely to share his comfort. Similarly, I rather dislike the emphasis placed here: 'Deronda could not utter one word to diminish that sacred aversion to her worst self—that thorn-pressure which must come with the crowning of the sorrowful Better, suffering because of the Worse.' Is this not making Gwendolen's experience too much a matter of moral hygiene, and diminishing the tragic reality? In the latter days of her marriage Gwendolen's will has been at the service of her conscience (a reversal of her earlier self) against her involuntary murderous desires. But the will is no more effective to alter events than when it served her ego. Gwendolen leaping away from herself, from her crime, when she 'saw my wish outside me' is the last and perhaps most startlingly vivid example of the inner self concentrated into gesture: the involuntary wish no longer holds back the will when its triumph is seen to be accomplished. Obviously guilt in the legal sense cannot be determined, and there is no temptation to call Gwendolen a murderess. But if *everything* had been different, if Gwendolen had not hated her husband, she would undoubtedly have thrown the rope, and even if Grandcourt had drowned the reality would have been quite different—we do not call every unfortunate death a tragedy.

This is not quite the end for Gwendolen of course. She still has to learn that Deronda's commitment to Judaism (the emphasis falls here rather than on his marriage to Mirah) will take him away from her for ever:

'That was the sort of crisis which was at this moment beginning in Gwendolen's small life: she was for the first time feeling the pressure of a vast mysterious movement, for the first time being dislodged from her supremacy in her own world, and getting a sense that her horizon was but a dipping onward of an existence with which her own was revolving. All the troubles of her wifehood and widowhood had still left her with the implicit impression which had accompanied her from childhood, that whatever surrounded her was somehow specially for her, and it was because of this that no personal jealousy had been roused in her in relation to Deronda: she could not spontaneously think of him as rightfully belonging to others more than to her.'

(Chapter 69)

In one sense, there is a rightness about this: that Gwendolen's experiences should not have effected a miraculous moral reversal. But I wonder whether any other readers share with me an irritation and resentment at George Eliot's talking, at this late stage, of 'Gwendolen's small life'? If we agree with Theodora in Henry James's 'Conversation' that 'she is extremely intelligent and clever, and therefore tragedy *can* have a hold on her,'[16] or with F. R. Leavis, 'So much pride and courage and sensitiveness and intelligence fixed in a destructive deadlock through false valuation and self-ignorance—that is what makes Gwendolen a tragic figure,[17] must we not feel that George Eliot's phrase is belittling? Of course Gwendolen's tragic experience does not bring her into conscious contact with the wider life of mankind, but is that the only sense in which a life can be large? For George Eliot it is, and that perhaps is why one feels some degree of uneasiness in describing her as a tragic artist. She is determined to put Gwendolen in her place.

In the opening lines of her most famous poem, which her friend Dr Congreve incorporated into a Positivist liturgy, George Eliot describes the Positivist's Immortality:

'O may I join the Choir Invisible
Of those immortal dead who live again
In lives made better by their presence.'

She bestows this immortality on most of her heroes and heroines—on Dorothea for example: 'the effect of her being on those around her was incalculably diffusive'.[18] Deronda is clearly destined for a high rank in this Paradise. What of Gwendolen? There is a suggestion of it in the letter which is the last we hear of her: 'I have remembered your words— that I may live to be one of the best of women, who make others glad that they were born' (Chapter 70). And what of Oedipus, Orestes, Othello, Macbeth? Public figures, of course, but isn't the largeness of their lives something quite other than this, and quite independent of whether they make other lives better? Perhaps one test of a tragic figure is whether one cares about such beyonds. In Gwendolen's case, I don't think I do.

Conclusion

Generations of readers have enjoyed and gained insight into George Eliot's novels with very little knowledge of nineteenth-century intellectual history, or of the circumstances of the author's life: it would clearly be wrong to say that this knowledge is essential. There is, moreover, the danger that in pursuing the intellectual foundations of her work, her struggles and achievements as an artist might be evaded, a distance placed between her and the reader, making of her a fossil in the history of ideas. But this is not a necessary or even a probable consequence of exploring the context of the novels. What makes George Eliot seem a very close figure to many modern readers is precisely that she was so much alive to certain aspects of her own time. In her the present has access to the past, and we learn also that the past is not separate from the present: the more real her novels are as historical events, the more real they should become as contemporary experiences.

Although I have discussed the novels chronologically, I have not been tracing an intellectual biography in the ordinary sense. George Eliot's career does not chart a development of ideas or beliefs that can be discussed separately from the novels themselves: her observable moral, intellectual and religious views remain constant from the time of *Scenes of Clerical Life* to that of *Daniel Deronda* (unless the suggestions of the supernatural in *Deronda* be taken more literally than I take them). But novels are acts of the intellect (although not exclusively so) and they are the conclusive evidence that George Eliot's was a great mind—and there are intellectual differences between the novels: differences in what they tell us about the ideas that lie behind them, in the relations between didactic impulsion and the imaginative invocation of reality. These are differences that exist only in the novels, and they are paradoxically more available to the reader than to the novelist herself. To take perhaps the clearest example: both *The Mill on the Floss* and *Silas Marner* are concerned with the doctrine of continuity, but critical reading reveals a considerable difference between the dogmatic assertion of past ties and the dependence of the moral life on obedience to them, in the earlier novel, and the co-operation of continuity with the past and trusting openness to the future which Silas's experience embodies. Critical analysis describes this difference in terms of the greater artistic success of *Silas Marner*, but it is equally an intellectual superiority, since George Eliot's art is the imaginative scrutiny of ideas. But it is not a development of formulated concepts existing outside the novels, and is possibly one of which George Eliot was unaware, since Continuity again assumes a dogmatic form in both *Romola* and *Felix Holt*, and perhaps more dogmatic than ever in *Daniel Deronda*.

Nevertheless, the development is not haphazard. With the exception of *Romola*, each novel presents a more remarkable triumph of the imagination than the last, a further advance in the understanding of humanity, while George Eliot always remains capable of writing as badly, thinking as dogmatically or sentimentally, as ever. And these weaknesses, artistic and intellectual, are not to be separated. While we frequently admire the power of George Eliot's mind in *Romola* or the Jewish part of *Daniel Deronda*, we are nevertheless admiring an inferior *intellectual* power to that of her artistic successes. *Silas Marner* represents a profounder thought about Continuity than the closing Books of *The Mill on the Floss* or Deronda's confrontation with his mother; the career of Gwendolen Harleth a profounder thought about egotism than that of Tito Melema. Effective thought about George Eliot's beliefs cannot, therefore, exist separately from critical thought about her art.

Notes

Introduction

1. 'She seemed to have a distrust or a distaste for all in life that gives one a springing foot. Then, too, she knew so well how to enforce her distaste by the authority of her mid-Victorian science or by some habit of mind of its breeding, that I, who had not escaped the fascination of what I loathed, doubted while the book lay open whatsoever my instinct knew of spendour. She disturbed me and alarmed me, but when I spoke of her to my father, he threw her aside with a phrase, "O, she was an ugly woman who hated handsome men and handsome women."' W. B. Yeats: *Autobiographies* (London, 1955), p. 88.

2. Gordon S. Haight, ed. *The George Eliot Letters* (New Haven, 1954-55), Vol. I, p. 162.

3. *Ibid*, III, p. 227.

4. Thomas Pinney, ed. *Essays of George Eliot* (London, 1963), p. 145. This essay was originally published in the *Leader* in 1855.

5. *Letters*, VI, p. 216.

6. Bernard J. Paris, *Experiments in Life, George Eliot's Quest for Values* (Detroit, 1965), pp. 38-9.

7. It is a serious weakness of Mr Paris's useful book that he takes the metaphor literally, treating events in the novels as if they were events in the real world and applying no criticism whatever to George Eliot's art. I shall be discussing the inadequacy of Mr Paris's method in one particular case, in my chapter on *The Mill on the Floss*.

8. *Essays*, p. 413.

9. *Essays*, pp. 289-90.

10. *Letters*, IV, p. 300.

11. *Letters*, III, p. 111.

12. *Letters*, I, p. 162.

13. *Letters*, III, p. 111.

14. *Letters*, IV, p. 364.

1. *George Eliot's Moral World.*

1. A more detailed discussion of Evangelicalism, with citations, is given in my chapter on *Middlemarch.*

2. Mr Brocklehurst was modelled on an actual Evangelical clergyman, the Reverend William Carus Wilson, proprietor of the Clergy Daughters' School, which the Brontë sisters attended. See Ford K. Brown: *Fathers of the Victorians, The Age of Wilberforce* (Cambridge, 1961), pp. 451-57.

3. Gordon S. Haight, *George Eliot, A Biography* (Oxford, 1968), p. 7.

4. *Letters,* III, p. 175. It was on an incident in this aunt's life that George Eliot based the relations of Dinah Morris and Hetty Sorrel, which were the first germ of *Adam Bede.* She insisted, however, that Dinah was *not* a portrait of Mrs. Samuel.

5. *Letters,* I, p. 9.

6. *Letters,* I, p. 46.

7. Apart from an early religious poem in the *Christian Observer.*

8. Cf. her comment on Henry Buckle, author of *History of Civilization in England* (1857): 'he is a writer who inspires me with a personal dislike—not to put too fine a point on it, he impresses me as an irreligious, conceited man.' *Letters,* II, p. 486.

9. Haight, *George Eliot,* p. 39.

10. Quoted from Edith Simcox's unpublished autobiography in K. A. Mckenzie: *Edith Simcox and George Eliot* (London, 1961), pp. 126-27.

11. *Letters,* I, p. 34.

12. *Letters,* III, p. 382.

13. *Letters,* II, pp. 422-23.

14. *Letters,* VI, p. 439.

15. *Letters,* I, pp. 143-44.

16. *Letters,* V, p. 31.

17. *Letters,* I pp. 125-26.

18. *Letters,* I, p. 254.

19. *Letters,* V, p. 387. One must note, however, that her correspondent here is an old-fashioned Tory. One should always be careful in using G. E.'s letters as evidence of her views, as she certainly adapted her expressions according to the correspondent. This is particularly true of the warmth of admiration for Comte expressed in the letters to Mrs Congreve, wife of the leading English Positivist. See the section below, 'Conservatism'.

20. Herbert Spencer *The Study of Sociology,* Chapter 14 (11th edition, 1883), p. 344.

21. *Essays*, pp. 55-6. I should add that at one stage in the 1840's she appears to have shared Bray's belief in phrenology — perhaps the classic instance of this kind of crudity — but it makes no appearance in her essays or novels; and although in a letter to Bray written as late as 1852 she appears to be construing Charles Dickens's character from the shape of his head, this is probably an example of the adaptation I have referred to (last note but one) in the letters to Blackwood and Mrs Congreve.

22. *Essays*, pp. 415-30. All Felix Holt's political attitudes in both the novel and the 'Address' (which George Eliot was persuaded to write by her Tory publisher) can more properly be called Positivist than Radical.

23. Auguste Comte, *A General View of Positivism*, translated by J. H. Bridges (London, 1865; second edition 1880), p. 246.

24. *The Birth of Tragedy* (translated by Francis Golffing, Doubleday Anchor Books, New York, 1956), p. 11.

25. *Letters*, VI, p. 32. This letter, to Mrs Bray, concerns the rejection of a children's story which Mrs Bray had submitted for publication to the Society for Promoting Christian Knowledge.

26. Martineau, ed. *Comte's Positive Philosophy* (second edition, London, 1875), Vol. II, p. 395. This work is a translation and condensation of the *Cours de Philosophie Positive*, approved by the author to be studied in preference to the original.

27. Auguste Comte *A Preliminary Discourse on the Positive Spirit*, translated by E. S. Beesly, (London, 1903), para. 56, p. 118.

28. See *A General View of Positivism*, p. 7; *The Essence of Christianity* translated by Marian Evans (1854), p. 303. Although it would be misleading to describe Feuerbach as a Positivist, this identity of attitude is one justification for discussing his influence under the same heading as Comte's.

29. With one important exception. In a passage quoted above Comte draws attention to the opposition between the principle of altruism and that of enlightened self-interest. In that passage he classes Utilitarianism as 'metaphysical'.

30. 'More Leaves from George Eliot's Notebook', Thomas Pinney, *Huntingdon Library Quarterly* 29 (August 1966), p. 373.

31. Auguste Comte, *A Preliminary Discourse*, para. 56, p. 119.

32. Evidence of George Eliot's mature attitude to Christianity abounds in her letters. I quote one instance here: 'I am the more inclined to think that I shall admire the book [*Christianity and Infidelity* by Sara Hennell], because you are suspected of having given undue preponderance to the Christian argument, for I have a growing conviction that we may measure true moral and intellectual culture by the comprehension and veneration given to all forms of thought and feeling which have influenced large masses of mankind—and of all intolerance, the intolerance calling itself philosophical is the most odious to me.' To Sara Hennel, 24/2/57; *Letters*, II, p. 301. See also III, p. 111; p. 231; pp. 365-66.

33. *Letters*, I, p. 162.

34. *A General View of Positivism*, p. 10.

35. *Letters*, III, p. 111.

36. *Letters*, IV, p. 333. The Congreves were among the followers of Comte who actually practised Positivism as a religion.

37. Mathilde Blind: *George Eliot* (1883), p. 213.

38. *Letters*, II, p. 153.

39. *The Essence of Christianity*. p. 14. (Refs. are to 1st edn.)

40. *Ibid.*, p. 15.

41. *Ibid.*, pp. 150-51

42. *Ibid.*, p. 156.

43. *Ibid.*, p. 154.

44. D. H. Lawrence, *Women in Love* (1921, Phoenix edition 1954), pp. 118-19.

45. N.B. George Eliot's use of this phrase ten years earlier, quoted p. 15 above.

46. *Essence of Christianity*, pp. 154-55. In a note to this passage Feuerbach points out that whereas the Hindus believe that a perfect man consists of three persons: husband, wife and son, and whereas the Adam of the Old Testament was incomplete without a woman, the New Adam, Christ, 'has no longer any sexual impulses or functions'.

47. *Ibid.*, p. 268.

48. *Ibid.*, p. 104.

49. *Middlemarch*, Chapter 68.

50. *Letters*, VI, p. 98.

51. *Letters*, II, p. 403.

52. *The Mill on the Floss*, Book 1, Chapter V. G. E.'s italics.

53. 'Looking Backward'; *Impressions of Theophrastus Such*, Chapter 2.

54. ' More Leaves from George Eliot's Notebook', Thomas Pinney, *Huntingdon Library Quarterly* 29 (August 1966), p. 373.

55. 'The Natural History of German Life'; *Essays*, p. 287.

56. Roughly speaking, pages 274-87 and 291-98 of the *Essays* are translated from or closely based on Riehl. I am indebted for this information to Mr Anthony McCobb. Some idea of the extent to which such ideas were current in George Eliot's intellectual world can be had by comparing Comte, *Preliminary Discourse*, pp. 145-46 and Spencer, *The Study of Sociology*, pp. 19-20.

57. *Essays*, pp. 287-88. G. E.'s italics.

58. Mathilde Blind, *George Eliot* ('Eminent Women Series', London, 1883), p. 174.

59. *Letters*, II, pp. 48-9.

60. Jerome Beaty, 'A Study of the Proof'; *Middlemarch, Critical Approaches to the Novel*, ed. Barbara Hardy. (London, 1967), p. 44.

61. *Middlemarch*, Chapter 21.

62. *Ibid.*, Chapter 24.

63. George Levine, 'Determinism and Responsibility in George Eliot', *PMLA* LXVII (1962), p. 271.

64. *Sunday Times Magazine*, 7th February, 1971, p. 11.

65. *Letters*, VI, p. 98; VI, p. 166.

66. 'Moral Freedom'; 'More Leaves from George Eliot's Notebook', p. 365. My italics.

67. R. H. Hutton, 'George Eliot'; *Brief Literary Criticisms* selected from the 'Spectator' and edited by E. M. Roscoe (London, 1906), pp. 179-81.

68. 'Evangelical Teaching: Dr. Cumming'; *Essays*, p. 166.

69. *Felix Holt*, Chapter 3.

70. *Romola*, Chapter 61.

71. *Ibid.*, Chapter 69.

72. *Ibid.*

73. *Letters*, IV, p. 104.

74. *Experiments in Life*, p. 51.

75. G. S. Carter, *A Hundred Years of Evolution*, p. 35.

76. *Experiments in Life*, pp. 207-08.

77. Auguste Comte, *Positive Philosophy*, II, pp. 73-4.

78. *Principles of Psychology* (1855, second edition 1870), I, p. 493.

79. Charles Darwin, *The Descent of Man* (1871, second edition 1874, reprinted 1909) p. 190.

80. *Ibid.*, p. 152n.

81. *Letters*, IV, p. 364.

82. 'More Leaves from George Eliot's Notebook', p. 373.

83. *Letters*, II, p. 85.

84. *Letters*, IV, pp. 333-34. George Eliot is often said to have invented this word, though *OED* cites one earlier use, in 1858.

85. J. W. Cross, *George Eliot's Life* (Tauchnitz edition, Leipzig, 1885), Vol. III, pp. 266-67.

86. See Haight, *George Eliot*, p. 195.

87. *George Eliot's Life*, Vol. III, p. 269.

2. *Scenes of Clerical Life*

1. See *Letters*, II, pp. 238-52.

2. See 'Silly Novels by Lady Novelists'; *Essays*, pp. 300-324.

3. *Letters*, II, p. 407.

4. *Essays*, pp. 158-89. 'Where is that Goshen of mediocrity in which a smattering of science and learning will pass for profound instruction, where platitudes will be accepted as wisdom, bigoted narrowness as holy zeal, unctuous egoism as God-given piety? Let such a man became an evangelical preacher' (pp. 159-60).

3. *Adam Bede*

1. *Silas Marner* is, of course, another exception, but more generally so in being George Eliot's one successful frank departure from her own canons of realism. There are also unsuccessful departures in *Romola* and *Daniel Deronda*. I argue that *Adam Bede* is not a realistic novel by the standards of *Middlemarch* but it is obviously not, like *Silas Marner*, openly 'romantic and symbolical', and was accepted as a work of realism by its early readers.

2. For an extended analysis of the novel as a re-working of the Fall myth, and comparison with *Paradise Lost*, see U. C. Knoepflmacher, *George Eliot's Early Novels, The Limits of Realism* (California, 1968), Chapter 4.

3. *The Mill on the Floss*, Book 4, Chapter 1.

4. We learn that in later years Hayslope took much less kindly to an Evangelical incumbent, Mr Ryde, than it had to Dinah; but Mr Ryde seems spiritually to have had less in common with Dinah and Mr Tryan than they with each other.

5. Raymond Williams, *The Country and the City* (London, 1973), pp. 165-81.

6 *Essays*, p. 269.

7. *Ibid.*, p. 271.

8. *Ibid.*, p. 270.

9. *Ibid.*, p. 280.

10. 'Looking Inward'; *Impressions of Theophrastus Such*, Chapter 1.

11. See Chapter 1, first section.

12. It has not, however, escaped Mr Irwine, whose morality, like George Eliot's, owes as much to Greek Tragedy as to the Gospels: 'Our deeds carry their terrible consequences, quite apart from any fluctuations that went before — consequences that are hardly ever confined to ourselves' (Chapter 16).

13. This is not a universal finding. Some critics have committed the vulgarity of attributing Hetty's characterisation to the 'ugly' George Eliot's hatred of beauty, or to an unconscious wish to punish herself for the 'immorality' of her relation to Lewes. There is no evidence whatever, either that she hated beauty or that she thought her life immoral. U. C. Knoepflmacher, who explicitly rejects such vulgarities, nevertheless refers to George Eliot's 'excessive efforts to denigrate her character,' and feels that she made Hetty 'far too repulsive' (op. cit., pp. 120-21). This seems to me naive:

Hetty is an uncompromising portrayal of a human possibility. The extreme nature of her egotism is due not to George Eliot's dislike of her (she is not after all a real person) but to a determination to face facts. Mr Knoepflmacher's belief that George Eliot's sympathy for Hetty is 'pretended' seems to me palpably wrong, and to miss precisely what is best in the novel. A pretended sympathy could not have produced the passage that I quote below from Chapter 37.

14. Compare the description of Eppie in *Silas Marner*, quoted below, Chapter 5.

4. *The Mill on the Floss*

1. *Our Mutual Friend*, Book 2, Chapter 15.

2. *The Mill on the Floss*, Book 5, Chapter 5.

3. *Our Mutual Friend*, Book 2, Chapter 15.

4. *The Mill on the Floss, loc. cit.*

5. Grahame Smith, *Dickens, Money and Society* (Berkeley, 1968), p. 204.

6. 'The Natural History of German Life'; *Essays*, p. 279.

7. Jerome Thale, *The Novels of George Eliot* (Columbia, 1959), p. 42.

8. *Ibid.*, p. 43.

9. *Letters,* I, p. 6.

10. F. R. Leavis, *The Great Tradition* (Peregrine edition), p. 51. I do not deny Dr Leavis's essential point, that the Dodsons differ from the Poysers in lacking 'charm'; but they are both more sympathetic and more formidable than the Waules and Featherstones.

11. *Ibid.,* p. 55.

12. Joan Bennett, *George Eliot* (Cambridge, 1948), pp. 120-21 and 127.

13. *Experiments in Life,* p. 165.

14. Charles Bray, *Phases of Opinion and Experience during a Long Life: An Autobiography* (L o n d o n, 1885), p. 75.

15. Contemporary protests were quite different and had nothing to do with this issue. The novel's first readers were appalled that Maggie should be attracted to such a creature as Stephen at all. Swinburne's article (reprinted in the 'Critical Heritage' volume, pp. 163-65) is an amusingly extreme example.

16. *Letters,* III, p. 317.

17. Gerald Bullett, *George Eliot: Her Life and Books* (London, 1947), p. 185.

18. See Haight, *George Eliot,* p. 541.

5. *Silas Marner*

1. As Q. D. Leavis points out in her splendid Introduction to the Penguin English Library edition of the novel (1967). However, while her discussion of the novel's sociological interest is typically scholarly and illuminating, I think that she places this interest too much at the centre, and attaches insufficient importance and value to the 'romantic and symbolical elements'.

2. A favourite phrase of George Eliot's. Pinney (*Essays,* p. 302n) cites nine references to it in her work, and calls it 'a key term in G. E.'s conception of realism'. The phrase is from *As You Like It,* I, iii, 12.

3. *Letters,* IV, p. 104.

4. *Daniel Deronda,* Chapter 4.

5. ' "Thought" and Emotional Quality'; *Scrutiny,* XIII, pp. 68-70.

6. F. N. Robinson, ed. *The Complete Works of Geoffrey Chaucer,* 'The Canterbury Tales' Fragment I, lines 229-32.

7. In this she resembles Shakespeare's Perdita. I have always thought that some elements in the novel—the function of the child, the sixteen-year gap — are strongly reminiscent of *A Winter's Tale.* Godfrey, un-

like Leontes, is denied re-union with the daughter he cast off: 'There's debts we can't pay like money debts, by paying extra for the years that have slipped by' (Chapter 20).

8. *Letters*, III, p. 227. The remark is apropos of the publication of Darwin's *Origin of Species*.

9. Auguste Comte, *System of Positive Polity*, Vol. IV, translated by Congreve (Paris, 1854), pp. 38ff. 'In the final religion we connect directly the maturity of the Great Being with its infancy'. Theology on the other hand is excluded. Comte's reason for thus singling out fetishism is that principle dear to George Eliot, 'the constant predominance of feeling over thought and action.'

10. See Chapter 1, first section.

11. 'I am writing a story which came *across* my other plans [for *Romola*] by a sudden inspiration.' *Letters*, III, p. 371; G. E.'s italics.

6. Romola

1. F. R. Leavis, *The Great Tradition* (Peregrine edition), p. 61.

7. Felix Holt

1. *ELH*, Vol. 18 (1951), p. 222.

2. *Letters*, VII, p. 44.

3. *Letters*, IV, p. 300.

4. Raymond Williams, *Culture and Society 1780-1950* (Pelican edition, 1961), p. 119.

5. *Ibid.*, pp. 116-17.

6. Leo Tolstoy, *Anna Karenina* (World's Classics edition), p. 271.

7. *Culture and Society*, p. 25.

8. 'It is the habit of my imagination to strive after as full a vision of the medium in which a character moves as of the character itself.' Letter to R. H. Hutton; *Letters*, IV, p. 97.

9. For example, Bamford's declaration at his trial—'I solemnly and firmly assure your lordships that I never again will advise my countrymen to exercise that degree of patience which I here did, until every drop of blood shed on that day has been amply and deeply atoned for.' *Passages in the Life of a Radical* (1844, Fitzroy edition, London, 1967), Chapter 80, p. 306—is quite likely the source of Felix's statement (Chapter 46) that there were circumstances in which he might assault a constable. Bamford suggests (Chapter 82, p. 313) that this declaration may have accounted for the severity of his sentence.

10. *Passages in the Life of a Radical*, p. 16.

11. *Ibid.*, pp. 200-201.

12. *Ibid.*, p. 116.

13. *Ibid.*, p. 70.

14. Jerome Thale, op. cit., p. 94.

15. W. J. Harvey, *The Art of George Eliot* (London, 1961), p. 183.

16. 'Notes on the Spanish Gypsy and Tragedy in general'; J. W. Cross. *George Eliot's Life*, pp. 266–67.

17. *Letters*, VI, p. 290.

18. *The Mill on the Floss*, Book 6, Chapter 14.

8. *Middlemarch*

1. *The Great Tradition* (Peregrine edition) p. 117.

2. *Victorian Studies I* (December, 1957), pp. 173–79; reprinted Gordon S. Haight, ed., *A Century of George Eliot Criticism* (London, 1966), pp. 306–13.

3. *Parl. Deb.* N. S. vol. xxii, p. 344; quoted by Elie Halévy in *A History of the English People in the Nineteenth Century* Vol. II: *The Liberal Awakening*, translated E. I. Watkin (London, 1926, revised edition 1949), p. 303.

4. W. J. Harvey, in his essay on the contemporary reception of the novel, points out that the reviewers 'really pounced on this passage'; the *British Quarterly Review*, the *North American Review*, the *Spectator*, the *Athenaeum* and the *Times* all pointed out the contradiction. The most pertinent comment seems to have been that of the *Fortnightly Review*, which suggested that Dorothea's society 'so nurtured women that their ideals cannot but be ideals of delusion.' *Middlemarch. Critical Approaches to the Novel*, ed. Barbara Hardy (London, 1967), pp. 133-34.

5. *Essays*, p. 58.

6. One of Comte's mottoes was 'Live without concealment'.

7. *Essays in Criticism, Second Series* (1888), p. 213.

8. *Experiments in Life*, p. 67.

9. R. H. Hutton, 'George Eliot and Mr Tennyson'; *Brief Literary Criticisms*, p. 191.

10. *Middlemarch. Critical Approaches to the Novel*, pp. 61-62.

11. *Letters*, VI, p. 166.

12. *Experiments in Life*, p. 178.

13. W. J. Harvey, 'The Intellectual Background of the Novel'; *Middlemarch. Critical Approaches to the Novel*, p. 36.

14. Thomas Wakley (1795-1862): Radical medical practitioner, founder of the *Lancet* 'with the primary object of disseminating recent medical information, hitherto too much regarded as the exclusive property of members of the London hospitals, and also with a view to exposing the family intrigues that influenced the appointments in the metropolitan hospitals and medical corporations' *(DNB)*. Wakley campaigned against the Royal College of Surgeons, was responsible for numerous medical reforms in Parliament, and became famous as an exposer of charlatans.

15. S. Squire Sprigge, *The Life and Times of Thomas Wakley* (London, 1897), p. 498.

16. The history of St John Long is to be found, together with that of Wakley's campaign for medical coroners, in Sprigge, *op. cit.*, Chapter 37. George Eliot found her information in *The Lancet*, her reading of which can be traced in *Quarry for Middlemarch*, ed. Anna T. Kitchel (California, 1950; supplement to *Nineteenth Century Fiction*, Vol. 4).

17. Jerome Beaty, 'A Study of the Proof ; *Middlemarch. Critical Approaches to the Novel*, p. 44.

18. *Letters*, VI, p. 98.

19. *Essence of Christianity*, p. 104.

20. Ford K. Brown, *Fathers of the Victorians*, p. 118. The quotations are from Wilberforce's *Practical View of the Religious System of Professed Christians Contrasted with Real Christianity*.

21. *Ibid.*, pp. 292-93.

22. *Ibid.*, p. 294. Brown remarks (same page) that 'no one then living who left any pertinent record of himself had so certain an understanding of the ways and intent of the Almighty.'

23. K. A. McKenzie, *Edith Simcox and George Eliot*, p. 88.

24. *Letters*, III, p. 227.

25. *Letters*, II, p. 301.

9. *Daniel Deronda.*

1. The famous opening to Chapter 5 of *Amos Barton* seems to me an example of this tendency: 'Depend upon it, you would gain unspeakably if you would learn with me. . . . '

2. *Letters*, VI, p. 290.

3. *Letters*, VI, p. 301.

4. See D. W. Harding on 'Burnt Norton': 'In this poem the new meaning is approached by two methods. The first is the presentation

of concrete images and definite events, each of which is checked and passes over into another before it has developed far enough to stand meaningfully by itself. That is, of course, an extension of a familiar language process. If you try to observe introspectively how the meaning of an abstract term, say "trade" exists in your mind, you find that after a moment of 'blankness, in which there seems to be only imageless "meaning", concrete images of objects and events begin to occur to you; but none by itself carries the full meaning of the word "trade", and each is faded out and replaced by another. The abstract concept, in fact, seems like a space surrounded and defined by a more or less rich collection of latent ideas. It is this kind of definition that Mr Eliot sets about here . . . '

5. *Letters,* VI, p. 98.

6. See Chapter 1, 'Determinism'.

7. See Chapter 1, 'Evolution'.

8. *Letters,* IV, p. 364

9. *Romola,* Chapter 14. See above, Chapter 5.

10. *Middlemarch,* Chapter 21.

11. *Letters,* I, p. 177.

12. *The Novels of George Eliot* (London, 1959, reprinted 1963), p. 47.

13. Haight, *George Eliot,* p. 496.

14. *The Great Tradition* (Peregrine edition). p. 121.

15. R. T. Jones, *George Eliot* (Cambridge, 1970), p. 85.

16. Reprinted in *The Great Tradition,* p. 292.

17. *The Great Tradition,* p. 124.

18. *Middlemarch,* 'Finale'.

Select Bibliography

1. *Works of George Eliot*
   Scenes of Clerical Life 1857-58 (begun 1856).
   Adam Bede 1859 (begun 1857).
   'The Lifted Veil' 1859 (written 1859).
   The Mill on the Floss 1860 (begun 1859).
   Silas Marner 1861 (begun 1860).
   Romola 1862-63 (planned 1860, begun 1861, begun again
       1862).
   'Brother Jacob' 1864 (written 1860).
   Felix Holt, The Radical 1866 (begun 1865).
   The Spanish Gypsy 1868 (begun 1864, resumed 1866-68).
   Middlemarch 1871-72 (begun 1869).
   The Legend of Jubal and Other Poems 1874 (written
       1865-73).
   Daniel Deronda 1876 (begun 1874).
   Impressions of Theophrastus Such 1879 (written 1878).
   The George Eliot Letters, 7 vols., ed. Gordon S. Haight
       (New Haven, 1954-55).
   Essays of George Eliot, ed. Thomas Pinney (London, 1963).
   'More Leaves from George Eliot's Notebook', ed. Thomas
       Pinney, *Huntingdon Library Quarterly* 29 (August,
       1966).

2. *Biographical, Critical etc.*
   Beaty, Jerome, *Middlemarch from Notebook to Novel*
       (Urbana, 1960).
   Bennett, Joan, *George Eliot* (Cambridge, 1948).
   Bissell, Claude T., 'Social Analysis in the Novels of George
       Eliot', *ELH* 18 (1951), pp. 221-39.
   Blind, Mathilde, *George Eliot* (London, 1883).

Bullett, Gerald, *George Eliot: Her Life and Books* (London, 1947).

Carroll, David (ed.), *George Eliot: The Critical Heritage* (London, 1971).

Cross, J. W., *George Eliot's Life* (Tauchnitz edition, Leipzig, 1885).

Haight, Gordon S., *George Eliot: A Biography* (Oxford, 1968).

    George Eliot and John Chapman (New Haven, 1940).

    (ed.) *A Century of George Eliot Criticism* (London, 1966).

Hardy, Barbara, *The Novels of George Eliot* (London 1959).

    (ed.), *Critical Essays on George Eliot* (London, 1970).

    (ed.), *Middlemarch: Critical Approaches to the Novel* (London, 1967).

Harvey, W. J., *The Art of George Eliot* (London, 1961).

Hutton, R. H., *Brief Literary Criticisms,* selected from the 'Spectator' and edited by E. M. Roscoe (London, 1906).

James, Henry,*The House of Fiction,* ed. Leon Edel (London, 1957).

Jones, R. T., *George Eliot* (Cambridge, 1970).

Kitchel, Anna T., *Quarry for Middlemarch,* supplement to *Nineteenth Century Fiction* Vol. 4, 1950.

Knoepflmacher, U. C., *George Eliot's Early Novels: the limits of realism* (Berkeley, 1968).

Leavis, F. R., *The Great Tradition* (London, 1948).

Leavis, Q. D., Introduction to *Silas Marner* (Penguin edition, 1967).

Levine, George, 'Determinism and Responsibility in George Eliot', *PMLA* LXXVII (1962), pp. 268-79.

Myers, F. W. H., 'George Eliot', *Century Magazine* XXIII (Nov. 1881), pp. 57-64.

Paris, Bernard J., *Experiments in Life: George Eliot's Quest for Values* (Detroit, 1965).

Stephen, Leslie, *George Eliot* (London, 1902).

Thale, Jerome, *The Novels of George Eliot* (New York, 1959).

Thompson, Fred C., '*Felix Holt* and Classical Tragedy', *Nineteenth Century Fiction* 16 (June, 1961), pp. 47-58.

Williams, Raymond, *Culture and Society, 1780–1950* (London, 1958).
The Country and the City (London, 1963).

3. *Historical and Intellectual Background*

Austen-Leigh, J. E., *A Memoir of Jane Austen,* 1870 (reprinted in the Penguin edition of *Persuasion,* 1965).

Bamford, Samuel, *Passages in the Life of a Radical,* 1844. (Fitzroy edition, London, 1967).

Bray, Charles, *Phases of Opinion and Experience during a Long Life: An Autobiography* (London, 1885).

Brown, Ford K., *Fathers of the Victorians, the Age of Wilberforce* (Cambridge, 1961).

Carter, G. S., *A Hundred Years of Evolution* (London 1957).

Comte, Auguste, *Comte's Positive Philosophy,* ed. Martineau, vols. II. (second edition, London, 1875).
A Preliminary Discourse on the Positive Spirit, translated by E. S. Beesly (London, 1903).
A General View of Positivism, translated by J. H. Bridges (London, 1865).

Darwin, Charles, *The Origin of Species* (London, 1859).
The Descent of Man (London, 1871).

Feuerbach, Ludwig, *The Essence of Christianity,* translated by Marian Evans, 1854, reprinted Harper Torchbooks, (New York, 1957).

Halévy, Elie, *A History of the English People in the Nineteenth Century, translated* by E. I. Watkin, vols. II, *The Liberal Awakening* and III, *The Triumph of Reform,* revised edition (London, 1949).

Hennell, C. C., *An Inquiry into the Origins of Christianity* (London, 1838).

Houghton, W., *The Victorian Frame of Mind 1830–1870* (London, 1957).

Ideas and Beliefs of the Victorians, BBC publication (London, 1949).

Kitson, Clark G., *The Making of Victorian England* (London, 1962).

Kolakowski, Leszek, *Positivist Philosophy*, translated by Norbert Guterman (Middlesex, 1972).

Lewes, G. H., *A Biographical History of Philosophy* (London, 1845-46).
    Life and Works of Goethe, 1855.
    Principles of Success in Literature, London, n.d.

Marvin, F. S., *Comte* (New York, 1965).

McKenzie, K. A., *Edith Simcox and George Eliot* (London, 1961).

Ruskin, John, *Praeterita* (London, 1886).*

Rutherford, Mark, *The Autobiography of Mark Rutherford* (London, 1881).*

Spencer, Herbert, *Principles of Psychology* (London, 1855, second edition 1870).
    Principles of Biology, 1864.
    The Study of Sociology, 11th edition, 1883.

Simon, W. M., *European Positivism in the Nineteenth Century* (Cornell, 1963).

Sprigge, S. Squire, *The Life and Times of Thomas Wakley* (London 1897).

Stang, Richard, *The Theory of the Novel in England, 1850-70* (London, 1959).

Strauss, David Friedrich, *The Life of Jesus, Critically Examined*, translated by George Eliot (London, 1846).

Willey, Basil, *Nineteenth Century Studies* (London, 1949).

Young, G. M., *Victorian England, Portrait of an Age* (Oxford, 1936).

* These books are included for their accounts of upbringings in, respectively, an Evangelical and a Dissenting environment in the first half of the nineteenth century. Ruskin was born in the same year as George Eliot (1819), Rutherford in 1831.

Index